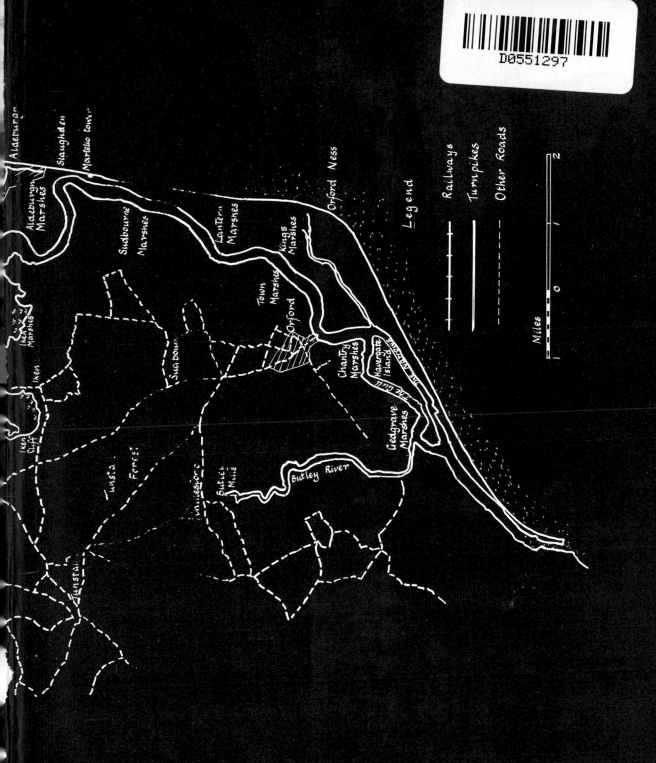

Aldeburgh

Slaughden

Martello Tower

Aldeburgh
Marshes

Sudbourne
Marshes

Lantern
Marshes

Kings
Marshes

Orford Ness

Iken
Marshes

Iken

Iken
Cliff

Sudbourne

Town
Marshes

Orford

Chantry
Marshes

Havergate
Island

THE NARROWS

Tunsta
Forest

Innicshore

Butley
Mill

Butley River

Gedgrave
Marshes

Tunstal

Legend

Railways

Turnpikes

Other Roads

Miles

2

1

0

Published by
TERENCE DALTON LIMITED
ISBN 0 86138 075 4
© Robert A. Whitehead 1991

Text photoset in 10/12 pt Baskerville
Printed in Great Britain at
The Lavenham Press Limited, Lavenham, Suffolk

Contents

Foreword

by
The Earl of Cranbrook

ROBERT WHITEHEAD has given us an anthology to cherish. His interest may focus most closely on Leiston, where his reputation stands on his role as "unofficial archivist and historian" of the Garrett Works (Chapter 13), but his subject matter expands outwards to cover, geographically, the middle Suffolk coast and sandlings; economically, the traditional crafts and industries of this area and communications within and beyond; and, socially, the personalities who have contributed most to the life and activity of this corner of our county these past 150 years. For sources he ably mixes solid archival evidence with more ephemeral documentation and, to great effect, the personal recollections of the many men and women with whom he has found fellowship in more than forty years of visiting this coastal district.

It seems to me a paradox of the English character that while freely moving about the country in pursuit of work, a home or other opportunities (as shown so often in the pages of this book) we nonetheless with equal fervour readily adopt the fiercest local loyalties. The visitor from elsewhere to the "beloved coast" will, I believe, find plenty in these pages to explain the how and why of what is here to be seen. But there also live among us newcomers in time, the children of this district born outside (or on the fringes of) the era of Suffolk history about which Robert Whitehead writes. I hope that they, too, will be fascinated by this book. For them he has stored the memories of parents and grandparents, recounting how this happened or that came to be, fixing in their minds the tales that there are no longer living lips to tell. These are the building bricks of local loyalty.

These are truly local stories, filled with the sense of place and person. Through the medium of the museums that the Long Shop has now become and the Moot Hall is in part, others in the locality are striving to save the material products of the past. There will not be room for everything; some objects, important in retrospect, may be lost by chance or choice. One most precious record of the past is the most vulnerable: the human memory. I rejoice that the pages of this book have saved so much from the experiences and memories of those who have gone before, to explain for all to come the true worth and meaning of the objects of this age that we preserve so carefully in our museums.

August, 1988   Cranbrook
(Chairman of the Long Shop
Project Trust)

Preface

THE PREFACE, as I have remarked in an earlier book, is the device whereby the author attempts to disarm his critics. In it he will, so far as modesty permits, suggest his qualifications for writing it at all and perhaps hint at his reasons. If he is prudent he will indicate how long an apprenticeship he has served at his subject.

In the latter connection one of the comments made by the late Allan Jobson to Frank Waddell comes to mind. More or less as a throw-away and as a mere aid to dating something else, he said: "When Queen Victoria died I was eleven." He was a native of Suffolk and, therefore, as an adoptive Londoner, an expatriate. I have no such claim to local connections nor, indeed, such astonishing longevity. Though my family came originally from East Anglia and my father lived the latter part of his life at Lowestoft I was born in Kent and I have known this strip of coast and its hinterland only as a visitor, for professional or recreational purposes, over a period of about forty years.

That period, however, has been sufficient to make a very large number of friends and acquaintances and, sadly, to have lost many through death. This book is dedicated to all those, living or dead, who have made the days spent in East Suffolk so memorable and enjoyable.

It is not a history book nor a guide book but a modest tribute to those who have peopled what a friend, in a felicitous phrase, once called "the beloved coast". I have appended a list, far from comprehensive, of those who contributed to it.

The companion of my days in Suffolk has been my wife Jean, always a good listener, a maker of notes, reader and critic of manuscripts and checker of printers' proof. If there is any credit to be ascribed for this book much of it is due to her, as are my sincere thanks.

The focus of our interest in the district has been the Garretts, whose name crops up again and again in the pages that follow. They had a hand in so many things and it was a sad day when the business at Leiston came to an end after running for two hundred years. For every avenue one explored in investigating the history of Leiston Works another presented itself, interesting and inviting, so that as we looked at area after area of the Garrett story others just as intriguing but not related directly to the main theme led off temptingly on every side. Some of these are looked at in greater detail in the pages that follow.

Nearly all that is written is of things and people. I do not think that I have the skills required to evoke the wide skies, the marshes and the heathlands of this incomparable piece of coast, from the draughty unpeopled bulk of Havergate Island to the gorsed sweep of the Minsmere Cliff. I never knew most of the people of whom I have written in these pages, but so often have their names and characters come up in conversations round the fire on a winter night, or in the reading of written or printed records, that though in many cases they were dead before my time their personal histories and characters seem to live.

Age does not confer a licence to pontificate but merely removes many of those who would otherwise have been in a position to contradict one. Though this book is not a work of erudition nor an historical record I have, nevertheless, used my best endeavours not to propagate misinformation nor to perpetuate mistakes that may have occurred elsewhere. Though a great deal of the information contained in the book is derived from either personal knowledge or primary sources, use has also been made of the published results of the researches of other writers, and these are acknowledged in the bibliography.

After all this had been said what is the reader to expect of the book? It contains fifteen essays on various aspects of the coast, some inter-related as, for instance, the chapters *The Beach* and *The Lifeboat*, others completely self-contained. I pictured to myself, when writing it, someone of like interests to my own, going there for the first time and wondering what lay beneath the surface. These are some of the things not immediately visible but, again, not much overlaid in the memories of those who live there. It is not complete, for there are many other topics that could have been written about but have not been—churches, country houses, and farming are three such subjects at random—mostly from considerations of length. Had I been writing a guide book they would have had to go in, but I was not, and these are therefore laid aside for some other pen—unless, that is, this volume finds such an enthusiastic public that my publisher invites a second volume! Why too, it will be asked, have I not mentioned two important matters, the 1953 floods and the Aldeburgh festival?

The festival, the means of making Aldeburgh internationally known, deserves, and is sure to find, a better chronicle than a compressed account in a few pages of this book, namely an account by a well-informed insider. The flood has already found such a chronicler in *North Sea Surge* by Michael Pollard. In short I do not consider myself qualified for the first task, and the second has already been admirably fulfilled.

Acknowledgements and Thanks

MY MOST sincere thanks are due to the Right Honourable the Earl of Cranbrook for the interest he has shown in the book and for having graciously agreed to contribute the foreword.

The staff of the County Archivist's Department at County Hall, Ipswich, have been very helpful at all times. I should also like to thank the late David Phillips and John Creasey (Curator and Librarian respectively) of the Museum of English Rural Life at Reading, and the Librarians of the Royal Institute of British Architects, the London Library and the Royal Academy of Arts. Mr A. J. (Tony) Errington and Miss Daphne Oliver of the Long Shop Museum, Leiston, have also been most kind, while the staff of the Museum of East Anglian Life at Stowmarket are perennially interested and helpful concerning any matter involving the past of Suffolk. John Morris of the Milne Museum, Tonbridge, helped with information on electricity supply.

The late Victor Garrett provided much information about the Garrett family and about Leiston and Aldeburgh in the first decade of this century. His son, Richard, and nephew, the late Peter Garrett, were also helpful. Many people connected with Leiston Works contributed to my researches but space forbids mention of all. It would be churlish, however, not to single out for mention Ted and Queenie Dunn, friends for nearly thirty years, and Alfred and Lorraine Wilshier. Ted, sad to say, died when I was about halfway through writing the book.

It was great good fortune to be introduced to Messrs Bob Burns and Dick Smith in Aldeburgh. Both are versed to an incredible degree in the recent history of Aldeburgh and both placed their knowledge at my disposal. Messrs Keith Cable, Nigel Saint and Eric Strowger provided information on Aldeburgh beach and the successive lifeboats. Messrs F. R. Corke and Trevor Hughes (Chairman and brickworks manager respectively of the firm of William C. Reade of Aldeburgh Limited) contributed information on the brickworks and brick-making, as did the late Alfred Rouse (formerly the brickworks manager), Jimmy Cracknell and Arnold Drew. The Landmark Trust provided information about the martello tower. Years ago Reuben Woods introduced me to the late "Jumbo" Ward and arranged for me to meet the late Tom Riggs. The latter introduction resulted in a most pleasant morning spent in his "Crows Nest" looking out over the Alde Estuary and the shore toward the martello tower. The Customs and Excise staff at Ipswich allowed the sight of registers containing Aldeburgh ships. Mr Charles Branch contributed reminiscences of the late Roy Watson.

Mrs Grace Walker, Mr Peter Free and the late Jack Titlow provided information about the Leiston Picture House. Peter lent me the minute books of the old company. Mrs Laetitia Gifford provided notes concerning the Aldeburgh Cinema and Mr Harry Archer on cinemas in Saxmundham.

The late Dr Ian Allen and Mr Frank D. Simpson both provided information on railways in the area. Frank also gave me notes on bus undertakings.

Several people contributed to my knowledge of mills in the area—the late T. B. Paisley, Mr Robert Wright (formerly of Friston windmill) and Mr Peter Dolman, a stern taskmaster who persisted in rooting out the shortcomings of my manuscript and who deserves my sincere thanks for keeping me on the right track.

A vast amount of help, both in direct information and in introductions to likely sources, came from the late Madge and Frank Waddell of Leiston. They were both great fun. We often stayed at their house in Leiston and there were seldom dull moments. John Waddell, their son, has kindly read and commented upon this book in manuscript and provided information for it.

Writing about artists of the coast was a particular pleasure. Mr Cecil Fry and Mr Michael Parkin kindly provided information concerning Cecil Lay. Information about the talented Rope family came from Mrs Doreen Rope, whose late husband Michael, a serving RAF officer, died with the ill-fated airship R.101; from Mr William Rope, from the latter's nephew Richard and his wife June, niece of Frank Waddell, from Mrs Mary Nottingham (née Rope) and from Mrs Irene Vaughan, an indomitable nonagenarian. Meeting these kindly and very helpful people was one of the pleasures of writing the book. My thanks are due also to Mr Peter Cormack of the William Morris Gallery at Waltham Forest, who has campaigned to achieve recognition for the stained glass artists of the Art and Craft Movement and who provided details of the stained glass work of both Margaret Agnes Rope and Margaret Edith Rope.

Some information about brewing activities came from my father-in-law, the late Douglas Pankhurst, who had a life-time involvement in the brewing trade, but much direct information on the local brewing scene came from a meeting with the late Gregory Wright, who arrived, aged twenty-one, in Aldeburgh at the turn of the century to be brewer at Flintham's Brewery.

Many other people have lent their assistance in the writing of the book and the researches that preceded it. Though I cannot list them all by name—indeed, in some cases I do not know their names—I thank them all most heartily.

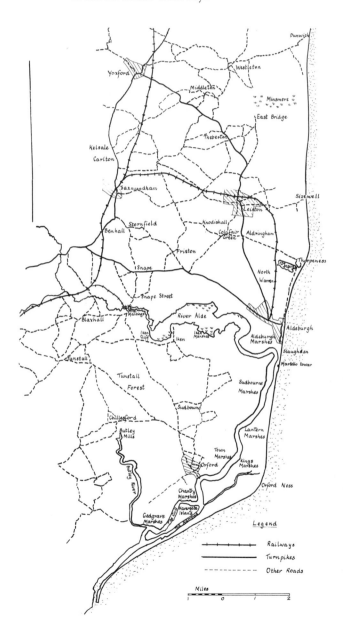

Places and Personae 1

INHABITANTS of the coastal strip of Suffolk which is to us the beloved coast were conscious of its being distinct from the territory that abutted it, although there was no hard-and-fast frontier between this area and the rest of Suffolk.

That engaging character "Owd England", written about by the late George Ewart Evans, was a farm horseman at Blaxhall, and he was aware of the division between his part of Suffolk and the rest of the county. He was once sent with his horses and a loaded wagon to Ipswich, where he stayed overnight, returning the next day. As he crossed the bridge at Farnham on the return trip he let out a sigh of relief and the comment "It's good to be back in owd England."

From south to north the area is bordered by the strip of shore from Havergate Island to the old coastguard cottages at Minsmere Cliff, with Saxmundham, Kelsale and Benhall as the most westerly points.

What is the area "enclosed"? Its actual physical extent is about 100 square miles, or 64,000 acres. In the days when the sailing codders put out from Slaughden, headed down the Alde and the Ore to the sea and thence to the sub-Arctic fishing grounds it represented roughly the catchment area from which they might have recruited their crews.

It is an area of gentle undulations. Its hills are all little hills, although when Garretts of Leiston wanted to give a steam wagon a good test they stopped it, fully loaded, on Choppings Hill in Aldeburgh to see how the wagon and its driver would cope with the 1 in 5 slope. Another definition of the area, by the way, would be to say that it covered the territory from which Garrett's habitually expected to draw the labour for their works, where agricultural machines, traction engines, steam and electric lorries and even trolleybuses were turned out.

Encountering this factory, which at its zenith employed 2,000 people and even made aeroplanes in the 1914–18 war, left the writers of guidebooks in a state of amazement, partly I suppose from finding such skills in a deeply rural situation and partly from seeing how little it had affected the rurality of the area and its people. The men who made machines by day retained the countryman's love of a garden, kept pigs or chickens and turned out to help with the harvest or hay carting, if required, in the evenings.

A Garrett group posed in the garden of the Works House. On the table in the centre is Tom Thurlow's bust of the third Richard Garrett of Leiston. Left of the table is Richard III's son Frank, and first left of the picture Lieutenant-Colonel Frank Garrett. Behind them are Frank's two other sons, Alfred (with the beard) and Victor. The man seated on the right was an auditor and behind him is W. J. (Billy) Marshall, a salaried non-family director. Courtesy RGE; photo by B. J. Finch

Those who made the mistake of patronising the man with a broad Suffolk accent whom they found taking a pint of beer outside a pub on a quiet summer evening were liable to find themselves confounded. Unlettered, even illiterate, some might have been, but there were those who had travelled all over Europe, and sometimes beyond, setting up engines for foreign buyers and teaching local men the best methods of driving and maintaining them.

The late Jack Newstead, for example, whose literacy ran to signing his name but little more, had travelled to France, Germany, Austria, Italy, Hungary, Russia (including territory that is now Polish) and the Baltic States. Unable to speak any language except English, he had nevertheless a talent for communicating with people by practical demonstration and for being liked wherever he went.

References to the Garretts themselves will turn up repeatedly. The senior members of the clan for four successive generations bore the name Richard. The last Richard never married and left no legitimate sons, so the practice ceased with him. The firm was started as a bladesmith's forge by Richard I at the age of twenty-one in 1778. It continued on a successful but minor scale until the time of Richard III (in control 1836–66), when it grew to

employing 600 men and enjoyed an international trade, and went on under his eldest and youngest sons, Richard IV and Frank respectively, to its zenith. Under Frank's son (also Frank) the company was liquidated in 1932 through a combination of the onset of the slump, an ill-judged attempt to join an engineering conglomerate (the Agricultural and General Engineers combine) and the decline in the use of steam engines as prime movers. It was reconstructed under new owners and continued until 1980.

Besides these actors on the Garrett scene there were other brothers in each generation. Richard III had two brothers, Balls, named after his mother's maiden name, and Newson, named from his grandmother's maiden name. Balls became the proprietor of an engineering business in Maidstone, Kent, and Newson developed Snape malting, owned ships and barges and took a prominent part for three decades in the affairs of Aldeburgh. In the next generation at Leiston there were two other sons besides Richard IV and Frank. The elder of these was John, progressive but hot-headed, who disagreed with his brothers as to how the affairs of the firm should be managed and went off to found a firm doing the same type of work in Magdeburg, Germany. The younger was Henry, well educated and socially agreeable but slack and self-indulgent. He too disagreed with Richard IV and Frank, mostly as to his standards of conduct, and took himself off elsewhere.

Frank in his turn had four sons, Frank Junior, Alfred, Stephen and Victor, all of whom took a part in running the firm. Alfred was a martyr to asthma, Stephen was killed in the first world war and Victor took over the management of the Eddison Steam Rolling Company at Dorchester, Dorset, in 1926.

Two of Newson Garrett's children achieved prominence. Elizabeth became, against tremendous odds, the first British woman to qualify as a doctor of medicine. Millicent was a notable figure in the Women's Suffrage movement, before the days of the Militant Suffragette. She married Henry Fawcett, the blind Postmaster-General, and Elizabeth became the wife of Stuart Anderson of the P & O line. Though the Garretts were decently well-off by middle-class standards, the Andersons were formidably wealthy; the inherent good sense of both husband and wife steered them clear of any vulgarly ostentatious brandishing of their possessions.

This characteristic of eschewing public flaunting of material wealth found an echo in the Ogilvies at Sizewell Hall. They first came to the district in 1859 when Alexander Ogilvie, who had amassed a large fortune as a railway building contractor, bought the house and began the assembly of the estate. His widow Margaret, who ruled over the 6,000 acres of which the estate eventually consisted (from her husband's death in 1886 to her own

3

in 1908), was often autocratic and sometimes eccentric, but few in the district had any real idea of the extent of the family fortunes.

Another family with major land holdings in the area were the Vannecks of Heveningham Hall, Yoxford and Leiston Old Abbey. Joshua Charles Vanneck, the fourth Lord Huntingfield, owned at the beginning of this century some 10,000 acres, though not all in the area which is our subject.

The Vannecks, again, never allowed their heads to be turned by the extent of their possessions. Some years ago my friends Ted and Queenie Dunn, of Leiston, who will be introduced in the course of the next few pages, went with a party of other keen gardeners to visit the gardens of Heveningham Hall. Ted engaged in conversation with a middle-aged man whom he found working on a flower bed. The man left what he was doing to accompany them round the grounds, drawing their attention to rare and exotic specimens, naming for them plants which they did not recognize and generally making their walk interesting. When they returned to where he had been kneeling he resumed work on the flower bed, and Ted took him to have been one of the gardeners. Later another member of the party remarked to him "You should be so lucky, having a conducted tour by his Lordship."

The character of a place does not come ultimately from its landowners and industrialists but from the people at large. It is here that the coast is at its best. Its natives are not generally chatterboxes, though of course a few are, and economy of the spoken word is proverbial. They are noted for a dry wit and epigrammatic utterances, as when Jerry Brown, the old labourer on Leiston Works boiler shop, described a tobacco pipe as having a fire at one end and a fool at the other; or when Lewis Chandler, who for years kept the staff registers there, commented against one entry "the man with the fast trotting daughters"; or, again, when the same master of the pithy comment remarked of a cocky apprentice "query grew too fast?"

Victor Garrett, Leiston born himself, remained very fond of its people all his life. He described the men who had worked for his father when he was a boy as being able to display independence without insolence.

The names of Ted Dunn and his wife Queenie will be found to crop up often in the pages that follow. He was the son of George Dunn, one of the Leiston barbers, and like his brother Dick chose to learn engineering at Garrett's rather than follow his father's trade. Dick ended his working life as managing director of Vincent HRD Limited at Stevenage, but Ted stuck to Leiston and when he retired was cost clerk in the works office. In the course of his life he learned two trades: when work tailed off badly at Leiston Works in the late twenties he turned to plastering, at which he became highly skilled. Many moulded cornices in houses and hotels in Aldeburgh came from his hand.

The attraction of the sea remains powerful to the young men of the district. Though the scale of inshore fishing is reduced from what it once was, there are still young men among those who follow it and Aldeburgh fishermen are as much in demand today as crewmen for the yachts of the wealthy at Cowes and elsewhere as they were in Edwardian times.

The names of farming families are also to be found in the pages that follow: the Ropes at Blaxhall and Leiston, the Sherwoods at Knodishall, the Borretts at Theberton. Percy Borrett

George Rope (1814–1913) of The Grove, Blaxhall, farmer and shipowner, known to his workmen as "The Old Gentleman".
Courtesy W. Rope; photo by B. J. Finch

served as a county councillor at the end of the last century. It was he who enlivened a meeting of the Education Committee during a debate on the introduction of pails to school closets. At one school the sanitary inspector had asked for a single pail. "Only one pail?" queried a member. "It must be a very small school." "Or a very large pail," rejoined Percy instantly. Percy's ready ripostes were a great aid in defusing pompous exchanges in both the County Council and the Leiston Urban District Council, of which he was also a member. Despite his readiness as a deflationary influence, he was well liked by Frank Garrett Senior, himself on occasions, not unaware of his own importance.

The Heritage Coast is rewarding on a visual basis alone, with its seascapes and riverscapes, its vistas of marsh and heath and, inland, its sweeps of arable farmland, but rewards become greater the deeper one becomes involved with it. The ties which bind its own people to it are able to catch and hold the affections of outsiders as well.

The Moot Hall, Aldeburgh, c1912, with, in the right foreground, "Russian Bob" Cable.
SPS

Aldeburgh Town 2

Until the passing of the Municipal Corporations Act of 1882 Aldeburgh was managed by an unreformed corporation composed of two bailiffs, elected annually, twelve capital burgesses, elected for life, and twenty-four inferior burgesses. Orford and Aldeburgh each had two Parliamentary seats until the Reform Act of 1832 deprived them of this privilege, one that was quite unwarranted by either their size or their importance and, sadly, corruptly exercised.

Membership of the old corporation was not taken over-seriously. Many of the members were not resident in Aldeburgh and either took no part in the administration of the town or participated only on such occasions as their interests were under debate or threat. The two bailiffs, elected yearly by the votes of the limited number of freemen of the borough, were the active officers, combining the offices of coroner and justice of the peace with their other functions. For some while in the middle years of the last century the incumbents of this office were Dr Samuel Randall, the Orford physician, and John Osborne, a retired naval captain.

Meetings and courts were held in the upper room of the decaying Moot Hall, in the lower floor of which was a small and very insanitary prison. The bailiffs had two macebearers, but otherwise they were served by part-time officers. P. B. Long, a solicitor in Ipswich, was town clerk and Henry Southwell, a Saxmundham solicitor, was clerk to the magistrates. William Hunt, the shipbuilder, was chief constable, while Horatio Salton, a boot and shoe repairer, was inspector of weights and measures. An administration organized on these lines achieved very little but had at least the merit of keeping down the rates.

The arrival of Newson Garrett upon the Aldeburgh scene in 1841 was the prelude to a period when he first aspired to and later succeeded in domination of the corporation. From 1841 to 1854 he lived at the Uplands, a stone's throw from the church and within sight and smell of the Albert Brewery, then owned by John Garrard. As soon as he had consolidated his control of his new business at Snape and set up his shipping interests he turned his eyes to local government. To become an inferior burgess was a simple matter of paying five pounds. Later he became a capital burgess.

In the corporation, as in most of his other affairs, Newson Garrett was soon involved in heated differences with his fellow burgesses, not least with the Reverend Henry Dowler, the vicar, who was also a capital burgess and for a time served as a bailiff. His displeasure with Mr Dowler was intermittent but extended over many years.

He had no illusions, despite his relative affluence, as to his social standing. He and Richard, as he well understood, were the brilliant but uneducated sons of a working blacksmith. Throughout his life he remained not far beyond the threshold of literacy. He saw the working people of Aldeburgh, accordingly, through eyes different from those of his fellow burgesses, who had had the dual advantages of middle- or upper-class birth and good schooling. In running his businesses he was a hard man and, in his belief that his own view of things was the only logical one for an intelligent man, arrogant. Nevertheless, by his ship-owning, his position of agent for Lloyd's, his acting as Receiver of Droits of Admiralty and his leadership of the Trinity pilots he was impelled to identify himself with the interests of the seagoing men of Aldeburgh. This affected not only his cerebral support of them but extended to physical courage, as when coxswain George Cable was swept to his death in front of Newson by the breaking of a rope in a chain of hands rescuing the crew of a ship cast onto the beach: without outward hesitation Newson Garrett took Cable's place, and did not leave till the rescue was complete.

He played a major part in establishing the two basic public utility undertakings of the town. It was mainly his money that financed the gas company, whose works began operation in 1856, and he had a large interest in the water company, set up in 1870. The water provided through the company mains was often derided for its unappetizing appearance and taste, but it was an infinite advance on the water yielded by the pumps and wells of the old town.

He had no part in the promotion of the pier, being committed to Slaughden Quay. Perhaps he also sensed it was a loser and he did not like bad runners. Newson's interest in the sea trade was, however, very real and more personal than mere commercial involvement. So long as was possible he kept his London sailing packets running from Slaughden to Bull Wharf at Queenhithe but switched to barges when he saw that the older types of sailing vessel had had their day. Though he had liked his ships he nevertheless became a railway shareholder when the East Suffolk Railway came into being.

Aldeburgh Corporation, having escaped attention under the Municipal Corporations Act of 1835, was finally reformed by the Act of the same name which became law in 1882. Despite his years

Newson Garrett stood for election, but he was defeated. His political opponents, who must have had personal affection for their impetuous old adversary, mollified him somewhat by appointing him to be the first mayor. Once he had taken the point that men who disagreed with him could still be effective in running the town, he settled down to working within the new arangements. After the creation of the East Suffolk County Council by the Local Government Act, 1888, he became the first county councillor for the borough and was made an alderman of the new council, an honour which touched and pleased him.

The Corporation continued to meet in the Moot Hall. It has been the fate of that ancient building to have been the subject of cyclic interest in its preservation and periods when apathy allowed its gradual decay. It reached a very low point in the eighteen-forties, from which it was retrieved by a restoration carried out in 1854–55 under the supervision of R. M. Phipson. The underlying problem with Aldeburgh, as with its neighbour Leiston, which became an urban district in 1896, was the minuscule proportions of its annual income. Though I do not have any figures for

Aldeburgh High Street, looking towards Slaughden, as it was in the first decade of this century. On the right Starling Brothers' clothing shop and behind it, on the other side of Choppings Hill, the premises of the now-defunct Aldeburgh Industrial Co-operative Society. SPS

Aldeburgh to hand as I write, I do have the figures for Leiston for the year ended 31st March, 1896, the first year of its existence as an urban district. On the income side it began with a balance of £191 13s 6d taken over from its predecessors. The second and principal item was the yield of the general district rate, which amounted to £466 5s 7d. The rent of allotment gardens brought in £2 17s 6d and there was ten pounds' worth of income arising from sewerage works, a grand total of £670 16s 7d.

The money was spent under ten heads:

	£	s	d
Sewerage works	1	10	0
Public lighting	81	5	6
Establishment charge	27	6	6½
Salaries	39	16	3
Sewage disposal works	85	0	0
Repair of roads	182	17	7
Irrecoverable rates	8	6	1
Election expenses	12	0	0
Interest on loans	29	2	10
Principal repairs	20	17	2
Balance	182	17	7½
	670	16	7

While it is easy to chuckle at the pluralism of some of the part-time officers of such bodies as Aldeburgh Corporation and Leiston Urban District Council, it becomes easier to understand the need for such economies when the limitations of income are understood. Robert Podd, Aldeburgh's assistant overseer at the time of the 1888 Act, was a tailor in the High Street. With a third hat he became the secretary of the water company. Harry Allerton, the town ropemaker in his commercial capacity, was the borough surveyor, its sanitary inspector, inspector of nuisances, inspector of weights and measures, serjeant-at-mace and town crier.

The water company was increasingly criticised for the poor potability of the water it delivered through its mains. The water was said to be brackish, and complaints were made about its muddy appearance. At Leiston in 1892 the part-time Medical Officer of Health (at an annual stipend of £20), Dr Robert Cook, described the well water used by most cottagers and householders as "partly-oxidised and diluted filth. Its only redeeming point is in its appearance; it is not unpalatable and neither in appearance nor taste does it reveal its unsavoury qualities."

Though Aldeburgh acquired a piped water supply in 1870, Leiston by contrast did not get one until 1901 and Saxmundham until 1922. In public electricity supply Aldeburgh also led its inland

neighbours. In 1912 the Aldeburgh Electric Supply Company Limited opened a modest power station, equipped with oil engines to power two generators, on a piece of land standing back from the south side of the Aldeburgh to Snape road, opposite the junction with the road to Leiston. Despite its name the company was not of local origin: the original grant of powers to build the station was made to Christy Brothers & Company Limited of Chelmsford, a company that built and equipped many similar small electricity undertakings and some larger ones.

Except for Woodbridge, which had a similar local power station, the rest of the area had to await the arrival of the East Suffolk Electricity Distribution Company Limited, founded in March, 1927, before it acquired a public electricity supply.

For much of the last century there was a marine observatory on the Terrace, near the top of the Town Steps, from which a lookout was kept on passing shipping. This was described by White (1844) as "one of Watson's General Telegraphic Stations. An account of all vessels seen from this observatory is sent daily by post to London." In the days before the arrival of the railway the post left Aldeburgh at half past six in the evening and was transferred at Saxmundham to the coach which left at 8.45 pm for Ipswich and London, which it reached early the next morning.

The view across the north end of the town c1908 from the top of the Town Steps. The look-out tower of the Down-towners beach company is visible above the houses. From it a continuous watch was mounted for ships in need of a Trinity pilot or of assistance in coping with an emergency. SPS

11

Watson was Barnard Lindsay Watson. Early references described him as a lieutenant, Royal Navy, but his name cannot be traced in Admiralty records. Watson first came to public notice as the surveyor of a visual telegraph line from Holyhead to Liverpool in 1826, employing his own design of semaphore. He continued to superintend the operation until 1839, when Liverpool Corporation paid him a lump sum to relinquish his post—an early example of a golden handshake.

About this time Watson moved to London, first to an office at 282 Regent Street and subsequently to 83 Cornhill, more conveniently situated in relation to the London shipping offices in the east side of the City. Watson's General Telegraph Association, as it was known, charged one pound a year for vessels of British or foreign registration to be entered in its list, in consideration of which the vessel so registered was reported off any of the stations owned by the association.

In addition to this activity Watson became the author of a semaphore line from Toppings Wharf, Bermondsey, to Kingsdown, giving communication with shipping in the Downs. It came to an end with a disastrous fire which devastated a large area around Tooley Street, bringing down the terminal tower at Toppings Wharf. Watson seems then to have abandoned his London ventures, but the Aldeburgh observatory went on for many years. Watson himself moved to Suffolk, dying at Monks Eleigh on 27th February, 1865.

The lookout on the Terrace was manned by ex-sailors. Though their names are largely lost, that of Bob Wilson survives, largely because Aldeburgh's distinguished daughter Elizabeth Garrett Anderson recalled his kindness to her when she was a child.

The other watchers on the coast were the coastguards, first organized as part of a concerted effort to suppress smuggling in the early years of the last century. Originally they were in effect shore-based detachments of the Royal Navy, organized on the same lines as any other naval shore establishment. For its first two years (1829–31) the coastguard was under the control of the Customs, but was transferred after the latter year to the Admiralty, with whom it remained until 1924. Within ten years of the establishment of the coastguard service smuggling was but a rump of its old self.

As established, the chain of coastguard lookouts was so arranged that each was visible, subject to the weather, from the next. No part of the coast was therefore free from surveillance. It was never a force of great numerical strength. In 1902 it had 4,200 men. At Thorpe, a typical station, Chief Officer Henry Kemp had command of five men. By 1922 his successor, Sidney Sworn, had control of one petty officer and three men. Over the years the force, at first a target of rancour and resentment to many, became widely respected and relied upon.

The basic functions of the coastguard were observation and communication. These remain in essence unchanged, though increasingly the observation is of small craft manned by amateur sailors, many of whom misguidedly attempt to evade the eye of the coastguard who might subsequently prove to be the means of rescuing them from the consequences of their own ignorance and ineptitude.

The onslaught on smuggling after 1815 made use in its early stages of the chain of martello towers erected around the coastline of southern, south-eastern and eastern England as an antidote to an invasion from France. The tower CC at Slaughden was the most northerly of this chain; a massive construction of brick dating from 1808–10, the building was arranged with four semi-circular fronts commanding the sea and the River Alde. When fully manned it had a garrison of a hundred men.

After the demolition of the battery at Fort Green the martello remained Aldeburgh's sole, and untenanted, fortification. Of the seven sister towers to the south of it only four remain, though others are still to be found beyond the Deben. In 1932 Aldeburgh's solitary tower was rescued from dereliction and converted to a holiday residence by Miss Debenham. A modern superstructure with steel windows was built on the roof, and the roof itself was made watertight by a coat of asphalt.

The martello tower, Aldeburgh.

After use in coastal defence during the 1939–45 war the tower once more became derelict. The onslaughts of the sea eroded the tongue of land on which it stood until the waves were lapping its seaward side, a process halted by the construction of new groynes and a concrete sea wall. It was bought by the Landmark Trust, who have spent a large amount of money in the conversion of the building to a home capable of use for holiday purposes while at the same time restoring the external structure of the tower to a state as near to its original condition as can be achieved.

Since the invasion fears of the Napoleonic era Aldeburgh has only once become the scene of internal military operations. The coast was, it is true, patrolled during the 1914–18 war, but it was not until the fall of France in the early summer of 1940 that anti-invasion defences on a massive scale were erected along the shore. Many inhabitants of the town, particularly the elderly and retired, understandably moved away to less vulnerable areas, and empty houses were requisitioned for use by troops, but there were not enough of these houses and some soldiers were in tents.

In the first world war there was a small airfield used by the Royal Naval Air Service on the north side of Snape Road to the west of the golf course; one of the buildings survives as a farm shed. It was connected by a narrow-gauge light railway to the brickyard jetty so that stores could be brought by sea.

The fashion among the wealthy and aristocratic for visiting or living at the seaside, for part of the year at least, in the last quarter of the eighteenth century rescued Aldeburgh from the decay into which it had appeared to be irrevocably sunk.

The last house to survive of old Slaughden was The Hazard, of which this photograph was taken in the late 1920s. At one time lived in by the marshman in charge of the Lantern marshes, it was latterly a private residence and was demolished soon after the second war.
Burns Collection

The Beach   3

IT WAS Basil Greenhill who characterized the wooden sailing
ship as probably the most dangerous vehicle ever developed by
man, remarking that "the losses, particularly of small sailing
vessels, in the coastal trades and fishing fleets . . . were appalling by
modern standards". The stretch of East Anglian coast of which
Aldeburgh is the southern limit and Cromer the northern has been
the target of the sea for centuries, during which the predominantly
southward longshore drift has eaten away headlands and filled
estuaries.

A hundred years ago the headland of Thorpe stood well out
into the sea and the scour was immediately to the south of it. The
Hundred River, entering the sea just to the south of Haven House
on the road from Aldeburgh to Thorpe, had an estuary wide
enough to warrant the building of a substantial timber bridge on
piles, opened in 1888 and known as the Jubilee Bridge. Within
thirty years the river was quite insignificant and the bridge, no
longer needed, was demolished in the nineteen-thirties; today,
unless one knows where to look, it is all but impossible to see where
it was.

The offshore shoals and banks made this coast a hazardous
place for the old sailing coasters, and the difficulties in which such
vessels found themselves gave rise in turn to the beach companies.
Aldeburgh harboured the most southerly of these, whose lookout
towers survive as mute evidence of an all-but-forgotten way of life.
The two companies were known respectively as the North
Company, the *Downtowners*, and the South Company, the *Up-
towners*. Each company was made up of longshoremen, mostly
engaged in fishing, banded together with the purpose of acting in
concert on salvage matters, to which end they subscribed in set
shares to purchase and equip suitable boats for their purpose and
to build the courts and towers from which they kept day and night
watch to sea to detect vessels in distress.

How long the Aldeburgh companies' history went back is not
known. The origins are, indeed, probably rooted in a process of
gradual evolution rather than instant spontaneous action. Inquiries
suggest that the Aldeburgh beach companies were moribund, if
not actually dead, by the opening years of this century, but as they
began by evolution so they faded away by the same process.

As the opportunities for salvage declined Aldeburgh waxed as
a seaside holiday resort. The beachmen who had been the

mainstays of the beach companies branched out into providing bathing machines and bathing rafts for visitors, with their attendant life-saver in his boat just off shore. Others engaged in taking off visitors who wished to spend a little time afloat or in rowing out amateur rod-and-line fishermen. The east coast, despite the efforts of Sir Cuthbert Quilter of Bawdsey, never became fashionable for the yachts of the wealthy, but men schooled in the hard conditions of the east coast came to be much esteemed as crewmen in the yachts of the wealthy at Cowes and elsewhere on the South Coast, and continue to be so regarded down to the present time. The beachmen also provided the crews for the successive lifeboats.

David Higgins' masterly study of the beach companies attributes twenty-six boats to the Aldeburgh beachmen, with a further six probables. Of these ten were gigs and all the remainder yawls, the essential tool of the beachmen. The qualities of a beach company boat were firstly the ability to live in devastating seas and secondly speed, partly because to be effective help had to arrive quickly and in part because the first company to reach the casualty secured the salvage. The yawl was constructed on closely spaced but slender steamed frames, giving a combination of lightness and flexibility with strength.

William Hunt built a number of yawls reputed to be very fast. His trade mark in fact was the head of a greyhound carved on the tiller fore-end. His yard at Slaughden was responsible for the building of the North Company's eight-oared gig *Dorothy*, notably successful in the Aldeburgh regattas of the eighteen-eighties, when the beach companies were still active but the builder's yard sadly in decline, mainly as a consequence of the fading importance of the cod smacks in the face of competition from steam trawlers. In 1844 there were fourteen smack-owners listed in Aldeburgh: Charles and Edward Burwood, Edward Burwood, Junior, John Cable, Tom Cable, Tom Cable, Junior, Sam Filby, Harry Finnery, John Green, George Self, Samuel Skeet, Harry Walford, Sam Ward and Robert Wilson. Forty years later there were only four: Harry Barley, Edward Coe, Daniel Harling and Harry Harling. Thirty years on again and only the two Harlings were left, and they had ceased to work the ships by 1914 at the latest.

Ships were traditionally owned in sixty-four shares. Many shareholders took no part in the active running of the ship. William Colchester, described as a merchant, of Grundisburgh Hall, was a prolific owner of shares in ships in the Woodbridge registers of last century. The smack *Eversfield* (1844) in the same register was mortgaged in 1893 to the late Hope Constable, of Penshurst, Kent, the noted builder of country houses, for £75 at an interest rate of five per cent per annum. The 35-ton cutter *Pilot*, launched from

One of the old Aldeburgh bathing machines on the beach by the Moot Hall. SPS

Aldeburgh yard in January, 1844, was owned in equal shares by Richard Garrett, of Leiston, and by Phillip Green, William Richardson and William Chattenden, all pilots of Aldeburgh. With the arrival of the railway Richard Garrett lost his interest in ships and shipping, selling out his share to his brother Newson in 1860. Subsequently two other pilots, James Gibson and George Kersey, took shares in the vessel in 1867, though since sixty-four is not equally divisible by six they cannot all have been equal share-holders. The *Pilot* was rebuilt and enlarged by Hunt in 1860.

In the early part of this century displaced cod smacks could be bought for very little. James Cable organized a group of fishermen to buy some of them for breaking. In all five were brought to

17

Slaughden, run aground on the North bank of the Alde and taken apart. One of the smacks, the *Ionia*, built at Grimsby in 1872, was not broken up but converted to a floating hostel. Before the 1914–18 war the ship was used by a London charity to give seaside holidays to poor girls from Greenwich. It survived into the nineteen-sixties, latterly let off for holidays, but eventually became too insanitary and unsafe to be used and was burned.

Not long before Hunt's yard closed for good the yacht *Sinclair* was built there for the Earl of Caithness. For a while there appears to have been some attempt to carry on at Slaughden by H. W. Tilbery, who had been apprenticed to Hunt, but he abandoned the task to take up employment with Arnold Hills at the Thames Ironworks at Blackwall, London, destined thirty years later to fall victim to the competition of the shipbuilders in the North-east.

The Hunts were the builders of the lifeboat *Rescue*, built by public subscription at a cost of £200 and presented to Joshua Chard at Sizewell beach on 19th May, 1870, an occasion attended, it is said, by some five thousand people. Though public subscriptions undoubtedly had a part in paying for the boat Victor Garrett used to say, on the authority of his father, that a good part of the money had been put up anonymously by Mrs Margaret Ogilvie, of Sizewell House, who had championed Chard's cause on other occasions.

A view of Aldeburgh, looking to the north, the Down-towners' look-out tower and court in the distance. The bathing machines on the right are more modern and the period may be just before 1914. SPS

Chard had his own beach company at Thorpe, using one boat wholly owned by him, crewed by Thorpe fishermen paid by him and allowed a share of salvage money. He began life as a carpenter, taking to a life based on the sea in the eighteen-thirties by selling provisions to passing ships on a part-time basis. After three or four years of this he had accumulated enough funds to purchase a fast boat of West Country origin, forfeited by a captured gang of smugglers.

Unlike most of his contemporaries Joshua Chard was able to read and write and kept a journal of what he did, commencing on 7th November, 1849. It is from this that most of the information came for the article on his life which appeared in the *Ipswich Journal* in 1869; this provides most of what is known about him today. Chard was dead, of course, before Victor Garrett was born but Victor's father had known him both in person and by reputation. His opinion, recalled by Victor, was that Chard was a man of modest demeanour and manly bearing not given to braggartry. During the course of his career he saved from the sea, by his own exertions and those of his company, more than a hundred people in circumstances of great personal gallantry. He met his death four days before Christmas, 1875, at the age of sixty-three, drowned at sea; his body was cast up on the shore at Thorpe.

The longshore fishing yields soles, cod, whiting, plaice, sprats

Aldeburgh's autumn harvest. Spratting might produce good catches at the expense of hard work, but the financial rewards were often derisory—a bucket of sprats sold for an old penny. In the bow is Billy Burrell, at the stern Pat Cable.
Burns Collection

and herring in due season. Until the overfishing of North Sea herring in recent times the Aldeburgh fishermen enjoyed an autumn season about October and a spring season. Sprats, on the other hand, were taken from mid to late November through until about the end of the year. Herring were largely salted, and many were dried or smoked. Small smoke-houses abounded in the towns and villages of the coast, some smoking only for their own households, others curing fish for sale to neighbours or for hawking in the public houses.

Sprats were often in glut, being eaten, on the whole, fresh. The arrival of the railway helped sales of sprats by enabling them to be sold outside the constricting confines of the district, but in a glut many were sold at derisory prices or carted on to the land as fertilizer. Ted Dunn recalled buying a bucket of sprats for one old penny.

Probably the most serious attempt to promote the welfare of the fishing population was the setting up of the co-operative Aldeburgh Fishermen's Guild. Some of the better-off residents of the town put their hands into their pockets to get it off the ground. George Constance, owner of the ironmonger's shop in the High Street, was a consistent supporter of the fishermen's efforts to improve their marketing and undertook the secretarial duties of the Guild for them.

There had been two earlier attempts to tackle the decline of the living that Aldeburgh derived from the sea. It was considered that the development of Slaughden as a port was hindered by the difficult approach through the estuary of the Ore, and an attempt to combat this disability was made in 1813 with a plan to cut through the shingle bank at the Crouch, across the river from the Orford town wharf, at the same time damming up the Lower Gull, with lock gates at Chantry Point. Nothing came of it, probably because no money was forthcoming.

There followed a long pause, with much complaint and little action. Then in the eighteen-sixties Peter Bruff, the Ipswich civil engineer, who had been heavily involved in railway building, proposed a plan for a direct connection 600 yards wide between the Alde and the sea, then about 100 yards apart, between Slaughden village and the martello tower, protected on the seaward side by two 200-foot piers bearing navigation lights. The Aldeborough Pier & Railway Act, 1864, granted powers to extend the railway down to the waterside, but again nothing tangible resulted.

Bruff was not easily put off. His earlier plan for unfettered communication between the sea and the Alde had been called into question by the time-lag between the tide in the Alde and that on the sea at the other side of the bank. In 1870 he came forward with a much more complicated but still abortive plan involving an outer harbour on the seaward side of the bank, with a ship lock between it and the Alde. It was proposed that the powers of the 1864 Act for the railway line be extended. There was yet a further proposal in 1884, this time for making a 200-foot cut 600 feet long through the Lantern Marshes south of the martello and constructing two piers into the sea to protect the entrance. The estimate for this scheme was put at £60,000, nearly half of which would have been taken up by the two piers.

In former times the Leiston Garretts might have been interested in putting money into such proposals, but the arrival of the railway at Leiston served them so well as to make the matter of no importance to them. Newson Garrett retained an interest in seaborne trade, but the shift in emphasis from brigs and schooners to the barge had made it of less interest even to him.

The quay at Slaughden was an estate held of the manor of Aldeburgh under the gift of a former Earl of Strafford in trust for the general use of the inhabitants. According to White (1844) "the premises were surrendered to new trustees in 1754 and again in 1808". The net income of the trust was applied to the education of the poor children of the town. For a period in the middle of last century the brothers Richard and Newson Garrett were joint trustees.

The trade of Slaughden continued to decline. The landing of coal for the gasworks opened in 1855 continued for nearly fifty years, but with a gradual decline until the last cargo was discharged in 1904. The local retail coal merchants had mostly transferred their allegiance to the railway. Only the brickworks continued to land the occasional coal cargo at its own jetty.

There had, however, been an altogether different attempt to promote Aldeburgh's links with the sea. The Aldeborough Pier & Improvement Co. Ltd was formed in the eighteen-seventies to construct a pier opposite the Moot Hall. As first designed the pier was to extend 145 yards out to sea at a width of 20 feet, with a clear height of not less than 13 feet above high water level. Work was begun on building the pier, but was dropped before the basic structure was complete. In 1884 the powers to build were extended, as was the intended length of the pier itself, to 204 yards. At the same time a pier pavilion, without which no self-respecting pier of the time was thought to be properly dressed, was authorized. The powers were transferred by the Act from the old company to John Hazel Fuller, who had an address in the City of London.

The new owner proved no more effective in completing the pier than was the old company. The uncompleted pier remained a rusty reproach. It was struck and damaged by the three-masted

The abandoned remains of Aldeburgh pier c1880–90.
Burns Collection

auxiliary steamer *Winifred*, which left behind as a memento the large iron anchor still to be seen on the beach near the Moot Hall. In 1892 Kelly noted that "a pier commenced and left unfinished has been since removed". Some indeed had gone, thanks to the *Winifred*, but the crumbling remains were not finally disposed of until Dr Elizabeth Garrett Anderson's period as mayor over ten years later.

Had the pier ever been completed it had been intended that it should serve as a landing point for goods and passengers as well as a promenade, as is apparent from the tariff appended to the Act. In fact the only sustained paddle steamer traffic to pass Aldeburgh was the Belle steamer service from London Bridge to Yarmouth. The ships were run by the London, Woolwich & Clacton-on-Sea Steamboat Company, which began its services in 1890 and was reconstituted as Belle Steamers Limited in 1897, by which time Aldeburgh Pier had long been abandoned to dereliction.

There have been no licensed pilots at Aldeburgh since the last, E. E. Gibbs, died in 1946 after twenty-four years as a pilot. When pilotage was at its peak in the first decade of the last century there were nearly fifty, but from about 1810 a decline set in.

In the eighteen-fifties and sixties and probably for some while after that Newson Garrett, as the agent for Lloyd's in Aldeburgh, had charge of the local pilots. In 1862 he and some others bought the forty-year-old smack *Two Brothers* (25 tons); Newson Garrett had ten of the sixty-four shares. The smack was lengthened, probably by Newson Garrett's own shipwright, John Felgate, at Snape. The vessel is believed to have been used to enable pilots to cruise off Aldeburgh in search of ships requiring pilotage.

The decline in pilotage, was, however, attributable to causes out of the control of the pilots themselves or of any person appointed to manage or lead them. Especially it was the result of the decline of the small sailing coaster in the face of competition on the one hand from sailing barges and on the other hand from steamers, while at the same time all classes of coastal ships were losing freights to the railway. Aldeburgh was not alone in losing its coastal trade.

Perhaps we may close the chapter on a lighter note. The annual regatta was essentially something belonging to the beach fraternity. By the nineteen-twenties it was beginning to totter sufficiently to make some of the non-seagoing townsmen feel that it needed a little extra support. A group, of whom the Butcher brothers Owen and Clifford were leading figures, decided that a street carnival was what was needed, and in 1927 this was put on. On one float Bert Ward was Father Neptune crossing the line while on another G. Reader was a drag Queen Neptune. The success of what initially began as a lark by a few spirited young men was so marked that in 1929 they were persuaded to do it again.

Cliff Butcher decided that if there could be carnival queens there could be carnival kings. That year, therefore, Aldeburgh had its first and only carnival king, but the next year habit reasserted itself and May Bottrill was crowned as carnival queen. The years 1931, 1932 and 1933 were overshadowed by the Slump and particularly by the closure of the Garrett works at Leiston, but in 1934 there was again a carnival, followed by another in 1936 and a third in 1938. In 1937, in the gap between two carnivals, there was a regatta sports.

The carnival had by then become established as a biennial event, but in 1940 there was no question of its being held, nor in 1942 or 1944 either, and it did not survive. But, as Dick Smith remarked, they were good carnivals while they lasted and their post-war successors have ably upheld the tradition they established.

A contemporary member of the crew of the James Cable and member of a long-standing fishing family, Eric Strowger, of Aldeburgh. Ron Smith

The Lifeboat   4

A SIDE from the private activities of the beachmen in saving life there have been four public lifeboat stations on the coastal strip, Sizewell, Thorpeness, Aldeburgh and Orford.

In one sense the lifeboat service derived from the activities of the beach companies. As to manning, seamanship and to some extent location of the stations, they could certainly be said to follow closely upon the companies, but as to finances and primary objectives they followed a separate path.

Since the beachmen received no remuneration for their work other than salvage payments, lifesaving was not their primary objective. At times gratitude on the part of those plucked from the sea may have led them to reward their saviours, but often the saved were penniless sailors rendered destitute by their shipwreck, so that it was to the salvage money that beachmen had to look for their livelihood.

Nevertheless there were numerous instances when they put to sea in the most impossible conditions, with no hope of earning salvage money but only of saving life; nor were cases lacking where they had been faced with the choice of a vessel or a crew and had without hesitation chosen to save a crew. In an age short on compassion, the conduct of the beachmen toward ships' crews in peril displayed a level of morality and certainly of personal courage that placed them well ahead of most of their fellow citizens.

The first attempt to design a lifeboat as such was made by Lionel Lukin, a London coachbuilder and a native of Dunmow, Essex. In 1785 he designed and subsequently patented what he called an "unimmergible boat", but it was twenty years before his first boat was in service. On the Suffolk coast a subscription was raised on the instigation of Mr Robert Sparrow, a wealthy summer resident of Lowestoft, and the Reverend Francis Bowness, rector of Gunton, to have a lifeboat built for Lowestoft. This was only the sixth to be built by Henry Greathead, a South Shields boatbuilder who was the first to produce boats intended specifically for lifesaving; the others were three for the Northumberland coast, one for St Andrews in Scotland and one for Oporto. Other promoters envisaged a similar boat at Bawdsey, and it was proposed that a third boat should be stationed at either Southwold, Dunwich or Aldeburgh.

It was unfortunate that the leaders in the project had failed to consult the men to whom they had of necessity to look for a crew, and who would have had the task of launching the boat from the open beach in the face of onshore gales. These men, who would put to sea in almost any weather in a yawl, would have no truck with the Greathead boat, which they considered unsafe and unworkable.

In the summer of 1807 Lionel Lukin happened to spend a holiday in Lowestoft, where, given his interest in the subject, the question of lifeboat design suitable for the Suffolk coastline almost inevitably came up for discussion between him and the local beachmen. Seemingly with help, judging by the degree of literacy displayed, the beachmen wrote a letter to Robert Sparrow (Mr Bowness having died in 1801), saying that they would be willing to serve in a lifeboat of Lukin's type, provided it had been proved in trials. With the sizable sum left from the original fund plus some new money a boat of Lukin's design was ordered from Batchelor Barcham, a Lowestoft boatbuilder, who built it under Lukin's supervision. This boat, subsequently named the *Frances Ann*, became very successful.

Meanwhile Robert Sparrow had been the main instrument in the inauguration of the Suffolk Humane Society, formed at a meeting in the public room of the King's Head, Kessingland, on 7th January, 1806. This society maintained lifeboats at Lowestoft and Pakefield until 1873, when control was handed over to the Royal National Lifeboat Institution (RNLI). Matters remained fragmented until the formation in 1824 of the Suffolk Association for Saving the Lives of Shipwrecked Seamen, designed to co-ordinate the volunteer lifeboats which by then existed at Land-guard, Bawdsey and Lowestoft. In the autumn of 1824 the association arranged for the management of its lifeboats to be by districts, namely Ipswich, Aldeburgh and Lowestoft, and before the year was out had decided to place a lifeboat at Orford. The association further took the decision to pay for service in the lifeboat at a fixed rate of half a guinea a day, or five shillings a day on exercises.

The Orford boat was built by Plenty of Newbury, Berkshire, at a cost of £168. It was delivered early in 1826 and launched formally from the beach in March of that year, when it was named *Grafton*. Unlike the boats used to the north the *Grafton* was not of the Norfolk and Suffolk type developed from Lukin's basic design, drawing upon the beachmen's yawls, but was of Plenty's own design. It was followed by a second and identical boat from the same builder, ordered for use at Sizewell Gap as a result of the successful trials of the *Grafton*.

Because of incomplete early records it is not possible to cite the tally of rescues accomplished by the two boats, though it is recorded of the Sizewell boat that in 1841 she rescued the crew of

the sloop *Catherina*, in trouble while carrying a cargo of potatoes from Goole to London; with help from Thorpe, probably by Josh Chard, she succeeded in taking the *Catherina* into Yarmouth. The *Grafton* was transferred from Orford to Woodbridge Haven some time before 1838; on 19th November that year she rescued the crew of four of the Newcastle sloop *Friendship*. The *Grafton's* sister boat continued in service at Sizewell Gap, but with the changing pattern of inshore fishing it became increasingly difficult to find a crew and the boat was accordingly transferred to Aldeburgh in 1851, founding a station that continues to the present.

The peripatetic *Grafton* served at Woodbridge Haven until 1853, when the station was closed. She was not withdrawn from service, despite having then been in use for twenty-seven years, but was used instead to set up a station at Thorpeness.

These changes were the result of the Suffolk Association for Preserving the Lives of Shipwrecked Mariners having passed over control of its services to the RNLI. The ex-Sizewell boat with which the Aldeburgh station was established, under Coxswain Sam Ward, was launched on Boxing Day, 1852, to attempt the rescue of the crew of eight of the Newcastle collier brig *Corinthian*, but the vessel

Lifeboatmen, clad in the old-type cork lifejackets, parading on the Crag Path during an Aldeburgh regatta.

27

broke up before the boat could reach it, and the crew were all lost. The use of the old Sizewell boat was a stopgap measure while a new one was under construction by Forrestt of Limehouse to Peake's self-righting design, 32 feet long; the new lifeboat was delivered in 1853. In 1860 she was sent back to her makers to be lengthened to 39 feet, but was sold out of service in 1870. For the last four years of her service she carried the name *Pasco*.

Immediately prior to rebuilding, the boat was involved in a serious accident while attempting to go to the assistance of a brig in a dangerous position just off the town on 21st December, 1859. Between half past two in the morning, when the first distress signals were seen, and daybreak three attempts were made to launch the boat, all ending in failure. As light dawned the fourth attempt seemed to be succeeding. By hauling hard on the haul-off warp the crew managed to get the boat as far as the inner shoal, only to have the boat turn broadside on to the waves as she passed over the shoal. While she was thus exposed a huge sea struck her, filled her with water and turned her over. Only one man of the fifteen on board managed to cling to a thwart and stay with her as she righted. Nine others flung into the sea nevertheless managed to climb back into her. One of the five left in the sea, named Pearse, was badly injured and probably had no hope; he was drowned. Of the other four, two reached the beach and were hauled ashore but Thomas Cable, grandfather of a later coxswain, James Cable, after whom the present boat is named, and P. F. Green, one of the Aldeburgh pilots, were carried north as far as Thorpe before they could be got out of the sea. Tom Cable was still alive when pulled ashore but died soon afterwards.

Notwithstanding the distrust of the beachmen for the "roly-polies" the *George Hounsfield*, which replaced the *Pasco*, was another self-righter. The new boat, built by Forrestt of Limehouse, lasted until 1890. It was in this boat that James Cable was appointed second coxswain to Charles Ward in 1880. After she was paid off Cable bought her and she lay on the beach at Aldeburgh for many years as a net store. He was appointed first coxswain in 1888 in succession to Charles Ward and was soon laying the foundation of a most distinguished career.

His first call was on 3rd November, 1888, to the barque *Flora* from Åland, then Russian but now in Finland. The crew were taken off by the Dunwich lifeboat *Ann Ferguson*, and the *George Hounsfield* returned, so to speak, empty-handed. She was soon to be involved in a rescue that demonstrated the mettle of her crew and the seamanship of her new coxswain. The vessel in distress this time was the German steamer *Sirius*, whose cargo of roadstone had shifted. Early on 4th November, 1888, the watch saw a flare from the Thorpe direction and the gun was fired to summon the crew of the lifeboat. Led by James Cable and the second coxswain Bill Mann, the *George Hounsfield* got off into heavy surf and inky darkness, but the sky lightened as they rowed north and they were able to make out the shape of a steamer on the seaward side of the outer shoal. While they watched, she was carried over the shoal and into the deeper water on the landward side. The Thorpe lifeboat *Ipswich* had also launched, but had insufficient depth of water to pass through the shoals. The outer shoal was very nearly the undoing of the *George Hounsfield*. As James Cable took her across, a gigantic sea submerged her and almost took the crew out of her. However, she survived and the coxswain faced the further task of getting alongside the steamer, which was sheering violently and already listing from the shift of cargo. By perseverance and the exercise of extreme skill it was accomplished. In the midst of the

Launching the George Hounsfield from the beach, 1872.
Courtesy Burns Collection; photo by Charles Clarke

drama and the tumult there came a rare moment of light relief. When the coxswain asked the number on board back came the answer "Sixteen—fifteen men and a cat", at which, tired and tense as they were, the lifeboatmen had to laugh. All were saved and the cat joined the household of one of the lifeboatmen.

The *George Hounsfield* was to answer a third call within a week. About eight in the evening on 7th November James Cable and Charles Ward were walking in the gale on the shore when they saw a light, followed by rockets, from the direction of Thorpeness. When the lifeboat reached the distressed vessel it proved to be the Swedish barque *Prudentia* on passage from Christiania (Oslo) to Bristol. The position and circumstances were almost identical to those in which the *Sirius* had been wrecked. The Thorpeness men were unable to launch and the coastguard had been unable to get a rocket line aboard owing to the distance.

The *Prudentia* was broadside to the sea, which was sweeping the decks. The first attempt to take off the crew was made by dropping an anchor to windward and bringing the lifeboat up to the weather side of the wreck, but this was defeated by the seas, one of which almost put the lifeboat on the *Prudentia's* deck and another of which hurled it against her side with such ferocity that James Cable was all but thrown overboard by the impact.

His second strategy was to run the lifeboat past the bows of the barque so that the seamen could drop into it from the jibboom, but this was broken. All the while the barque was being driven closer and closer to the shore. This encouraged the coastguard to make another attempt with the rocket apparatus, and as the lifeboatmen picked up their anchor they were nearly struck by a rocket which hit the water a few feet from the *George Hounsfield's* stern.

Shaken but undeterred, Cable took the boat closer to the shore and again anchored, veering down toward the *Prudentia* but keeping well to the lee of her for fear the gale would carry away a mast on to the boat. When he judged he was in position to come alongside the barque's quarter there was a final great effort to get it into position for the ship's crew of ten to jump. The first man to jump accidentally kicked a lifeboatman in the face, fortunately without breaking his nose. When all had been taken off the lifeboatmen hauled in the anchor, got up the sails and as the anchor was weighed sailed clear of the broken water close hauled on the starboard tack. Once in deep water Cable came about and headed back to Aldeburgh on the port tack, arriving on the beach after midnight.

The boat with which James Cable was most identified, however, was the ill-starred *Aldeburgh* (RNLI ON 304). Yielding to the opinions of the Aldeburgh beachmen the RNLI commissioned as a replacement for the *George Hounsfield* a Norfolk & Suffolk type, longer and broader than its predecessor, with fourteen oars instead of twelve. The builder was J. H. Critten of Yarmouth. The boat was used under Coxswain James Cable and Second Coxswain Bill Mann. By the day that brought her career to an end the *Aldeburgh* had had fifty-four launches on service and had saved 152 lives.

The day of her end was 7th December, 1899. Cable and Mann were both ill at home but turned out when they heard that guns could be heard at sea to the southward. Notwithstanding his influenza Cable was in his oilskins putting on his lifebelt when seen by his doctor and told, in terms sufficiently forthright that he obeyed them, to go home. His place was taken by his immediate predecessor, Charles Ward.

The other places in the boat were eagerly contested, and another former coxswain, Charles Crisp, raised a laugh by climbing on to the shoulders of one of the crowd and being passed over their heads to the boat. Though the launching party got the boat off successfully, the crew were unable to haul her over the inner shoal by means of the haul-off warp and in consequence had to set sail while she was still within the shoal. Because of the size of the seas they had trouble as they endeavoured to sweat the foresail up tight. At the south end of the town Charles Ward decided to cross the shoal, gradually working the boat through the broken water almost broadside to the waves as they broke over the shoal. When they were on the outer part of the shoal two or three exceptionally heavy seas broke into the boat. The acting coxswain shouted a warning to the crew to hold on as a further and even larger wave approached the boat.

The Aldeburgh *lying on Aldeburgh beach after the 1899 disaster in which seven men were lost. The hole cut in the hull in an effort to release those trapped underneath can be seen, as can a spar used in an attempt to lever up the heavy boat. RNLI; photo by Clarke of Aldeburgh*

Cable, despite the doctor's instructions, had remained on the beach, following the boat southwards. He saw the great wave crash on to the boat, totally submerging her. Under the huge weight of water the starboard padding sank deeper into the water and in slow motion she turned over. For an instant she lay with her sails level with the water, then the masts parted and she rolled right over. Cable saw it all and was later to give a precise account to the Board of Trade inquiry.

Charles Ward had sprung up as the boat went over and flung himself clear, but six men were trapped under the upturned boat as she drove ashore. The others, by one means or another, either swam or floated clear in that brief pause before she turned right over. The waves cast Charles Ward in his cork lifejacket up on to the beach, in his own words "like an old cork fender". His only thoughts were for the rest of the crew. Dragging off the lifejacket, he went back into the water to assist in the rescue. Coxswain Cable tried to extricate the men caught under the boat. While other men, and at least one woman, pulled the survivors from the sea, spars and capstan bars were used in an endeavour to raise the boat, but it weighed thirteen tons and the effort was in vain. Cable had a hole hacked in the bottom of the boat but it, too, was a vain effort. One man was got out from under the fore part of the boat too far gone for the doctor to revive him. One of the rescued men died three months after the accident from the effects of that night. None of the six trapped under the boat survived, and it took several hours of hard work to extricate the bodies.

Charles Ward's bravery and dedication earned him a second service clasp to the Silver Medal for gallantry which he had been awarded in 1894 for having climbed into the rigging of a sunken ship to lower down a crewman marooned there by a broken leg. A fund was set up in the town to help the dependants of the dead men; the RNLI gave £1,350, besides rewarding some others who had done well at the rescue.

The work of the station had to go on despite the accident. To take the place of the *Aldeburgh* the RNLI sent another Yarmouth-built Norfolk and Suffolk type, a year older than the lost boat and built by Beeching for the RNLI station at Winterton. It was in this boat that the Aldeburgh men went to the succour of the steamer *Hylton*, of London, barely two months after the disaster. Not only was the launch made in the shadow of the disaster but also into the heaviest seas remembered up to that time on the Aldeburgh station, seas which, moreover, extended as far out as could be seen from the shore. James Cable had thought that he might have had trouble getting a crew. In the event there was no hesitation on the part of any.

The boat commissioned from Thames Ironworks to replace

the *Aldeburgh* was possibly the apotheosis of the improved Norfolk and Suffolk type and the largest sailing lifeboat in service. There can have been few better boats afloat in her time. Forty-six feet long and fourteen in the beam, with twelve oars, she cost the then unprecedented sum of £2,640, raised by a special lifeboat fund in Winchester. On 23rd July, 1903, the new boat was named by Lady Winchester *City of Winchester*; she had in fact been in service since the previous year, known only by her number, ON 482.

Five boats served at Thorpeness after the *Grafton*. That which followed the *Grafton* in 1855 was a self-righter built by Beeching in 1852 and transferred from Boulmer. Before arriving at Thorpeness she was rebuilt (1854–55) by Forrestt.

In 1862 she was replaced by the first of three boats to carry the name *Ipswich*. A self-righter, like all the boats stationed at Thorpeness, she was from Forrestt's yard at Limehouse, but in 1870 her place was taken by the former *Leicester*, another Forrestt-built boat previously at Gorleston from the time she was built in 1866. After only three years at Thorpe she was once more transferred, this time to Skegness, and her place was taken by the third *Ipswich*, again from Forrestt but a larger boat. When her turn

Launching the City of Winchester *by the haul-off warp (left) assisted by a push pole (right) pushed by the beach party.* Burns Collection

46686. ALDEBURGH: LAUNCHING THE "CITY OF WINCHESTER"

came for replacement in 1890 the new vessel, the *Christopher North Graham*, also came from Forrestt. By 1900, with the decline in inshore fishing and pilotage at Thorpeness, it had become very difficult to crew the boat and the station was closed. During its period of operation the Thorpeness station saved ninety-three lives.

For three years, 1860–63, Thorpe had been able to support a No 2 boat, a small self-righter built by Forrestt in 1855 and previously at Newcastle, County Down. Much smaller than her contemporary on No 1 station, she was only 26 feet long.

In 1903 the station at Dunwich, which had like Thorpe begun to experience a shrinking of the pool of working fishermen from which it had drawn its crew, was closed. Thus Aldeburgh to the south and Southwold to the north were called upon to provide cover which had previously been provided by the two intermediate stations. Southwold already had two boats and the decision was taken to provide a second boat at Aldeburgh also. Out of a legacy from the will of Edmond Dresden of Mayfair, London, the RNLI commissioned a Liverpool type boat from the Thames Ironworks which was given the name *Edward Z. Dresden*, that of the father of Edmond Dresden.

The pattern of the shipping passing Aldeburgh in the first decade of this century had changed markedly from fifty years before. The trend was to fewer and larger vessels, and these were on the whole more seaworthy than the brigs and snows and other small sailing ships that had contributed on such a lavish scale to the toll of wrecks on the East Anglian coast. By way of balance, however, as the number of smaller commercial sailing craft declined there was a yearly increase in the numbers of small sailing yachts.

An era of another sort and of great distinction came to an end in August, 1917, when James Cable retired from his position as Chief Coxswain of the No 1 boat. His place was taken by Charles Mann, who had been second coxswain since the death in 1903 of his father, Bill Mann, the previous holder of the post. James Cable was the type of man from whom legends arise. Apart from his work with the boat, which had earned him three RNLI Silver Medals, the Norwegian Silver Medal and the Royal Humane Society Medal for Life Saving, he had in addition three times been awarded the Royal Humane Society Thanks on Vellum for saving life from the shore.

He was a prodigious swimmer. On one occasion he rescued a young woman, cook at a house in the town, who had gone bathing against his advice and got into difficulties. When she called for help he was working on the beach and dived in fully clad, including even his deck boots, to make a successful rescue. He had already, on separate occasions, saved from drowning each of the three daughters of the young cook's employer.

After his retirement from the position of coxswain James Cable served as a member of the Aldeburgh station committee.

The *City of Winchester* remained in service until the end of 1928, when she was withdrawn with a record of forty-three missions and forty lives saved. Temporarily the station received the *James Leath* (ON 607), another Thames Ironworks boat, dating from 1910, similar to but at 42 feet in length and 12 feet 6 inches in the beam smaller than the *City of Winchester*. This boat had already seen a lengthy period of service at Caister. In 1929 the *Edward Z. Dresden* was withdrawn from No 2 station, the temporary replacement being again a Thames Ironworks product, the *Hugh Taylor* (ON 629), built in 1912 and previously in use at Pakefield. When the permanent replacement arrived at No 1 station the *Hugh Taylor* was transferred to Kessingland and the *James Leath* became Aldeburgh No 2 boat.

Although all the earlier Aldeburgh boats had been sailing and pulling types the policy of the RNLI was to use powered boats as replacements wherever possible. The question mark over Aldeburgh was whether or not a motor lifeboat, necessarily heavier than a pulling and sailing boat, could be launched successfully off the beach. The RNLI wisely concluded that practical experiments

Reserve No 1 ex Margaret *on No 1 station 1899–1902.* SPS

35

should be carried out, and a 43-foot Watson class boat, the *William MacPherson*, formerly stationed at Campbeltown, was sent to Aldeburgh, arriving on 10th February, 1930; a series of launching trials conducted in diverse types of weather resulted in the broad conclusion that a powered boat at Aldeburgh was feasible.

The information gathered was used as the basis of design for a new class of motor lifeboats known initially as the Aldeburgh class, later changed to the Beach type, designed specifically for stations which had to launch from the beach. The first of the type arrived on the Aldeburgh No 1 station on 12th December, 1931. Forty-one feet overall and 12 feet 3 inches in the beam, she was not a self-righter. She was fitted with two 35-horsepower AEC Weyburn petrol engines which made her capable of seven and half knots in favourable seas. She did not have to wait long for an opportunity for a launch in service. On 9th January, 1932, the Swedish steamer *Polaris* ran ashore on Sizewell Bank and the new lifeboat was launched to render assistance; the ship was successfully got off the bank.

The cost of the boat was met out of a bequest in the will of Mrs Jane Elizabeth King, of St Leonards-on-Sea, Sussex. Her son-in-law, Abdy Beauclerk, a regular visitor to Aldeburgh, had been much moved by witnessing the launch of the *Aldeburgh* in

The William Macpherson, *temporarily stationed at Aldeburgh in 1930 to ascertain the feasibility of launching a motor lifeboat off the beach. The crew are (left to right) Dan Wilson, Hector Burrell, unknown, Billy Green, "Cork" Burrill, unknown, George Chalton.*
Burns Collection

circumstances of great bravery on the part of the crew to go to the assistance of the Russian barque *Venscapen* on 20th November, 1893. Abdy Beauclerk had had a campelling desire thenceforward to bestow a new lifeboat on Aldeburgh, but his premature death in 1912 frustrated his efforts. It was thus Mrs King who provided the boat.

The new lifeboat, as well as the crew and the town, were honoured when His Royal Highness Prince George, later to be Duke of Kent, agreed to name the new boat *Abdy Beauclerk*. The service of dedication, followed by the naming ceremony, took place on 27th May, 1932, and the Prince later went afloat in the lifeboat with the coxswain, J. H. Pead, who had been one of the crew of the *Aldeburgh* at the launch which had had such an effect on Abdy Beauclerk.

The *James Leath* survived as Aldeburgh No 2 until 1936, when she gave place to the *Baltic* (ON 665), a Liverpool-type boat with fourteen oars built by S. E. Saunders of Cowes in 1916 and previously in service at Wells. By the time war broke out in 1939 Aldeburgh was one of only two East Anglian stations still equipped with sailing and pulling boats; the other was Caister. The end came at Aldeburgh with the delivery from Groves & Guttridge of Cowes in 1940 of the 35 feet 6 inches motor Liverpool-type boat *Lucy Lavers*.

The *Abdy Beauclerk* performed the first war service by any lifeboat in Britain a week after war broke out when the 8,640 ton *Magdapur*, of the Brocklebank line, struck a German mine which broke her back and left her in a sinking condition. When the *Abdy Beauclerk* arrived on the scene a dozen survivors were still in the sea or in one of the ship's own boats. These men were picked up, covered in black oil. The other survivors had been taken aboard three steamers that were standing by and were taken ashore by the lifeboat, together with the body of the second officer, one of the six killed in the incident. A fortnight later the 3,500 ton French coal carrier *Phryne* was sunk on her way from Immingham to Bayonne and the lifeboat picked up the twenty-four-man crew from the ship's boats.

The injured from these two incidents were tended by Dr Robin Acheson, the honorary surgeon to the Aldeburgh lifeboat station, but when the lifeboat was called out on 23rd November in response to a message that a man was floating in a lifebuoy about two miles off Shingle Street it was his wife, Doctor Nora, who went out in the lifeboat in case medical help was needed. Sadly no one was found, only floating wreckage being located.

Both the boats took part in the excavation of Dunkirk in the opening days of June, 1940. The *Abdy Beauclerk* and the newly delivered *Lucy Lavers* were handed over to crews of Royal Navy

The Abdy Beauclerk
*(1931–1959) in the
centre of a peaceful
scene. At any time, day or
night, the firing of the
maroon would have
transformed it into urgent
but orderly activity.*

men at Dover. In all seventeen RNLI boats took part in the transfer of British and French forces from Dunkirk to Britain, but no details survive of what the two Aldeburgh boats actually did.

Once back on station the *Lucy Lavers* was called out to her first service on 11th August, 1940, when the London tanker *Oil Trader* was set on fire in an attack by German aircraft about seven miles to the south of Aldeburgh. It was also the *Lucy Lavers* that saved Bob Roberts and his crew of two from the boomie barge *Martinet*, taking in water in a south-south-easterly gale and very heavy swell off Orfordness. The barbed wire and scaffolding shore defences on the beach impeded the launch and had to be cleared to make way for the boat. The coastguard reported the distress signals at 5 am on 27th February, 1941, but because of the shore defences it took an hour and a half to get the boat away. Meanwhile the crew of the *Martinet* worked desperately at the pumps to keep her afloat, as Bob Roberts was to relate years later in a radio programme, when he recounted also the total relief they had felt as the lifeboat approached.

It is not only in wartime and in stormy weather that lifeboatmen face danger. It was during the hauling up operation after a practice launch on 2nd November, 1955, that the *Abdy Beauyclerk* became involved in an accident with potentially serious consequences. During the launching operation the main securing chain, used to hold the boat on its cradle at the head of the beach, became fouled under the keel. It was freed and the operation of hauling the boat up the slipway went ahead, but unknown to the crew a link in the chain had been damaged. As the boat was hauled on to the cradle of the turntable at the head of the beach she was secured by bow and stern wires and the turntable was rotated so that the bows of the boat pointed seaward. All this was standard procedure. Once it was done the main securing chain was attached to the stern, the bow wire was let go and the boat was eased forward a short distance so that she was poised for the next launch, with the load taken by the securing chain.

As the chain took the full load of the boat the damaged link parted and the boat relaunched herself. The launching party, in the second or two available, did everything they could think of to stop her, but to no avail. With great presence of mind sixteen-year-old John Sharman, one of the helpers and son of Horace Sharman, the boat's motor mechanic, hung on to one of the lifelines as she entered the sea and managed to haul himself aboard. Had the boat gone afloat unmanned she would have been in danger of striking the groynes, but John steered her seaward and northward until the No 2 boat could be launched to put some crew on board with him. The *Lucy Lavers* then towed the *Abdy* clear of the groynes and beached her. Through John's action there was only superficial damage from bumping a groyne. Subsequently the RNLI sent him a letter of appreciation of his courage and determination and an award in cash.

Probably the most extraordinary service performed by the *Abdy Beauclerk* in a career full of incident was in connection with the Norwegian fishing vessel *Jenco II*. It began with a telephone call not long after midnight on 8th August, 1957, from the coastguard to the late Tom Riggs, the Aldeburgh honorary secretary of the RNLI, reporting that the *Jenco II* was adrift near the Shipwash Sands (which lie on a north-south line from a point off Bawdsey to the entrance of the port of Harwich), with three men aboard, one of whom was the skipper, drunk and armed with a pistol. The police were called and at 1.58 am the lifeboat was launched, carrying with her Sergeant Tukesbury of Aldeburgh and Inspector Moore and another policeman brought by car. Coxswain John Burrell took the *Abdy Beauclerk* alongside the fishing boat so that the three policemen could board it. The captain was in the wheelhouse, still drunk but not violent, and they were able to coax him below to the cabin. At the request of the police Billy Burrell,

*Billy Burrell,
undoubtedly one of the
great lifeboatmen of the
east coast.*
Photo by Wendy Turner

then Second Coxswain, took the wheel and with another member of the lifeboat crew on board set course for Harwich, accompanied by the lifeboat. Even after their arrival at 6.30 am the incident was not over, as they spent another three hours or so transferring police to or from the *Jenco II* before being free to return to Aldeburgh, where they arrived at twenty minutes after midday.

During the summer of 1958, on 26th July, the *Abdy Beauclerk* performed what was to be her last service when she went out to the Shipwash Sand to assist the yacht *Scylla*, which was lying alongside after colliding with a French trawler. The yacht's bows were considerably damaged and holed, but it was decided to plug the hole with a spare sail and escort her into Lowestoft.

When the *Abdy Beauclerk* was withdrawn from service at the end of 1958 she was sold for service as a pilot cutter in Cork Harbour. During January an electric capstan was installed for hauling up the new boat, though the old manual capstan was left as a standby. More importantly the decision was taken to abolish the No 2 station once the new boat arrived.

The new and as yet unnamed boat (ON 946) was, like her predecessor, a product of the yard of J. Samuel White at Cowes, but whereas the *Abdy Beauclerk* had cost £6,384 the replacement cost nearly five times that sum. Apart from an increase of a foot in the overall length the new boat was similar to her predecessor, but she was equipped with twin 48-horse-power Gardner diesel engines instead of petrol engines.

The day after the new boat came on to the station the No 2 boat *Lucy Lavers* departed to join the reserve fleet, leaving Aldeburgh, for the first time in nearly fifty-four years, as a single-boat station.

For the first half of 1959 the new boat, provided out of a legacy under the will of Mrs Patience Gottwald, of Southport, was without a name; on 15th July she received at the hands of the Countess of Cairns the name *Alfred & Patience Gottwald*. She was a well-liked boat to which the crew readily adapted, probably because her characteristics followed so closely upon those of the *Abdy Beauclerk*. At the men's specific request, however, she was provided with a mizzen sail for the purpose of steadying her in rough weather. During her career she was launched eighty-four times on service, saving thirty-one lives.

A very memorable service occurred on 10th April, 1972, when the weather and sea conditions underwent a rapid deterioration. All the beach fishing vessels were accounted for bar the 18-foot *Ocean Pride*, with three men on board. When she had still not returned by 10 am Coxswain Reuben Wood and Second Coxswain Billy Burrell, themselves both fishermen of great experience, became very anxious as to her safety in the face of the south-south-easterly wind, already at force 7 and continuing to increase, with frequent squalls, and visibility often no more than 250 yards. At five past ten they fired the maroon and at ten past the boat was launched, turning southward towards where the *Ocean Pride* was expected to be found.

About a mile south of the town they came up with her and passed lifejackets to the crew. With the wind by that time up to force 9 Reuben Wood decided to keep close while the *Ocean Pride* crossed the shoals, above which the seas were particularly violent. Closely followed by the lifeboat she passed over the outer shoal successfully, but as she tried to cross the inner shoal she was overwhelmed by a very large wave. From the lifeboat Reuben

41

Wood saw her first lost to view by reason of the wave and then with her bows flung high into the air as she went down by the stern.

Because the lifeboat was following closely only seconds elapsed before she was on the spot where two of the *Ocean Pride's* complement could be seen in the water. In order to create a lee for them he swung the boat until her bows pointed seaward. In the turmoil of the sea the lifeboat was battered violently, momentarily grounding several times because of the shallowness of the water, but the coxswain was able to hold her till the two men were safely aboard and he could attempt to reach the third, thirty yards away and closer to shore. Because the beach was so close he decided that the only possible approach was to take the lifeboat in stern first, notwithstanding the alarming manner in which she was rolling, using the engines to keep her head to sea. A lifebuoy was thrown to the man in the water, but he was too far gone to take it. Despite the imminent danger of running aground and imperilling the boat and crew, Reuben Wood backed the boat up to him until he could be manhandled aboard, the seas meanwhile raking the lifeboat from stem to stern.

As soon as he was sure the rescued man was aboard he took the lifeboat out to deeper water while Nigel Saint, the motor mechanic, gave the nearly drowned man artificial respiration. It was later estimated that he was but a couple of minutes from death when he was pulled from the water. The lifeboat was beached safely and the rescued men were taken to hospital, where they all recovered. For this magnificent feat of seamanship and for his great personal courage Reuben Wood was awarded the RNLI Bronze Medal. Nigel Saint received the RNLI Thanks on Vellum.

Each of them had a record of distinguished services, but what made the service to the *Ocean Pride* special to them above all others was firstly that the lives saved were those of fellow members of their own close-knit beach community and secondly that it had been the result of the intelligent anticipation of events displayed by the coxswain and second coxswain. When Reuben Wood retired in 1978 he had a record of twenty years in the office of coxswain, only exceeded by the period of service of James Cable. Appropriately his successor was Billy Burrell.

Since 1963 the RNLI had been progressively introducing a new and additional type of inshore lifeboat to deal with incidents which demanded instant reaction and high speed and which were capable of being dealt with by a vessel of more modest capabilities than a full-scale lifeboat. These inshore rescue boats were inflatables, fitted with a 40-horse-power outboard motor and capable of about 20 knots, operated by a helmsman and one other. Such a craft, D-111, was sent to Aldeburgh in July, 1977. Before the crew had had time to complete their training on 17th August it had its first service and, moreover, in very onerous conditions.

About a quarter past eight in the morning the coastguard reported a yacht in trouble and firing red flares about half a mile out to sea. Heavy seas were running and it was decided to launch the *Alfred & Patience Gottwald*. The maroon was fired and the crew assembled, but because of the very low water the lifeboat failed to clear the beach on launching and was caught by the surf and swung round until she was bows to shore. While the urgent recovery operations were in progress fresh flares were fired by the yachtsman.

There was an immediate conference on the beach, as a result of which it was decided, despite the conditions being worse than those stipulated as the inshore boat's limitations, to launch it to assist the yacht. John Marjoram, the helmsman, with Douglas Cook as second man, and a number of other crewmen and helpers took the boat down to the water, the saturated shore party holding it head to sea until a moment's pause in the breakers enabled the boat to be got away, the two-man crew using oars to get it away from the beach. The seas were filling the boat as the engine was started, fortunately at the first attempt. John Marjoram took it some distance south between the inner shoal and the shore before crossing the shoal and heading for the yacht, which they reached about nine o'clock.

It proved to be the 24-foot *Spreety*, with the owner and his eleven-year-old son aboard. The lifeboatmen brought their boat alongside and took off the boy, who was shortly transferred to a helicopter alerted after the *Alfred & Patience Gottwald* had become immobilised. The inshore boat stayed with the yacht to help. The Harwich lifeboat *Margaret Graham* had been called, but as things turned out she was not needed. At a quarter past nine while the work of recovering the *Alfred & Patience Gottwald* was going on she was lifted by an exceptionally heavy sea. Sizing up the chances in an instant, Reuben Wood put both engines full astern and drove the boat clear of the beach, albeit with the aft cockpit filled wth water. He swung her round and followed the inshore boat southward, reaching the *Spreety* at five to ten. Getting a line aboard, he took the yacht in tow into the River Ore, the inshore boat and crew staying with the yacht until she was in safe water.

This exploit earned a Bronze Medal for John Marjoram. Douglas Cook and Reuben Wood each received a framed Letter of Thanks and a general Letter of Thanks was sent to the crew and shore party who had enabled the inshore boat to get away. It was to be Reuben Wood's last major service before his retirement. The *Alfred & Patience Gottwald* continued under Billy Burrell until 1979; in May that year the RNLI announced that Aldeburgh was to be equipped with a new Rother class self-righting boat from the yard of William Osborne at Littlehampton, Sussex, paid for partly by the Civil Service and Post Office Lifeboat Fund and in part by moneys raised locally in Aldeburgh by the Mayor's Appeal.

For the two years until the arrival of the new boat the duties of the station were carried out by another boat paid for by the Civil Service Fund, the *Charles Dibdin (Civil Service No 32)*, generally similar to her predecessor but fitted with radar. She had previously seen service at Walmer and Eastbourne. The formal hand-over date was 4th August, 1979, after which the *Alfred & Patience Gottwald* joined the relief fleet. Five days after arriving on the station the *Charles Dibdin*, under Coxswain Burrell, saved three men from the cabin cruiser *Cresta* off Sizewell.

On 7th June, 1982, the new lifeboat was delivered to Aldeburgh. His Royal Highness the Duke of Kent had agreed to perform the formal launching ceremony and to name the new boat, as his father had done with the *Abdy Beauclerk* over fifty years before. Whereas, however, in 1931 the formalities observed had

The James Cable, *tenth and latest (at the time of writing) occupant of the No 1 station at Aldeburgh.*
R. Smith—Aldeburgh

been almost entirely to do with protocol and security had taken the form only of a limited police presence, in 1982 protocol rode with a very light rein but the security aspect had to be attended to with considerable if discreet thoroughness. At the ceremony on 20th September the new lifeboat (ON 1068) received the name *James Cable*, honouring the station's celebrated coxswain. William Burrell continued as coxswain until May, 1985, when James Churchyard took over.

Up to the spring of 1988 the *James Cable* had been launched in service twenty-seven times, many of them to help yachts in trouble, though on seven occasions local fishing boats were helped. Lifeboat services are not always to ships or yachts. On 24th October, 1984, she was called to rescue twelve men from the services platform off Sizewell power station, where they had been marooned by the seas resulting from a force 8 south-south-easterly gale. Getting the boat alongside was very difficult; she was damaged and holed, with the

The Dutch schooner Voorwarrts *ashore at Sizewell, 17th January, 1912. The crew were taken off by the Southwold lifeboat.* Courtesy Alfred Corry; Photo by J. S. Waddell

pulpit rail torn off. All twelve men were eventually taken on board, though one man suffered a badly broken leg in the process.

The *James Cable* was the last Rother class boat to be built. When boats of the Rother and Oakley classes come up for renewal they will be replaced by a new class with a higher maximum speed, one of which was sent to Aldeburgh for launching trials in May, 1990.

It would perhaps be appropriate to close this chapter with a necessarily brief mention of shore-based lifesaving equipment. Many wrecks happened directly on the shore, separated from it by the surf but potentially within reach of a line. On some occasions it was possible to get a line aboard by means of the heaving-cane carried in the lifeboat. Such a rescue was made from a brig ashore south of Aldeburgh by James Cable and Charles Ward with a large party of fishermen on 19th January, 1881. There they got their heaving-cane across to the ship, pulled ashore a large rope belonging to the ship herself and then secured it while the beleaguered crew came down it to the beach.

The same morning a schooner ran ashore between the first wreck and Aldeburgh town. The rescue here was made possible by the personal courage and sheer toughness of Cable himself. The ship's crew put a ladder over the side made fast to a line. Cable set out from the shore with a line attached to his body and held by some of the rescue party. As he put it, "I managed to reach the ladder." The line was secured to it, a heavier rope was pulled in by the lighter one and the crew came down it to the shore. The feat of wading and swimming so modestly described was performed in a raging sea in temperatures so low that the River Alde had been frozen over.

Many vessels ashore, however, were too far off to be reached by such methods and in these cases the line-throwing mortar, brought to a practicable form in 1808 by Captain George Manby, an artilleryman and barrack master at the time of Yarmouth, was sometimes used with good effect. This apparatus, placed in the hands first of the Preventive Service and then of the coastguard, which followed it, proved a valuable means of saving lives.

Rockets came into general use as a replacement for the Manby-type mortars about 1855. The first suggestions for the use of rockets to carry lines aboard a wrecked ship had ante-dated Manby's work on the mortar, but the practical foundation of lifesaving rockets had been laid down by John Dennett of Newport, Isle of Wight. The type of rocket subsequently adopted by the Board of Trade for issue to the coastguard and rocket brigades was a two-stage type, the invention of Colonel Boxer; two rockets were combined in one case, the first to lift the appliance to its full elevation, the second to give boost and, consequently, greater range.

Trading and
Tradesmen 5

IT USED to be said that it was always possible to know that one had done a really hard day's labour if a wooden box seemed a comfortable seat at the end of it. Plain wooden seats were the countryman's rule, for farmer and labourer alike. Stools of elm or yew or beech, mostly locally made, were widely used in conjunction with settles and forms. Plain wood was cheap and strong and gave no harbour to vermin.

Other ranks of society, however, fell gradually to the lure of upholstery. By the eighteenth century the great master chairmakers were providing the houses of the prosperous with padded seats and cushions to their chairs, the fashion being speedily taken up by their lesser followers.

Many of the new buyers of upholstery looked for the outward forms of the expensive padded furniture that had been created for the upper classes, but at a price they could afford. Factory-made textile coverings proliferated, and horsehair, which had become the traditional material for seat pads, was eked out by the use of other animal hair, by flocks, by vegetable fibres and even, in the cheapest pieces, wood shavings.

Vegetable fibres on the whole lacked resilience, tended to become brittle and broke up too soon, as well as containing leaf material which deteriorated into dust. It was discovered, however, that the dried fronds of eel-grass, *Zostera marina*, a marine plant growing in the Alde, gave a fairly durable fibre that could be formed into pads suitable for the arms and backs of chairs and sometimes for seats. Dried eel-grass, described in the trade as "alva", was in appearance not unlike a coarse shag tobacco.

Alva formerly occurred in large quantities on the north bank of the Alde in Friston parish. *English Botany* (1869), edited by John T. Bowell Syme, noted that it was common and generally distributed, growing "on sandy and muddy seashores in bays and inlets and at mouths of rivers near or below low water mark". As far as the Alde and most of the coast of Suffolk is concerned, it has now totally disappeared. F. W. Simpson in his *Flora of Suffolk*, 1982, considers this is probably the result of disease. *English Botany* says of it:

The leaves are very tough and flexible when dry and are collected on many parts of our coast . . . for a stuffing material for mattresses, cushions, etc. for which purpose they answer well for a time, but are not durable and absorb moisture from the air.

Only the best of the alva that was harvested went into upholstery. Inferior grasses were used in large quantities for packing around earthenware and china in transit.

For many years, certainly as far back as the eighteen-eighties, the Alde alva harvest was in the hands of Robert Watson, who farmed Rushmere Lodge at Friston. The trade was of sufficient importance for him to describe himself as "farmer and alva merchant". So far as is known the harvesting of alva was dropped during the 1914–18 war and not resumed.

Other trades in the area were less exotic and did not attract notice outside the district, though the Leiston tailor Charles Geater enjoyed a wider reputation for his "patent waterproof Roquelaures for gentlemen and Capes for ladies" during the eighteen-sixties and seventies. A roquelaure was a cloak reaching to about the knees popular in the eighteenth century, in decline by the second half of the last and hastened to all but extinction by the Burberry raincoat and its imitators. The Geater business, originally Gooch and Geater, was already listed as making "waterproof garments" in 1845. Aside from his activities as a tailor and inventor Charles Geater and his daughter were noted for their amateur musical talents.

Another Leiston village craftsman who attracted notice, if not in some quarters approval, was Nathaniel Andrews, the shoemaker. Nathaniel lived and worked at a cottage in Foundry Lane, now renamed Dinsdale Road. Like many of his craft Nathaniel was in his politics a firebrand, and his home was a focal point for the political radicals of the district, prominent among whom was Joseph Belmoor, a Garrett wheelwright and a founder of the Leiston Co-operative Society. Belmoor, whose daughter had married Nathaniel's son Francis, also employed at Leiston Works, had been a prominent figure, along with his son-in-law, in the 1871 strike at the Garrett works which sought and failed to obtain the introduction of the fifty-four-hour working week. All three were admirers of Joseph Arch, whose attempt to unionize the agricultural workers of East Anglia as a step towards improving their precarious standards of living failed, just as the Garrett strike had failed.

Agriculture continued its slow decline until 1879, the worst summer known to any then living; the weather was cold and wet throughout the critical months and much of the East Anglian harvest was never taken at all. There followed a twenty-year slump in farming when poor prices for crops compounded the trouble brought about by a series of summers of indifferent weather.

Politically much blame was heaped upon the successive Liberal governments for their policy of unfettered free trade, which admitted low-priced foreign grain without hindrance. Despite this the Eye division, to which Leiston belonged, doggedly voted Liberal. The policy that depressed farming provided cheap cereals for the industrial population and hence secured itself a broad political base. With the introduction of refrigerated ships this competition spread to perishables, particularly meat and butter.

The ability to transport meat on long sea voyages and to store it safely in industrial-scale coldstores on land did not solve the problems of local distribution. In the warmer months meat taken out of the coldstores began to thaw quite soon, and once thawed it had a very limited life. The only refrigeration available to retailers was the ice box, an insulated small coldroom kept cool by the slow melting of block ice, a method not over-efficient in itself and circumscribed in its application by the availability of block ice.

In the eighteen-seventies block ice was imported from Norway. Butchers with village shops found ice out of their reach either by reason of the initial cost or of wastage in transit or a combination of the two; they relied on a cool cellar or a thick-walled outhouse to preserve their meat. Their defence in the hot weeks was to turn their stock over quickly.

Of the nineteen villages in the district, only six had a butcher's shop in 1883, namely Aldringham, Kelsale, Knodishall, Orford, Tunstall and Westleton. Of the larger settlements Saxmundham had five such shops, Leiston and Aldeburgh three each. Families who required meat in villages with no shop were served by the butcher's cart. Competition was intense and a good customer would expect daily deliveries, with perhaps an early call to receive orders into the bargain.

Aldeburgh, with its disproportionately high percentage of the middle classes and its summer visitors, gave the opportunity for the best class of trade, but with the disadvantage that it was seasonal. Saxmundham, closely tied to the state of farming, had a trade related to the country houses, parsonages and farms of the area for the better cuts and the trade of the villagers for the cheaper cuts.

In Leiston, by contrast, the state of employment, though still cyclic, was regulated by forces not directly related to the state of local agriculture. Between April and October, 1870, for instance, the number of men employed on the works declined from 548 to 413 as a result of the numbing effect of the Franco-Prussian War on the trade with the Continent, upon which the Garretts depended for a substantial part of their business. In the eighties trade with Austria–Hungary, also important to them, declined because of the protectionist policies introduced there to foster native industry.

In some respects Leiston remained the Suffolk village it had been seventy years before, but in others it began to take on some of the aspects of a northern company village. So far as the meat trade was concerned the comfortable family trade, as seen in Saxmundham, co-existed with the cow-beef butchers—in trade slang the "keg-meg men". The former category was exemplified by George Morling's shop opposite the Works House and later by Joseph Challis's shop in Sizewell Road, the latter by the open-fronted shop of Herbert Cockerell in Crosses Lane (now Cross Street) or later by the shop of Tender & Good in the High Street, lit by gas until late on a summer Saturday night and set to attract the tipsy or half-tipsy men tumbling out of the pubs, with the intention of "clearing the shop", knowing that most of what they had would not survive the weekend if unsold.

When I began taking a serious interest in the past of Leiston and of Garretts, just on thirty years ago, there were many people alive who recalled the town at or soon after the turn of the century. Mrs Elsie Wilshier, who had lived in the town all her life, wrote a list of all the tradesmen she could remember from the days when she was a young housewife in 1911, which she allowed me to copy.

There were plenty of butchers. Beside Challis and Tender & Good, already mentioned, there were P. F. Wheeler and R. C. Balls, both in the High Street; the latter described himself as "established 1833", against which Mrs Wilshier commented tartly "not in Leiston". Then there was William Catling (afterwards Emsden's) in the High Street, near where the Picture House was soon to be erected on his meadow. By contrast there was only one fishmonger, Jimmy Smith.

There were grocers a-plenty, ranging from George Gunthorpe's large shop on the corner of High Street and Valley Road, formerly Gundry Neave's, who traded as both wholesaler and retailer, to various smaller businesses such as Fish & Company in Market Place (Sizewell Road) and Leeming's in the High Street, opposite the Black Horse, Rivers' in the Market Place and John Waddell's establishment in Haylings Road. Grocers in the small league were Teddy Peake, on the corner of Paradise and Haylings Road, who doubled as a dancing master, and Dan Masterson, who sold groceries and sweets and a great many odds and ends in High Street. He was a noted violinist and played in the string orchestra of the Baptist Chapel on Aldringham Common.

Milk was sold by Robert Smith (Milky Bob) who lived in one of a pair of big cottages between the works Tally House and the Works Institute. Both have now vanished. Milk was also sold, of course, by some of the farmers. The oldest of the bakers was Charles Westbrook in the Market Place and High Street, a business already in 1911 with fifty years of trading behind it (and over fifty

*Two Christmas displays, 1910, by Leiston butchers, (**above**) William Catling, and (**left**) P. T. Wheeler.*

more to come). The shop, in fact, trades still, having been taken over by Harold Smith, whose shop in Aldeburgh, at the corner of Crespigny Road, was once the Aldeburgh Co-operative Society. Another baker was E. B. Maple, who had the shop, now demolished, opposite the Tally House in Main Street. There was also Fred Last in Sizewell Road. Lastly there was J. List in Haylings Road, "Baker, Pork Butcher and Coal Merchant—Speciality! Home-made Bread". Even in a district where pluralists were common this was an unusual combination of trades.

The only real ironmonger's shop, then as now (Mrs Wilshier's words), was Titlow's in the High Street, but there was also Potter and Wightman's, who declared themselves to be cycle agents and repairers, repairers of any machine from a sewing machine to a motor car, gas, heating and hot water fitters, fixers of electric bells, suppliers and repairers of gramophones, gunsmiths, and capable of carrying out "general repairs". Cycles obviously attracted men in vaguely compatible trades. Harry Moss, who worked as a gas fitter, copper, tin and zincsmith and general sheet metal worker from his house at 65 Crown Street, also sold and repaired bikes. George Archer, another man who traded in cycles, worked from his cottage at Coldfair Green.

In Station Road Stanley Cooper doubled up the business of jeweller and clock and watch repairer with that of cycle dealer and hirer, offering new cycles from four guineas. Apart from Titlow's, who sold wines and spirits along with their ironmongery, there was

Titlow's ironmonger's shop, Leiston. The diversity of the goods displayed is enormous— four sizes of children's beach spades, a mangle, buckets, birdcages, kettles, baskets, balls of string, garden tools, lamps, carpenter's tools, paints and varnishes and, not least, wines and spirits. It was the only ironmonger's in the kingdom with a licence to sell them.

one wine and spirit merchant, T. Storey & Son, at No 1 Cheapside, though most of the public houses dealt as off-licences also. Griffiths the tailor had his shop in the High Street, undertaking also repairs, cleaning and dyeing; he catered, as he hoped, for the upper part of the market. Those with less to spend went to Tom Welch, who had a shop in Sizewell Road and would make suits to measure from twenty-two shillings and sixpence. He would, moreover, sell them on deferred terms; many a Leiston man was married in one of Tom Welch's suits, paid for at a shilling a week.

There were two chemists, T. Pratt Gooch, MPS, at 58 High Street, "Family recipes carefully prepared", and Charles Hardy, MPS, at the shop at the north end of High Street near what is now Baker's men's outfitters, then carried on by Fred Cuthbert. Tobacco was sold in the pubs and also by Harold Hillen, who had the little shop by the level crossing and whose wife was a "teacher of pianoforte, theory and harmony" at their home, 2 Ashmere Villas, Carr Road, on the north side of the railway. Another tobacconist was E. E. Holley, whose shop on the west side of High Street opposite Hardy's was soon to be demolished to make way for an extension to the Garrett works. He specialized in tobacco for chewing, especially the most prized brand, "Negro's Head".

High Street, Leiston, about 1908, showing Tom Welch's clothing shop. Tom would sell suits on credit, repaid in weekly instalments, and many a young Leistonian was married in a new Tom Welch suit bought on credit.

Smoking was forbidden on the works and many men chewed as a substitute. Miss Helen Alcock had a little cottage shop in Dinsdale Road, doubling the role of tobacconist with selling sweets in ha'porths and farthing's worths to the local children, and odd items of grocery and household goods, carded pills, pencils, marbles, bottles of ink and the like.

Another establishment noted by Mrs Wilshier and also remembered by Ted Dunn was Miss Last's fancy bazaar next to his father's barber shop in Sizewell Road; there she sold toys, crackers and fancy goods. Ted remembers her as a curious, gruff old lady who used from time to time to drop toys over the fence for him and his brothers and sisters, excusing her action by saying they were old stock or damaged. Ted's father George, newly established as a master man, helped out the income from hair-cutting and shaving by repairing umbrellas, a combination of trades also practised by another Leiston barber, A. J. Parsons, in the High Street, who noted with pride that he had been established since 1880. Poor George, by inference, was an upstart but a popular man nonetheless. When he worked as a journeyman for Smith, the barber opposite the works entrance, he used to open up the shop every morning before a quarter to six so as to be able to serve hot coffee at a penny a cup to men arriving to start work at six o'clock. The third Leiston barber was Walter Shippon in the High Street.

Charles Ives was the leading boot and shoe salesman, and also a men's outfitter at 23 Sizewell Road. Later he was to move to London House on the corner of High Street and Sizewell Road, then occupied by Miss M. R. Barrell as a ladies' outfitter's. The business stayed there until his grandson John moved it to Woodbridge in the nineteen-eighties. Fred Clarke, in the High Street, mended boots and shoes and made boots to order, a fast-dying trade. Bespoke boots had a life expectancy far in excess of factory-made boots because of the superiority of the stitching, but at double or even treble the prices of factory boots and usually of clumsy appearance they were in 1911 in the last stages of a losing battle.

The main newsagent was A. H. Weston at 4 Cheapside. He also sold stationery, birthday cards, wrapping paper, sealing wax and similar items, besides all of which he was a picture framer. Anyone wanting business stationery, such as ledgers, journals and account books, had to go to Crisp's in Saxmundham, who had supplied dozens, if not hundreds, of the stoutly boarded and leather-bound books in which Garrett's had kept their records and accounts. Fairweather & Morling ('phone number 13) did supply some items of that kind, produced letterheads and business heads, printed the *Leiston Observer* when it began and did various other types of jobbing printing.

Greengrocery and flowers were sold in Sizewell Road by a man named O'Dell, and a little further on was a similar shop kept by Mrs Swallow, whose husband was a chimney pot and flower pot maker at Carrs' brickyard. By the most grinding thrift managed to scrape together the money to build not only the shop but also the terrace of cottages known as Coronation Cottages a little way down towards Sizewell.

The longest established of the builders was George Partridge, established as such in 1880; his yard was in Eastward Ho. Arthur Gibbs was in Waterloo Avenue (he was a telephone subscriber also, number 9). H. W. Beaumont was in Valley Road. He was also a wheelwright and an undertaker, and helped to make the coffins for the German crew of the Zeppelin shot down at Theberton. W. Barker in Carr Road was more of a speculative builder, offering "freehold residences" for sale. G. A. Smythe, whose business began in 1862, was both a builder and a house furnisher at 104 High Street, in that part of the High Street which until a few years before

O'Dell's fruit and flower shop in Leiston, a business combined by the proprietor (in the doorway) with an agency for the Liverpool & London Insurance Company.

55

had been known as Aldeburgh Road. J. Cutts & Son in Cross Street also did funerals as well as building work. They were proud of the fact that they were, or had been, contractors to the War Office, the Board of Trade and the Admiralty, and they offered their "improved steps", a design with a folding strut between the next-to-bottom step and the cross member of the hinged leg in lieu of the usual cords.

Since nearly everyone cooked and heated their houses by burning coal there were several coal merchants. The Carrs, William and Talbot, were the largest. They were also in business in Ipswich and Chelmsford. Besides being coal merchants they owned the Leiston brickyard. Bob Coleman carried on his coal business from the same yard in Eastward Ho as his father John Coleman, the jobmaster and cab proprietor. Frank Forsdike was in the same street. Other coal merchants were Smith in Valley Road and Frank Moss at 17 Prospect Place. The other "black-faced" trade—blacksmithing and farriery—was predictably well represented. A. W. Hammond had his forge and shoeing traverse at 38 Prospect Place while J. Balls and Sons had theirs in High Street not far from W. E. Rowe, who offered his services besides as a machinist.

J. Balls' forge and farrier's shop in Leiston, about 1910.

Smith, Moss, Forsdike and the Colemans doubled up as cartage contractors. Freddy Garrod at the north end of the High Street also did cartage, combining it with a slightly better class of jobmastering than John Coleman's—so he averred—and offering funeral and wedding carriages. He, too, believed in the telephone, having the number Leiston 8.

There was, however, only one laundry, carried on by Fred Baxter in Market Place, opposite Joseph Challis's butcher's shop. Domestic laundering was mostly done at home with the wash-tub and the copper in the scullery or outhouse. Those who could afford it often sent out their washing to washerwomen who did the work in their own homes. Dyeing and cleaning of otherwise non-washable material was rather different. Men's suits and ladies' coats were usually cleaned by washing in highly inflammable benzine, and this was mostly done in the large works of the old-established dyers. Pullar's of Perth and Achille Serre of London were prominent in this trade, with agents all over the country who sent and received hampers daily by rail. Achille Serre's agents in Leiston were K. & M. Sawer, who had a cash drapery, millinery, and dress shop on the corner of Cheapside (Sizewell Road) and High Street opposite to Miss Barrett's. The Sawers were prominent Quakers. Further along towards Sizewell F. H. Adams, also a draper and milliner, was agent for Pullar's. A. G. Smith, the other Leiston milliner, of High Street stuck to the one trade and was agent for no-one.

C. Stephenson, the jeweller and watch and clock maker, was based in Aldeburgh but had a branch shop in Leiston High Street. Leiston residents, on the whole, did not have the funds needed to make a good-class jeweller's shop flourish. Also, perhaps surprisingly, there was no saddler in Leiston, despite the number of horses in use; none, in fact, nearer than Andrew Webster, opposite the forge in Thorpe Road, Aldringham. There were a few other trades with only one representative each. Harry Holley was solitary as the town signwriter at 42 Eastward Ho and W. Norman was the sole ironfounder (apart from Garrett's works). He had a small foundry facing the green at Knodishall, and his chilled plough-shares were locally celebrated.

The Leiston Co-operative Society, founded on 28th June, 1861, had expanded by the time of which Mrs Wilshier wrote. A branch had been opened in Aldeburgh and others were to follow in Saxmundham and Orford. In the early days of the society it was the custom to hold an annual summer tea for the members, for which purpose the Works Hall was loaned by the Garretts. The tea was followed by a concert and hymn singing. Six hundred or so people attended the concerts in their early years. The teas cost sixpence, a substantial sum in the context of the time and place, but for it the bill of fare included bread and butter, sandwiches, rusks, cheese, ham, plain cake, currant cake and plenty of tea to drink. Admission to the tea did not qualify the ticket holder for entry to the evening concert, which cost a further threepence.

The annual general meeting of the shareholders of the society was a quieter affair held in the store itself in Sizewell Road. Membership fluctuated in its earlier years around or a little below the one hundred and fifty mark and the annual turnover at near £3,500. The annual dividend seldom fell below a shilling in the pound and on at least one occasion (1964) reached one and threepence.

To receive a pound in dividend at the end of the trading year was a useful addition to a family's income, but membership of the society turned as much upon political outlook as upon mere economic advantage. Belmoor and his co-founders were drawn from the radicals of the village, and men who wished publicly to dissociate themselves from radicalism made a pointed avoidance of the Co-op. John Cornforth, the smith's shop foreman at Garrett's, was a rigid Conservative and kept away from the Co-op. Ishmael Girling, of the thresher shop, was a radical and was a leading member of it.

Leiston's Co-operative Society maintained its independence until well after its centenary but in the nineteen-seventies found itself at a disadvantage in its wholesale buying compared with the supermarket chains. The Yoxford shop, which had long been of dubious value to the organization, was closed and sold, producing some improvement in the trading position, but in the end amalgamation into a larger unit came to be accepted as the only long-term solution and in 1984 the business was joined to that of the Ipswich society.

Two family businesses in Leiston that passed down the generations were those of Westbrooks, the bakers, and Titlow's, the ironmonger's, whose shop had the distinction, as we have seen, of being the only ironmonger's in the country to possess a wine and spirit licence. Started in 1869 by W. D. Titlow, it was owned for many years in this century by Ted Titlow, one of the founders of the Picture House, passing to his son Jack. On his retirement it was joined to the business of G. Constance Ltd of Aldeburgh, though the name has been kept along with the shop. With his inheritance Jack took over the services of William Beddingfield, generally referred to in the years I knew him as "Old Beddingfield" or "Old Bill". He used to preside in a pontifical manner over the counter on the left of the door, and was possessed even in his late eighties of a very nearly faultless memory for the minutiae of the trade, perhaps tinged by a hint of *folie de grandeur*. Jack once confided, in a wry aside, that he sometimes felt uncertain as to which of them was employer and which employee. Beddingfield was, nevertheless, a very remarkable man, quite absorbed in the trade, and like many men thus engrossed scarcely survived his retirement. When he retired he had worked for the Titlows for seventy-six years.

The Westbrook business was started by Charles Westbrook in 1860 and remained in the family, father to son, for three generations until 1976, when it was sold to Harold Smith, already a well-established family baker in Aldeburgh. Joseph Gibbs was the Leiston baker in the earlier years of the last century, though whether or not his actual business was taken over by Charles Westbrook is not known.

Saxmundham also has a very old-established ironmonger's shop, William Wells and Sons. This was certainly in business, on the evidence of White's directory as early as 1844. There was in Saxmundham also a branch establishment of Richard Garrett and Sons, carried on there under the management of William Backhouse. An early invoice, which was kept in the works safe up to the time of final closure, described the firm as "Iron merchants, oil and colour men, nail, chain and chaincable makers, smiths, founders, braziers and agricultural implement makers". Surviving ledgers from that period show sales of table cutlery, kettles, coal scuttles and similar items for domestic use, making it clear that the business was truly that of a large country general ironmonger.

Another trade which has undergone radical changes in the last hundred years is that of the village blacksmith and farrier, for the two skills commonly went as a pair. In 1883 there were twenty-three blacksmiths in the villages of the coastal strip. Aldeburgh and Saxmundham had two each, while Leiston had four; and there were, of course, also blacksmiths on the maintenance staffs of the various landed estates and of the agricultural implement dealers and repairers. In the latter category came the Heffers of Farnham, three miles down the road to London from Saxmundham, another father-to-son succession that came to an end on the death of the last incumbent, "Harbut", in the nineteen-seventies. His works was on the east side of what is now the A12, on the country side of the bend the George, the keeping of which was also in the Heffer family. The Heffers were owners and repairers of threshing tackle, repaired implements, sold engine stores—cylinder oil, packings, mudhole joints and the like—undertook general engineering and blacksmithing and provided the kind of back-up to general village life that is now sadly missed.

For instance when Frank Waddell had despaired of finding a replacement link for the long-obsolete delivery chain of the old Wharfedale printing machine at the Leiston Abbey Press it was H. H. Heffer who was able to find a suitable replacement link in his stock of scrap. "Harbut" was a great character, totally without airs or conceit, and oblivious to or contemptuous of appearance or attire, while at the same time not having much patience with those who were preoccupied with their own importance.

When the Richard Garrett works was bought and reopened by Beyer Peacock and Co. Ltd, of Manchester, after the crash of the old company in 1932, Arthur Bamborough, a Mancunian accountant, was appointed general manager. Though of irreproachable integrity and very hardworking, he was perhaps not unaware of his own status, and since "Harbut" was a long-standing customer of the works it was probably inevitable that fate should arrange a brush between them.

H. H. H. was of such undoubted probity that it would not have crossed the mind of anyone on the works to deny him credit—no one, that is, save the new General Manager. Herbert was, like many men of his type and generation, no great hand with the pen and his debts tended to be paid when he chanced by the works. Thus small sums often stood against him for months at a time and such a small debt—perhaps thirty shillings or so—was discovered by Bambrough and commented on adversely in one of his inspections of the ledger.

Besides being a sculptor Tom Thurlow was a pioneer photographer. The photograph from which this engraving was made was taken from Leiston windmill.

Leiston Works Established in 1778.
from a Daguerreotype taken by Tom Thurlow of Saxmundham about the year 1847.

Some time afterwards Heffer came to the works for a few requirements, which were attended to by Cyril Thurston. While they conversed in the lower yard not far from the Tally House Thurston saw the General Manager striding down the yard in the black jacket and pinstriped trousers which he customarily wore. Though not straitened in his circumstances, Herbert Heffer was quite heedless about how he dressed. That day he wore nondescript trousers and jacket and a particularly worn and greasy old raincoat.

Prompted perhaps by a sense of duty, or even a sense of mischief, Thurston introduced the two men. Bambrough looked at "Harbut" with a lack of cordiality, if not actual distaste. "Am I right in supposing", he said, "that you are the same Mr Heffer who has owed the company a sum of money for many months past?" "That's quite right, Mr Bambrough", agreed Heffer, "wholly sorry I am but I expect to sell a machine or two shortly and then I'll be able to pay."

He took the hem of Bambrough's neat jacket in his fingers. "That's a very nice jacket you've got on, Mr Bambrough, and, as you can see, mine's not up to much. Do you happen to have an old jacket at home you could spare I'd be wholly grateful for it, or an old raincoat either, for mine's past its best." Bambrough turned on his heel with an audible snort and stalked off into the office. "Whoi", said "Harbut", turning to Cyril Thurston with a grin, "he don't seem to hev no sense o' hoomer."

Harrod in 1864 had described Henry Heffer as a "drill maker" at Farnham, though Smyths of Peasenhall were the most noted drill-makers of the area from the opening years of the last century through to the nineteen-sixties. Garretts were also makers of drills, beginning a little after the Smyths, probably in the eighteen-thirties, but though their drills achieved an eminence equal to that of their neighbours and rivals the commercial importance of drills declined as that of steam engines increased at Leiston, and Garretts sold out that part of the business in 1914 to the Rayne Foundry Company in Essex. In their time both Smyth's and Garrett's achieved world-wide sales of drills, vying with each other in improvements to them.

Both Smyths and Garretts establishments grew from forges, the former in general smithing, the latter specializing in blades——mostly reaping hooks. It is easy to understand the progression from blacksmith to implement maker, just as it is to see the logic of Charles Turner being both the Saxmundham miller and also one of the town's bakers. It is not so simple to see why David Brown, who was a pork butcher in Westleton in the eighteen-eighties, should also have practised the craft of hay-trusser, nor is there any very evident logic in James Barber, the Iken traction engine and threshing machine owner, being a horse-breaker as well.

The name that most engages me in Iken, however, is that of his contemporary George Chambers, described as a potmaker. One of the products of the Iken pottery was the earthenware bottle or costrel, designed with lugs for a carrying cord and used by reapers and hay-mowers to carry cold tea or beer to the field. Another apposite name from the same period was that of William Last, the bootmaker at Saxmundham. There was also Robert Coleman, the Leiston coal merchant, in Eastward Ho, Leiston, though he was a little later. John Coleman, his father, was, as mentioned earlier, a jobmaster, hiring out horses and vehicles and keeping a livery stable of sorts. He had the second Christian name of Nollar. Unusual though that was, it was surpassed, at least in my eyes, by Henry Page, the Saxmundham chemist, who had the second name of Skikelthorpe.

Reverting for a moment to the subject of pork butchers with a second and completely disparate occupation, it is perhaps worth remarking that in pre-refrigeration days few, if any, ate pork in the hot months, May, June, July and August. The pork purveyor needed a secondary trade to tide him over those months. A second element to be borne in mind in this connection is the cottager's pig. Many village people in the last century kept a domestic pig, or pigs, fattened on kitchen waste, gleanings, acorns and any other food that could be mustered. Slaughtering and preparing these pigs provided an occupation, at least part-time, for some of the men listed by the directories as "pork butchers". Like many part-time trades it was often combined with that of publican or beer-house keeper. James Chaston of Leiston was one such in the eighteen-sixties. During the day when the licensee was out at work what trade there was would be looked after by his wife, but during the evenings he would be at home attending to the bar or tap-room.

Other trades than pig-killing were combined in this way with the keeping of a public house. To be a carrier fitted in quite well, as did the craft of woodcutter or hurdlemaker. Hurdles were in requisition for penning up sheep grazed upon the commons and sheep walks of the coastal strip. Some publicans owned horse cabs for hire or kept livery stables of a sort. From keeping live horses it was an easy step to dealing in dead ones: at least one publican known to me was a horse-slaughterer as well. It must not be imagined that in the days when all local traffic depended upon the horse the average specimen was a magnificent animal; mongrel specimens abounded, and they were sometimes allowed to deteriorate further as a result of age or neglect, the latter often in reality underfeeding.

It was a constant complaint by the Army veterinary inspectors that the calibre of cart and van horses was so inferior that they did not constitute a good enough reserve for the Army to draw upon in the event of war. In April, 1914, the War Office, having surveyed its potential sources of horses, admitted to being "appalled at the number of animals which by faulty conformation or obvious unsoundness are quite unsuited for hard work".

Even in the limited territory under our review the horse was of such importance that his accoutring supported, in the early eighties, no fewer than six saddlers. By 1933, with horse traction a shadow of what it had been fifty years before, there were only two. Horse feeding-stuffs, particularly hay, were a prop of the rural economy. Because of its bulk in relation to its weight hay did not suffer from foreign imports to the same extent as cereals, nor so soon. Only after the introduction of the power press for baling hay in the early eighteen-eighties did imports make any advance into the home market. It was the shortage of home-produced hay by reason of drought in 1892 and 1893 that opened the British market to imports.

In the coastal district, in common with most of Eastern England, crops of only twenty per cent of normal were common—5 cwt per acre where 25 cwt might have been expected. In consequence rather more than 60,000 tons of hay were imported in 1892, followed by two years in which the imports topped a quarter of a million tons. Thereafter, with an improved home crop and resultant lower prices, imports went down to about half that level. Since hay production in the years immediately prior to the drought had been of the order of nine million tons, a quarter of a million tons of imports was not a major threat, but the possibility of importing hay had become established and acted as a restraint on prices.

The hay scarcity, moreover, gave an uplift to alternative types of horse feed. Horse carrots, once an important crop on the sandlings flanking the coastline of the district, underwent a revival in the nineties so that there was by about the mid-nineties a perceptible easing of the depression that had held agriculture in its grip since the terrible rain-drenched summer of 1879.

But as farming revived a little the long-established fleet of cod smacks sailing from Aldeburgh finally declined to extinction, vanquished by the steam fleets based in the major fishing ports further north, notably Grimsby and Hull. The end of the smacks meant the end of trades that had depended upon them. Large quantities of the common whelk had been purchased as bait, and the loss of this trade was a blow to the longshoremen who had dredged them. Similarly salt suppliers suffered a shrinking of demand as the fleet was reduced, for although the smacks were welled only the choicest fish were kept alive in the wet well, all others being split, gutted and salted. Basketmakers too felt the pinch. For many years in the last century Stephen Mann made baskets at Aldeburgh, while in Saxmundham there were two further makers, William Cousins and Ezekiel Markwell; with the decline in fishing basketmaking disappeared.

So far as Aldeburgh itself was concerned the increasing importance to its economy of the summer holiday visitors helped to cushion the loss of the Iceland cod fishing. Homes all over the town began to take in summer lodgers, while the hotels expanded and prospered. The vigorous shaking up of the town's sanitary arrangements, inaugurated during Dr Elizabeth Garrett Anderson's period of office as mayor, doubtless assisted this trend by reassuring visitors. Not only boatmen and bathing machine proprietors but also the town tradesmen benefited from this development—grocers, bakers, fruiterers, butchers and, of course, launderers and washerwomen.

The doyen of laundrywomen was undoubtedly the golden-hearted if raucous-voiced Susette Pettit, daughter of James Pettit, the miller of Fort Green mill. Susette (1871 to 1955) had her hand laundry on the seaward side of the mill and her drying ground on Fort Green. Town boys found attempting to play football near her washing lines were treated to a vigorous tongue-lashing. Hearing her holding forth in this way, anyone who was foolish enough to

The north end of Aldeburgh High Street, pre-1914. The tall building is the old Post Office, the victim of a German bomb in the second war. Further up the street the Great Eastern Railway's horse and dray is delivering goods whilst on the right is Walter Hill's outfitters shop, now Aldeburgh Book Shop. SPS

dismiss her as a rough-tongued hoyden was sadly mistaken; Susette was a woman of enormous public spirit and great kindness of heart.

She began her laundry in 1894 when in her mid-twenties and ran it until it was finally overwhelmed by the sea in 1938. In 1899 when still only twenty-eight years old she was instrumental in the setting up of a district nursing service in Aldeburgh. She played a prominent part, too, in the establishment of the Aldeburgh Cottage Hospital in 1921 and supported it both with her own money and also by her fund-raising efforts until it was merged into the National Health Service in 1948. She was a good friend to travelling showpeople visiting the town, and after the regatta fair had been banned from its old site at Oakley Square she lent her land at Fort Green for use as a fairground, leaving it on trust in her will to continue to be used for that purpose.

The ladies who did the washing and ironing in Miss Pettit's laundry must have been made of pretty durable stuff. Several of them came from Snape, walking to and from work each day by way of the Sailor's Path through the Blackheath estate, parallel to the River Alde. The path is said to have acquired its name from the days of the Slaughden smacks: the masters, mates and seamen of these vessels, concerned with the working of the ships, were full-time professionals but the crew also included a proportion of men known to the professional seamen as "greenhands" and recruited from the farm and village labourers of the coast, and it was from such men, walking home to Snape and the nearby villages, that the Sailors' Path took its name. While it is difficult to trace in the villages such individuals who had one foot, so to speak, ashore and the other afloat, the staff registers of the Garrett works, which I was allowed to inspect during my researches for *Garretts of Leiston* and *Garrett 200*, kept for many years in the last century and the opening years of this by Lewis Chandler, record many instances of men coming on to the works who had been fishing and others of men leaving to go fishing.

The men who thus made the break with what, in reality, was the drudgery of life ashore for the exacting life afloat were usually young men looking for adventure or fleeing from misadventure —the imminent arrival of an illegitimate child or the consequence of answering back an overbearing employer or repressive foreman, or some similar happening which made it expedient to be absent for a while. Often they found themselves cooped up for a long period with a master or mate with harsh or sadistic tendencies. As Mr C. Alp, writing to Edgar March of his experiences as a smacksman, commented, "there were some good ones and a lot of bad ones".

Herring were also fished from Aldeburgh and Orford, though

not on the scale of Lowestoft or Yarmouth, nor for that matter of Southwold. Mention of herring calls to mind barrels, and barrels, in turn, coopers. Not all the locally made barrels, of course, were for fish handling. The local brewers must also have been customers, and there was a trade in wooden pails, killed off by the increasing use of iron buckets.

Since coopering as a local trade declined with the local fishing fleet it seems fair to conclude that the two events were not unconnected. By 1912 the last working cooper in the area was James Baldry of Leiston, but thirty years before he had as fellow practitioners of the ancient craft Robert Berrett of Saxmundham and Robert Wade at Orford. Aldeburgh, too, had at one time its own cooper, John Garrod, but his business seems to have ceased in the middle years of the last century. In 1844 White mentions Jonathan Taylor as a cooper at Leiston.

Besides having its share of the rarer trades the coast has never lacked a good number of rare characters in conventional trades. One well remembered from the recent past is R. J. Ashford, who had his jeweller's or watchmaker's shop in Aldeburgh High Street. He was a merry soul, partial to his liquor, and an avid duckshooter, a pastime which he had in common with Charles Clarke, the town photographer, a few doors south on the opposite side of the street.

Fred Last's baker's and confectioner's shop, Leiston, c1908.

When R. J. felt bored with business, which was a fairly frequent occurrence, he would simply take himself off after lunch on to the marshes. Charles Clarke, somewhat older, was not so cavalier toward his customers. Since Garrett's abhorred the Liberal politics of Leiston's only photographer, John Smellie Waddell, they used Charlie Clarke to take the numerous photographs made of the works products. He was a good photographer, but erratic. The works albums contained more than one photograph printed with the plate reversed, so that engines had the flywheel on the right instead of on the left.

When Victor Garrett was a young man, early in this century, it was to Charles Clarke that his father, Frank Garrett, entrusted the task of instructing Victor in the arts of wildfowling. A careless shot had cost Frank Garrett the vision of one eye when he was himself a young man and he considered, according to Victor, that Charles was likely to inculcate a thorough grounding of sound shooting practice into his youngest son.

Recalling when in his eighties the nights and early mornings he had spent with Clarke in quest of duck, Victor remembered him with great affection. He also recalled that despite Charles Clarke having shot some thousands of duck in his lifetime he never ate any of them in his own house. Mrs Clarke loathed duck and refused point blank to cook them or have them in the house, with the result that it was only in the homes of friends that Charles could eat what he had shot.

It would not be fitting to leave the subject of tradesmen without a mention of Tom Thurlow of Saxmundham. Tom was the stonemason and monumental mason of the town in the middle years of the last century. He was a contemporary and friend of the third Richard Garrett of Leiston Works and of Newson Garrett, and though he never matched Richard in either worldly wealth or influence, in his own way he was as remarkable a man as his more famous friend. In his capacity as a master mason he was responsible for the design and execution of the stone reredos in Saxmundham Church, erected in memory of John Charles Crampin. He is believed also to have carried out the mason's work in the reconstruction of Leiston Church, to the cost of which the Garretts contributed.

Apart from this, he was a noted sculptor, though only in his own district. His works include a bust of his friend Richard Garrett and also the bust in Aldeburgh Church of the poet Crabbe, honoured in the town whose people he often denigrated. Besides this Thurlow was an enthusiastic pioneer photographer, using the daguerreotype process, and was responsible for the running of the Saxmundham gasworks, of which he was secretary and superintendent.

The talented Tom Thurlow's bust of his erstwhile school-friend Richard Garrett III. Tom was a monumental mason by trade and a self-taught sculptor.

Brothers in Brewing   6

THE BUSINESS of Richard Garrett & Sons at Leiston as a large engineering establishment was effectually created by the third Richard Garrett of Leiston (1807 to 1866), something of a business prodigy who took effective control of it from his father at the age of nineteen. His two younger brothers Newson and Balls (after his maternal grandfather's surname) found no place on the works.

The Garrett attitude to inheritance was distinctly of the Old Testament. That is to say the eldest son was expected to succeed to the estate of his father. In Richard III's case he had largely created the inheritance into the bargain and thus had an added disincentive from sharing power with his brothers. Balls took up engineering and ironfounding, setting up a business in Maidstone which was carried on with moderate success. So far as is known his exclusion from the Leiston scene produced no rancour and he remained a welcome if rare visitor to Carlton Hall, and later Aldringham House, until his death.

With Newson (1812 to 1893) the case was rather different. Though six years younger than Richard he was equally headstrong and ambitious, almost as able a businessman and quite determined to show that he was as well able to succeed in his endeavours as his eldest brother had been. Hence there was a constant struggle to match achievement with achievement. Joint ventures were rare, though they did agree for some years to be joint lessees of the wharf and buildings at Slaughden quay, an uneasy partnership from which Richard withdrew as soon as the coming of the railway had made the use of coastal shipping unimportant to him.

Richard's grandson Victor maintained that there was rivalry but no enmity between Richard and Newson. They could, however, not be in each other's presence for long without debate developing into argument, often heated. Their wives Elizabeth and Louisa (née Dunnell) were sisters and remained on affectionate terms with each other throughout their lives, damping down as necessary the sparks thrown off by their spouses' differences.

Louisa was not only called upon to compose Newson's differences with Richard. He had quarrels, sometimes in quite intemperate terms, with neighbours, fellow townsmen and business associates, some mere transitory tiffs forgotten within days but others going on for weeks, months or even years. Mrs Garrett declined to become enmeshed in such matters, maintaining equable contacts with the other parties to the quarrels and with their wives.

How the two brothers became interested in brewing is not known. After finding no acceptable niche in the management of Leiston Works Newson had taken himself off to London, where he became a pawnbroker at 1 Commercial Road, Whitechapel, seemingly with considerable success as by 1838 he had taken over the management of a larger and better class of pawnbroking shop at 142 Long Acre, near St Martin's Lane and in the environs of Covent Garden. His father had died in 1837 and, though the business had passed to his brother Richard, Newson had received under his will a quarter share of "the stock, implements and interests on hand".

Perhaps Newson hankered for a more constructive trade than that of pawnbroker, or possibly he found the squalor of Central London a poor exchange for his native Suffolk. Equally possibly the conjunction of his commercial success at pawnbroking with the funds inherited from his father's estate, payable in instalments, provided the means and the incentive to contemplate a move. At Snape Bridge, where the parish of Snape meets the boundary of Tunstall, there was a small port and the first bridge over the Alde. On the south bank, in Tunstall parish, there was a coal and corn merchant's business earlier owned by Osborne and Fennell but by the eighteen-thirties by Richard Fennell alone.

In 1840, with the onset of what was to be his terminal illness, Fennell offered the business for sale. It is said that Richard told his brother that the business was coming onto the market, but it must not be overlooked that their father-in-law, John Dunnell, was only some ten miles away at Dunwich and could also have played the part of messenger. Certainly Jo Manton, who had access to the family papers of the Newson Garrett branch of the family, records that John Dunnell put up some capital to supplement that of Newson and Louisa for the purchase of the business. Early in the autumn of 1840 Richard Fennell died, but it appears that Newson could not or did not find the capital to take over Fennell's sloop *Margaret*, built at Hunt's yard at Aldeburgh only the year before; this became the property of Newson's brother Richard.

Despite the fact that under Newson Garrett's control the business at Snape Bridge was developed so as to make him a very well-to-do man the growth was not on a scale to match that of Leiston Works under the control of Richard, nor did it bring him the international acclaim achieved by the latter. Whether rivalry or simply his own irrepressible ambition was the spur, he seems to have looked for a logical development of his handling as a merchant of East Suffolk malting barley. In the early eighteen-fifties he took over the Bow Brewery in London, probably with its own malting.

A view under the entrance arch of the Maltings, early this century. Before the arch is a turnplate so that railway wagons coming down the track from the foreground of the picture could be turned at right angles onto the lines parallel with the front of the building.   SPS

In the eighteen-fifties the malting trade burst out of its urban fetters and, as the London printers were to do thirty years later, relocated itself in the country. This move brought it close to its then sources of barley and placed it amid the more plentiful and cheaper labour of the Eastern Counties. In this move Newson Garrett was a pioneer, setting up his first malting at Snape in 1854 and expanding it so rapidly in the next three years that at the end of that period the output was at the level of 17,000 quarters annually. Clearly an output of this scale was not taken up by his own brewery; one of the London customers for his malt was his friend Joseph Wood of the Artillery Brewery, Westminster. The growth of the traffic in malt and malting barley, together with the coal required for firing the malting, triggered off Newson Garrett's interest in ships and in securing a freight branch of the East Suffolk Railway to serve Snape.

What prompted his brother Richard to venture into brewing is perhaps a more complicated speculation. Simple rivalry may well have been the spur for both Garrett brothers turning to brewing about the same time. It is, indeed, not possible to say which was the first venture. The brewery bought by Richard was the Camden Brewery, Hawley Crescent, Camden Town, London, NW, where he traded as Garrett, Whittaker & Co. He already knew quite well the Ipswich brewer and banker J. C. Cobbold, with whom he was soon to be associated on the board of the East Suffolk Railway, and this may have prompted in him an interest in brewing as a profitable outlet for his energies.

Having by the mid-fifties built Leiston Works into an energetically managed and profitable concern, in the management of which three of his sons, Richard, John and Henry, were involved, Richard Garrett Senior made a determined effort to distance himself from the day-to-day burdens of running the factory. The agreement between him and his sons, which came into operation on 12th May, 1856, rewarded them with half of the net profit, and the purchase of the brewery may have been intended to provide a source of income to recoup this diminution in the moneys he drew from the works.

In practice he used the brewery to provide a niche for his son-in-law, George Grimwood, husband of his daughter Betsy Maria, who lived at Shern Hall, Walthamstow; in the days before the brick tide of East London had flowed over it this was a desirable residence in the country. Though the day-to-day management may have been left to George Grimwood, Richard took a house in St John's Wood so as to be able to give the brewery personal attention and to be able to take a greater part in the meetings of the Royal Agricultural Society and of the Royal Society of Arts, in both of which he was involved.

Thus Newson had returned from London to East Suffolk and Richard had swapped residence in East Suffolk for a life in London, albeit a more salubrious district of the capital. He did not, however, give up Carlton Hall, Saxmundham, his Suffolk house, which he retained as a country residence.

Richard may have been motivated in part by a third consideration not connected with commercial factors at all. The middle years of the last century saw the resurgence of the social conscience of the middle classes. Richard was not a great social reformer, certainly not in the way of his youngest son, Frank, whose interests were better housing for his workmen and the fostering of higher elementary education, but he had a well-developed sense of fair play; one of the targets of his ire was the dishonest tradesman, the purveyor of adulterated or impure foods. The standards of many brewers at that period were suspect. The four standard ingredients of the sound brew, malt, hops, yeast and water, still the norm in contemporary German beer, were being undermined by adulterants, especially added sugars and bittering agents other than hops. Charles Knight (1859) lists some of the iniquities practised upon the unsuspecting beer drinker of the eighteen-fifties:

*

A few flavouring and sweetening ingredients are required and allowable in brewing; but much of the beer retailed in the public houses of London and other large towns is scandalously adulterated. It has been ascertained, by chemical examination, that quassia, gentian, wormwood, broom-top are added to impart bitterness; capsicum, ginger, coriander, orange peel, carraway, to give pungency; opium, cocculus indicus, nux vomica, tobacco, poppy, henbane, to intoxicate; molasses, sugar, treacle as substitutes for malt; sulphuric acid, alum, vitriol, salt, to impart various properties: some items in this numerous list are generally to be found. The Excise authorities have battled hard against these fraudulent dealings; but the subject is a difficult one to manage.

*

Richard had inveighed against Edward Gooch of Leiston White Horse for behaving, as he put it, "illeberally"* toward his customers and may have considered that ownership of his own brewery, besides keeping him apace of Newson and making a profit, might also enable him to see that the brew was sound.

*See *Garrett 200*. Richard was always a poor speller!

The brewery pursued an uneventful life under George Grimwood and later under his son, Tom, characterized by Victor Garrett as "a charming fellow but no business man". Eventually it fell into the net of Watney Combe Reid & Co. Ltd during their expansionist period in the twenties of this century, passing to their control in 1925.

While the two Garrett brothers were jousting for position in brewing Richard Junior fell in love with his cousin Louisa, Newson's eldest child. Accounts differ as to what followed. According to Sir Alan Garrett Anderson, Louisa's nephew, she refused Richard's proposal. Richard's nephew Victor, son of his youngest brother Frank, maintained however that Louisa returned Richard's love but that the match was vetoed by the two sets of parents on the grounds of consanguinity. According to Victor's father, Louisa was the only true love of Richard's life. Richard became thereafter a noted philanderer, being once described by Frank as a "freelance sire" and having a number of natural sons, some of whom were employed on the works. Frank, who had seen little of his father, kept much from home by his multifarious activities, including the brewery, turned to his eldest brother as a substitute in many respects for his father, and held him in great affection in consequence.

In 1857 Louisa married James Smith, the brother of one of her schooldays friends. This circumstance in itself could hardly have endeared James Smith to the younger Richard, who referred to him contemptuously as "Linen-draper Smith". In due time Smith became a partner of his father-in-law in the Bow Brewery, which became known as Garrett, Smith & Co. Mortal offence came after John and Richard Garrett had quarrelled irremediably and John had taken himself off to Germany, where he had set up a works in Magdeburg in direct opposition to Leiston, whose markets he poached upon thereafter and whose reputation he denigrated whenever opportunity arose. James Smith put capital into John Garrett's venture, a gesture that was as salt into an already painful wound.

The circumstances of John's defection were felt by the two Richard Garretts at Leiston, father and son, to be disgraceful and were a cause of lasting bitterness, especially to Richard Junior. The other brother, Henry, had already had differences with them and removed himself from Leiston. The backing given to John by James Smith coming after his marriage to Louisa, was a further affront to the younger Richard. Death removed Richard Garrett Senior in 1866 and the blameless and beautiful Louisa, centre of the turbulence, died of appendicitis some three months later in February, 1867. The fourth Richard Garrett took over control of Leiston Works in association with his younger brother Frank.

When Richard IV died in July, 1884, and Frank became the sole proprietor of the firm of Richard Garrett & Sons John Garrett circularized all the firm's customers claiming that Frank was using the firm's title as a usurper and that the title properly belonged to him and to Henry's son, another Richard, who had joined him at Magdeburg.

Victor was brought up in an atmosphere that had no good thing to say about the Magdeburg establishment, but he never recalled being received other than with great kindness at his great-uncle Newson's homes at Alde House, Aldeburgh, and at Snape, and his relationships with his cousins of the Newson Garrett clan were cordial. Victor, of course, was only eight when his great-uncle Newson died, but his cousins once removed, George and Sam Garrett, lived on many years into his lifetime, and he knew them well and liked them.

Of their famous sister Elizabeth, the first woman to gain access to what had been the male citadel of medicine in this country, he saw little until she retired to live at Aldeburgh in her old age. He and his brothers knew her as Cousin Lizzie. He thought her to have been rather taken advantage of by the militant wing of the Suffragettes and led into actions which she might have been better spared. Elected Mayor of Aldeburgh, she made a notable success of her term of office, which left the town in a distinctly improved condition; in her terminal years her formidable intellect was undermined by hardening of the arteries, but until then she worked hard to promote the sanitary improvement of the town. Like her father and Uncle Richard she could not abide sloth and disliked impositions by artful traders upon the poorer inhabitants.

Though the Garretts were interested in maintaining or improving the standards of brewing they did not carry their interest in the subject to the point of joining the crusade for pure beer headed by Sir Cuthbert Quilter (1841–1911), of Bawdsey. Quilter took over the Coach and Horses Brewery at Melton, just outside Woodbridge, and renamed it the Pure Ale Brewery, from which he supplied a small number of public houses, one of them in Orford. Two of the other Orford public houses were owned by the Ropes and supplied from their own brewery until it closed in 1912.

Though it may well have been the case that the Coach and Horses Brewery supplied beer freer from adulteration than that sold by Rope's there is no evidence that it was better liked. The late Gregory Wright, the brewer for Flintham Hall & Co. Ltd at the Albert Brewery, Aldeburgh, who took over Rope's houses in 1912, had no very high opinion of village beers and thought that many were esteemed merely because there was no standard of comparison. He considered the Melton brewery brews not to have been significantly different in palatability from those offered by its

MELTON BREWERY PURE BEER.

Sir Cuthbert Quilter's pure ale brewery at The Coach and Horses, Melton. The muddy road was the county road from London to Lowestoft (later to be the A12 until the Woodbridge by-pass was built). SPS

neighbours, nor did he think that the public houses supplied with his own beers, including the Three Mariners at Slaughden, attained a very high standard.

Gregory had arrived in Aldeburgh in 1901 at the age of twenty-one to become head brewer for Flintham's. As he commented to me over seventy-five years later, it was not a very exalted position. The only other employee was a man named Howard who stoked the boiler, looked after the horse and helped with the general work of the brewery. Between them they did everything from brewing to bottlewashing, and also delivered to the firm's five licensed houses in Aldeburgh. Total production in summer was of the order of twenty barrels a week, but in winter only half that. The

bulk of the production was in mild and bitter, both sold as draught or bottled. There was also a bottled stout and a very strong draught old ale, mostly for winter sale.

If the beer was indifferent, so was the manner in which it was served. Glasses and pots were washed, if that is the appropriate term, by a perfunctory swirl in a bowl or bucket of cold water, used hour after hour. The Three Mariners had the advantage of drawing its water from the pure supplies of the Aldeburgh Water Company. Elsewhere it mostly came untreated from shallow wells situated in the same garden plot in which the publican disposed of slop water, the household excreta, the drainage from the men's urinal and probably the seepage from the stable.

The steam barges Katherine *and* Gladys *(nearest the camera) alongside the old engineers' workshop at Snape Maltings on the River Alde, the photo taken from the Stone Quay on the opposite bank.* J. S. Waddell

77

Doubtless, however, the bargemen, fishermen and maltsters of the Alde had like Mithridates acquired immunity by continuous exposure to the hazards of this water since infancy. Certainly they seem not to have been deterred by either the state of the pots or the source of the beer from partaking of the wares of the publicans.

Besides the three Orford houses and the Three Mariners at Slaughden they were served at one time by three further public houses, the Anchor and the Boot at Iken and the Plough and Sail on the Tunstall side of Snape Bridge. Of these only the Plough and Sail remains. Since Iken was a stronghold of the Rope family presumably it had been beer from their Orford brewery that was sold at Iken, perhaps at Snape also. "Alex" Alexander, who was brought up at Tunstall in the early years of this century, recalled the Plough and Sail being kept by an elderly maiden lady, Ellen Ann Gooch, last of a succession of licensees of that name since at least the sixties, whose methods were perhaps best described as basic. Her hostelry was nicknamed the Sow and Pail; as Robert Simper relates, bargemen would press barley grains into the dirt filling the cracks in the table tops, where, watered with spilt beer, they soon sprouted.

After Newson Garrett died the malting was continued by his son George, who had been involved with it since he was a young man. As he had grown older Newson Garrett had gradually relinquished control of the business to his son, who had the formal title of manager from 1882. Victor Garrett remembered him as a kindly, relaxed man, shrewd in matters of money, who did well with his investments, notably with British companies involved in public utility undertakings abroad; tramways and railways were prominent in his shareholdings, but he is said also to have put money into gas companies. In 1908 he began the building of a new house in Snape, Green Heys, to which he retired in 1910, leaving the management of the business to his nephew, Maurice Cowell. Maurice was the son of his elder sister Alice, who against her father's wishes had married Herbert Cowell, QC, a barrister practising at the Indian bar.

Maurice Cowell joined the army in the 1914–18 war and his uncle returned to the malting, at first on what he considered a temporary basis. His return acquired permanency when Maurice was killed in 1916.

George Garrett had been a shareholder since the previous century in an equally well established firm of maltsters, S. Swonnell & Sons, which owned the large malting at Oulton Broad. At the close of the war he arranged the sale of the Snape business to Swonnell's, by whom it was continued until the voluntary liquidation of the business in 1965. The last manager at Snape was J. G. Wood, a great-grandson of Newson Garrett.

Mills and Millers 7

OF THE TWENTY or so windmills that once dotted the area, only two remain intact, the three-pair postmill at Friston and the ertswhile grist mill that once stood at Aldringham but was removed to Thorpeness in the winter of 1922–23. The former mill, no longer worked, remained a corn mill, but Aldringham mill was converted to pump water at the time of its move to Thorpeness. Apart from these two the old tower mill at Fort Green at Aldeburgh still stands, petrified into a house on the edge of the beach, and the former smock pumping mill from Minsmere has been dismantled and re-erected at the Museum of East Anglian Life at Stowmarket.

The Thorpeness mill, dating from 1824, was originally sited on Mill Hill behind the Parrot and Punchbowl at Aldringham. As the Sizewell Hall estate was assembled by Alexander and Margaret Ogilvie the mill and its site were added to it. The earliest miller I am able to name was James Crane, there in 1844. The miller in 1864 was John Waller, and after him came Samuel King. A later miller was Francis Skoulding, one of the family who had mills at Kelsale and whose name also crops up in connection with the mill at Coldfair Green, Knodishall.

After being acquired by the Ogilvies the mill was used by the estate for grinding animal provender under the management, at least from 1906, of John Oxborrow, a member of another old Suffolk milling family. Edward Oxborrow, until he died in the late eighteen-seventies, had been the miller at Bredfield, while Thomas Oxborrow had Hasketon mill. John Oxborrow continued to serve the Ogilvies for a considerable number of years, but in the winter of 1922–23 the mill was transported to Thorpeness by Amos Clarke, a member of a local family of millwrights, and re-erected as a pumping mill to pump water to the adjacent water tower. Ted Friend, another millwright then employed by the Ogilvies, also took part in this transfer and the final setting of the mill to work. Billy Knights was the mill-keeper.

One of the more difficult aspects of the work was the boring of the central post from end to end to provide a way for the pump drive rod.

There is evidence that a mill once stood in Knodishall itself, but the mill in the parish which worked during the period of our narrative was a post mill with a roundhouse that stood adjacent to the Green on a piece of ground subsequently incorporated into

Fort Green mill, Aldeburgh, soon after it was converted to a house. SPS

Robert Norman's engineering works. Its dates are uncertain. It was there by 1836 and was demolished *c.* 1908. The only miller whose name is known to me was Francis Skoulding.

Windmills suffered from wartime regulations imposed in 1914–18; applying to all types of mills alike, they required the production of a fixed percentage of white flour, and posed problems for stone mills, which leave more flour with the bran than do roller mills. The regulation was the cause of many stone mills dropping out of use for flour milling at that time. Some continued to grind grain for animal feeding, but many simply ceased to work altogether. The further decline in farming and the reduced arable acreages that followed the war completed the ruin of most windmilling enterprises.

In the district we are considering there was the further problem that a high proportion of the mills were post mills. In order to make a windmill into an effective working machine it is necessary that it should be possible to "wind" it; that is to say, it must be possible to present the sails to the direction from which the wind is coming. In a post mill the whole body, or buck, to use the East Anglian term, of the mill is caused to rotate about a large central post, supported at its base on brick piers through strong horizontal members (the crosstrees) and angled struts (quarter-

Theberton tower mill as it was in the time of Watson Cole. The post-mill buck in the foreground came from Glemham.
Peter Dolman Collection

bars), morticed and tenoned together and secured with iron gibs and cotters. The head of the post forms the bearing for the crown tree, the main horizontal cross member below the milling floor, and there is sometimes (though not usually in Suffolk) in addition a collar on the post at the level of the bottom floor of the buck which carries part of the weight. The mill was turned into the wind by a long tailpole extending from the base of the buck down to a little above ground level. In a mill of any size this had a wheel at its base, running on a circular level path called the tramway. Finally came the improvement of turning the mill mechanically by means of a fantail and gearing.

In the oldest mills the staircase had to be raised clear of the ground before winding. Later the stairs were often fitted with wheels; in a mill with a fantail the staircase and the framing bearing the fantail were one structure, stayed to the buck and with the wheels running on a circular tramway. The details of this arrangement varied from mill to mill and from master millwright to master millwright.

By its nature a post mill was a timber structure, boarded against the weather. Traditionally the structural timber was oak, though some mills were built of sweet chestnut, which has characteristics very close to those of oak. A few of the later Sussex

81

post mills had posts of pitch pine. The weatherboarding required tarring or painting at intervals and regular inspection so that splits or cracks in the board and any incipient rot could be dealt with before serious penetration by the weather developed. All this constituted an expense which millers found hard to bear.

Often the trestle of a post mill was protected by a circular brick structure, a roundhouse, with a conical roof projecting up under the buck. In addition to keeping the weather off the trestle the roundhouse provided storage space for grain or flour. The surviving mill at Friston is a post mill with a brick roundhouse, while the Thorpeness mill has a square concrete roundhouse.

By contrast the pumping mill formerly situated at Minsmere, and now re-erected at Stowmarket, is a smock mill, and the mummified mill at Fort Green, Aldeburgh, is a tower mill. In principle the smock mill is identical to the tower mill; both have structures that are static, with only the cap containing the windshaft being capable of rotation to wind the mill. In a smock mill the static portion is a tapered timber structure, boarded against the elements, and hexagonal or octagonal to give clearance to the sails. A tower mill is built, as a rule, circular on plan and

The mill at Thorpeness.

tapered. Most Suffolk tower mills were of brick, possibly tarred. A fine intact tower mill in Suffolk is at Pakenham.

Probably the ultimate in post mills is represented by Saxtead Green Mill, only just to the west of our defined area. Here the mill is made very lofty, in order to raise it above trees and buildings which denied it wind, by raising the trestle upon high brick piers, making the roundhouse a very substantial structure. Sweffling High Mill, long gone, was of similar design. Rex Wailes has said that when Sweffling was dismantled about 1912 the external stairs went to Saxtead Green for use there.

Alfred Aldred kept the Saxtead Green mill going commercially as long as he could, using a Garrett steam tractor to power the machinery through an external pulley when the wind failed.

The post mill at Darsham, moved there in 1801, was run by the Robinson family for over a hundred years, passing from father to son, all confusingly named William. Finally it went to Rose, widow of the last William, from whom it passed to a man named Holmes, and at the end of its life it passed to F. N. Simpson, of Yoxford. It was still listed as working up to 1928 and was not finally destroyed until 1937.

The two-pair tower mill at Theberton ceased to work at about the same time, and only the stump of the brick tower remains. For many years the miller at Theberton was Watson Cole, who had succeeded Thomas Geater and whose widow carried it on after his death, with Fred Keeble running it. After Mrs Cole gave up Fred Keeble and his brother Monty took over as millers for a few years. Queenie Dunn, whose parents lived at that time in the Mill Cottage, has happy memories of Fred and Monty. As a small child she found the mill a fascinating place, especially after dark on a winter afternoon, when it was lit by candle lamps that cast moving shadows as the machinery turned. Fred Keeble had a little wall desk, with a locker beneath, on which he kept the records of his milling. One day he opened the locker and took out one of the small rounded eggs sometimes laid by pullets coming on to lay.

"You know my rooster, Queenie", he said, "well, he laid an egg today and here it is. Just you take it in to your mother and ask her to cook it for your tea."

By the opening of the twenties rural milling was near the end of its long battle with the big dockside roller mills. Fred Keeble eked out his income from the mill by working a smallholding, but by 1924 milling at Theberton had ceased altogether and the mill fell slowly into disrepair; it was taken down in the early thirties.

Competition from steam mills was of long standing. The first steam mill, in London, dated from 1784, but the menace which finally encompassed the ruin of the country wind or water mill was the introduction of roller milling, in which the grain was crushed between iron rollers instead of being ground between upper and nether millstones.

The first effective roller mill was erected by Hefenburger at Rorschach in Switzerland in 1820 and the use of roller mills spread steadily out over Europe. By 1840 Hungary, whose wheatfields of the Danube plain produced much of the grain for the Austro-Hungarian empire, awaking from its long traditionalist slumber on the accession of Franz Josef I, had its first roller mill. In 1862 the method was introduced to Britain, a country in the grip of free trade; as the wheatlands of the American Middle West and Central Canada were opened up by railways high tonnages were shipped to the United Kingdom, soon followed by wheats from Australia. The table below shows how this trade expanded from 1872 to 1900.

United Kingdom Annual Imports of Wheat and Flour (in Quarters) set against home production (source G. J. S. Broomhall–*Corn Exchange Year Book*)

Year	Import	Home Production
1872	9,469,000	11,481,438
1882	14,850,000	10,115,225
1894	16,222,000	7,588,000
1895	25,197,000	4,785,000*
1896	23,431,000	7,281,000
1900	23,196,000	6,790,000

*A drought year in UK.

Large industrialized roller-milling establishments at the dock-side were very well placed to deal with these imports, though they were not the only channel through which imported grain reached the market. Much was distributed to older corn mills if they were conveniently placed to receive it. Grain was transshipped at the major ports from ocean-going ships into lighters or barges for transport to waterside mills and maltings, but little or none reached the windmills dotted over the countryside. Consequently, as British corn-growing declined in the face of imports, so windmills declined with it.

The decline was made worse by the contrasting products of the two systems. Flour milled in a roller mill has a different character from a stone-ground flour. It is in the first place whiter, and capable of being rendered whiter still by bleaching, as can be done in a large establishment with agene. Secondly, it takes up more water in use, giving, weight for weight of finished loaf, a greater economy in use. Thirdly, much less of the natural oil of the wheat is retained in roller-ground flour and there is less tendency for the bread made from it to develop a rancid flavour on keeping. In the past ten years public opinion, reacting to an increased awareness of the value of dietary fibre, has moved pronouncedly back toward stone-ground flour, but from 1870 until at least the early nineteen-seventies it was white roller-milled flour which stood first in the esteem of both bakers and their customers.

Some local millers bowed to demand and put in roller mills driven by a steam engine. Sometimes these supplemented the output of the old windmill or watermill; in some places the original power source dropped out of use. Others refused to compromise and stuck determinedly to stone grinding. William Ezekiel Markin, one of the two millers at Snape, had problems over the spelling of his name, varying it from Markham to Markin, but no internal conflict at all on the merits of stone grinding, which he upheld without deviation to the end of his life. Markin and his wife kept the mill, built in 1800, from the eighteen-seventies. When the old lady died at last in 1908 her obituary shook a last defiant fist at the hated enemy:

> Markin, on May 11th, Hannah Matilda died in her 87th year, wife of the late W. E. Markin, stone flour miller, Snape. Established 1800. No rollers.

Markin's mill, an open-trestle post mill, was painted in oils by George T. Rope in 1897. It is not known when this mill last worked, but it was demolished in 1922 and has now totally vanished. A second post mill, with its trestle hidden within a brick roundhouse, owned or worked by Harry Hudson and before him by Joseph Lee, stood on the opposite side of the village. This mill was afterwards worked by E. Barnes and Son and from 1925 by Frederick Wilson; it ceased work in 1933. The site had had a mill since 1668, and the mill that stood on it latterly was built in 1797 by Thomas Butcher of Wickham Market for William Ship and John Hunt of Parham for £210. When closed the mill stood idle for a while until the buck was dismantled by the late John ("Tiny") Brown, of Leiston. The stones were stored in the roundhouse and were still there in 1936, when the 3 foot 6 inch runner from Snape was taken to replace the 4 foot 4 inch stone at Saxtead Green Mill, in order to lighten the load at the latter. The roundhouse at Snape still stands as part of a house, into which it was converted for use (1937–47) by Benjamin Britten, to the designs of Arthur Welford, the architect, father-in-law of Britten's sister. Britten composed his operas *Peter Grimes*, *The Rape of Lucretia* and *Albert Herring* at the mill.

For many years the tower mill on Fort Green, Aldeburgh, dating from about 1800, was worked by James Pettit (or Pettitt), who farmed at Red House Farm on the Leiston Road and whose

Markin's mill, Snape,
from a painting in oils by
G. T. Rope, 1890.
Courtesy W. Rope;
copied by B. J. Finch

daughter Susette ("Dovey") owned the hand laundry at fort Green. Before him the miller was Thomas Mayhew and before him in turn Henry Sawyer. James Pettit is first mentioned in 1885. Milling had ceased by 1902 and the mill was converted to a house in that year to the designs of R. W. Briggs.

The 1851 harbour proposals show a second mill for drainage on the edge of the marsh not far to the south-west of the old gasworks site in Park Road, opposite the school. A third mill in Aldeburgh was Flintham's mill, owned by the proprietor of the Albert Brewery and standing well back from what is now called Victoria Road, on the seaward side of the station. A post mill, this was known as Station Mill.

When Flintham took his chief clerk, Hall, into partnership and the business was converted into a limited company as Flintham Hall & Co. Ltd the mill was one of the assets taken over by the company. The miller in charge of the mill was a Mr Hayward. Milling had ceased by 1919, when Roy Watson took over the premises, and the mill was taken down in 1924. Initially the work was given to local men to ease distress among the fishermen, but in the end "Tiny"

Brown had to be called in to finish the job.

In all Aldeburgh is said to have had nine mills. In addition to those we have already discussed, there is said to have been a mill on the terrace on the site now covered by the Roman Catholic Church and a smock pumping mill (demolished in 1900) on the marsh to the north of the town. As to the situation of the other three, one was on the edge of the sea roughly midway between Aldeburgh and Thorpeness, another lay inland from this point about half way between Sluice Cottage and the old railway line, while the third was in the town where the East Suffolk Hotel (now the Festival Office) stands. The first two were pumping mills, the latter a corn mill of great antiquity which disappeared early. The other two had also gone by about the turn of the century.

The nearby Friston post mill, at 51 feet to the ridge the tallest surviving post mill in the country, was built in 1811–12. After having several early owners the mill was sold in 1837 to Joshua Reynolds. He was succeeded by Caleb Reynolds Wright, his nephew, who died in 1929, when his executors sold the mill to his son of the same name. Under the Wrights' regime a small steam-

Station mill, Aldeburgh, in its working days when Mr Hayward was the miller and Flintham, the brewer, owned it. The station, with its "all-over" roof, is dimly visible in the left background.
Burns Collection

87

driven mill was set up in the roundhouse of the post mill. Friston was the last mill in the district to grind corn commercially by wind, and is believed to have done its last milling in 1955.

One of the mills at Kelsale, a post mill with a roundhouse, stood at Dorlays Corner on the high ground to the north of the village. There were two further mills in Kelsale parish, at Carlton, close together. The oldest, another post mill with a roundhouse, said to have come from Aldeburgh, was at Kelsale at least by 1800. Close by it was a tower mill built by Whitmore and Binyon of Wickham Market in 1856. These were owned in the eighteen-seventies and eighties by the Skoulding brothers, Thomas and John, whose brother Francis was the miller at Aldringham as well as at a third mill at Cold Fair Green. The Skouldings were succeeded by William Chambers and Sons and then by W. E. and J. J. Maulden, who installed a steam engine. The post mill was demolished about 1895 but the tower mill worked by wind until around 1910, though the steam mill in the tower continued after that; the tower still stands, now used as a house. The mill at Dorlays Corner was worked for many years by William Andrews, who transferred to the tower mill about 1916; the mill at Dorlays Corner was not finally dismantled until 1923–24.

William Waller's Albion Mill at Saxmundham on the hill just to the west of the railway line was earlier owned by Charles Turner and earlier still by Robert Reynolds. A post mill, it was supplemented early this century by a steam mill in the roundhouse. The windmill ceased work soon after the fitting of steam power and was taken down to the roundhouse in 1907, though the firm was continued as Henry Waller & Sons, wine, spirit and corn merchants. Two miles to the south on a knoll overlooking the green on one side and what is now the A12 on the other stood Robert Bloomfield's mill at Benhall, demolished down to the roundhouse in 1921–22 after being taken over by his son, J. G. Bloomfield. The Bloomfields had the mill between them for some sixty years, but latterly an oil engine was used. Benhall Mill, built in the late eighteenth century, had the distinction, according to Rex Wailes, of being built mainly of sweet chestnut. At one time Benhall had a second mill, of which I have no details.

At Leiston a timber smock mill stood on the ridge shared by the railway, a little to the south-east of the station. The earliest miller of whom I have record was James Bedwell, who seems also to have had a mill at Sweffling, though this may have been worked by another miller of the same name. After his death it was carried on for a while by his executors before being sold to Henry James Lambert, by whom it continued to be owned until milling by wind finally ceased; the mill was dismantled in 1917 by "Tiny" Brown. Lambert and his sons had a steam mill built alongside it, and part of the buildings still stand, now used as a store. The Lamberts had a local reputation for being very canny with their money, which they invested in various pieces of cottage property in the town. The Lamberts business suffered from the opening of Hayward's steam mill in Carr Avenue *c*1912, and this may well have been the principal cause of the decline of the smock mill establishment.

Out of the village there was at one time, though not in the memory of any now living, an open trestle post mill referred to as the "Monastic Mill". The mill stood until about 1870; there had been a mill on the site, possibly the same mill, for over 250 years.

At Westleton the oldest mill was Rouse's post mill on an open trestle at the Moor, dating from the first third of the eighteenth century. Like so many mills this was lost by fire. Ralphs Mill, a smock mill built perhaps fifty years later, stood until 1969, when it was demolished, but the most recent of the Westleton mills in terms of building date was the post mill with roundhouse which stood on the mill mound in the centre of the village. It dated from 1842–43, and was taken down as unsafe about 1963.

At one time there was a post mill at Tunstall. It was certainly there by about 1815–16; later William Ford was the miller. It ceased work about 1928 and in 1928–29 was demolished by "Tiny" Brown. At Blaxhall the post mill had the distinction of reputedly working four pairs of stones. The miller in the middle years of the last century was William Cockerell. The mill suffered a disastrous fire in 1883 and was never rebuilt; what remained after the fire was demolished so thoroughly that it is difficult to find any traces.

Another mill that is all but forgotten stood at Middleton. The miller there in the opening years of this century was John Newson Junior, one of the numerous clan of Newsons who were also brickmakers, farmers and coal merchants. John carried on until *c* 1910, when he was succeeded by Walter Hatcher, but the mill is said to have ceased work and been demolished about 1913.

The area did not lend itself so readily to the use of water mills, but there were a number. The best preserved surviving example is Butley Mill, which stands on the back road from Butley into Chillesford; it is nearer to Chillesford than to Butley village, but it takes its name from being at the head of the Butley River. It is said that in the past the river was navigable up to the mill, but it is certainly not so at the time of writing, although according to Robert Simper barges penetrated to a jetty 500 yards downstream from the mill until the first world war. Paul's barge *Eaglet* was used to deliver maize for stock feed in this way.

The mill has had a chequered history. There has been a mill on the site since 1535, but the present buildings probably date in the main from the early nineteenth century. The wheel was undershot, following the common practice in East Suffolk.

Tunstall mill.

The millers at Butley are the Hewitts, owners of the mill for generations. At one time a post mill stood on the rising ground behind the water mill, having been brought from Woodbridge to replace an earlier mill, fallen into decay. The replacement was lost in the late nineties by fire, the traditional enemy of the windmill, and was replaced by a brick-built roller mill on the river bank next to the water mill; the roller mill is still standing and working as a provender mill. The water wheel in the older mill was taken out about 1962.

At one time the Hewitts were commercial growers of lupins, which were harvested and sent by barge to Belgium for the manufacture, it is said of natural dye for carpet making.

Only five miles from Butley Mill across the fields is Little Glemham. The watermill there, on a tributary of the Ore, is a little smaller than that at Butley, though with three pairs of stones. The date of the present building is uncertain, but probably late eighteenth century. The wheel is undershot as it was at Butley. The miller at Little Glemham in 1858 was George Geater, who continued for several years afterwards but was succeeded by the Stannards. William Stannard worked the mill until the nineteen-twenties. At one time Little Glemham had an open trestle post windmill, the buck of which was dismantled and taken to Theberton.

The present lessee of this water mill is Dennis Thorold, who

*The Leiston smock mill in
the early years of this
century.*
Courtesy J. S. Waddell;
SPS

came across it by chance when walking. Being attracted by the buildings, even in their state of near-dereliction, he made inquiries as to what was to happen to them. He heard with horror that they were unused, unwanted and, in consequence, likely to be allowed to collapse, if not actively nudged into a fall. After lengthy negotiations he became the leaseholder and set about restoration. The first step was to restore the envelope to a state of wind-and watertightness, and he then began to resuscitate the machinery. At the time of writing this is still incomplete and the wheel awaits rebuilding.

The third water mill in the territory of this book was at Watermill Farm, Middleton, driven by the Minsmere River. Though it is possible to pick out where the mill must have been, little is left to identify what it was like or to attempt to date it. It is said to have been of great antiquity and to have vanished by the eighteenth century. There was a post mill with roundhouse at Middleton dating from the late eighteenth century. It was still working in 1883, when the miller was Charles Pretty, but how long it continued to grind after that I have no means of knowing.

There was possibly a tidemill at Orford in medieval times. The village mill was an open trestle post mill dating perhaps from the beginning of the last century. The miller was Robert Martin, landlord of the King's Head. Later and for many years it was run by Sarnder Osbourne Markin. References to it as a working mill cease by the nineties of the last century and it was demolished in 1913. Out of the village at Lodge Farm was Orford Black Mill, a wooden smock mill dating from the first quarter of the last century and burned about 1886. In 1844 the miller was William Field; later George Leach had this mill.

To be a windmiller requires total commitment. The mill must be watched day and night, particularly at times of high wind. Speeding can lead to overheating or the striking of sparks off the stones and may well result in a fire, to which windmills are, in any case, prone. Such a mill is labour intensive when at work but vulnerable to involuntary idleness when the wind is coy.

The reward for effort made was very poor, moreover. As the old race of millers gradually dropped away into retirement or death few could be found to succeed them. A combination of circumstances conspired to destroy mills. Poor financial returns, the farming slump of the twenties, the ever-increasing cost of repairs, growing scarcity of millwrights, and the greater cost of labour in the inter-war years combined with the disappearance of the millers themselves to snuff out the mills. Today only Friston windmill remains intact and original on our territory; thanks to the Ogilvies Thorpe mill remains, now cared for by the county council, in its altered role as a pumping mill.

Brickworks and   8
Brickmakers

THE ART of the stonemason in East Suffolk relied upon imported material, whereas the evidence of the local brick-maker's craft is widespread and self-evident. Brickearth occurs all up the coast, but the only worthwhile building material used direct from the pit was flint, and even this was usually stiffened and bonded by quoins and band courses of brick and by brick jambs and arches to door and window openings.

A brickyard in its simplest form needed very little fixed investment. Bricks are still made at Aldeburgh and Cove Bottom. Within living memory, or almost there were yards at Chillesford, Benhall, Orford, Tunstall, Snape, Carlton and Leiston, and two other yards are known to have existed in Aldeburgh, at Kings Legend and what is now Park Road. The yard off Park Road that appears on the deposited plans of the 1870 Aldeborough Harbour Act was situated in a fold in the land to the west of an imaginary line drawn from Alde House to Albert House and equidistant by about 300 yards from cither. Most of them, no doubt, began as clamp burning yards; indeed, only at Aldeburgh, Leiston, Snape and South Cove is there clear evidence that the working method progressed beyond that stage.

For clamp burning the requirements were simple; all that the brickmaker needed was a flat and drained site. The paving in a working yard was usually of defective bricks from previous burnings, but with a new site presumably such bricks had initially to be brought in from working yards elsewhere. The prepared floor would be higher than the surrounding ground to help keep it dry. Above the base came the fire holes, a grid of flues built dry and covered with two courses of bricks laid on edge diagonally and about two inches apart.

The fire-holes were packed with faggots of gorse or brush-wood, sometimes supplemented with dry hedgebrishings, and the clamp builder then filled the space between his diagonal bricks with sifted cinders, breeze or small coals. He next laid a close-packed course of unburned bricks on edge, followed by a seven or eight-inch layer of fuel and another course of green bricks. After this came another bed of fuel about half the thickness of the first, another layer of bricks and a further spread of fuel, this time only about two inches deep. This structure formed the bottom of the clamp and contained all the fuel needed for the burning. The rest of the clamp consisted of raw bricks built in thin walls with space between to allow the heat to circulate. The top of the clamp was usually protected with discarded bricks from previous burnings or with boards or old corrugated iron.

A finished clamp would be some fourteen feet high. As to its other dimensions, this would depend upon the scale on which the yard was trading. Clamps of up to a hundred thousand bricks were common in the brickfields of the Thames and Medway estuaries, but it seems likely that the coastal brickyards set their sights rather lower. A clamp of a hundred thousand bricks would cover an area of perhaps 45 feet by 180 feet, but certainly smaller clamps than this were prevalent in East Suffolk.

Once the faggots in the fireholes were ignited, usually by lighting straw in the openings facing the prevailing wind, the burner hoped that the fire would spread slowly and evenly through the fuel in the clamp. In windy weather it might be burned out in a fortnight, but in a calm and sultry spell burning might take up to six weeks. The clamp subsided in the process of burning; if the fire had spread evenly the subsidence would be relatively orderly, but too rapid or uneven burning produced collapses inside the clamp.

A gale was the brickmaker's dread, with the fire inside the clamp drawn to white heat and flames dancing on the top. A clamp burnt in this way would have a high proportion of wasters, mostly bricks vitrified and fused into lumps, known to the brickmaker as burrs. The proportion of overburnt bricks in clamp burning generally was high, both misshapen and sound. Sound overburnt bricks were saleable for use in foundations, but many of the misshapen specimens were too distorted to be of any use other than to be broken up for the bottoms of roads and yards. Burrs mostly found their way to the same destination, though some were built into ornamental garden walls and rockeries.

There were yet other hazards to the clamp-burnt brick. Heavy rain upon the hot bricks on the outsides of the clamp or even a sudden spell of cold wind would produce bricks with surface or deeper cracking. These were called chuffs, and again were not usually capable of being sold except as hardcore.

Some builders bought bricks "unsorted from the clamp". Indeed, the brickmaker himself was often a builder and hence the user of the bricks he made. Leiston brickworks was worked for several decades by the Garretts, yielding bricks for building and enlarging Leiston Works, and the Aldeburgh Hall brickworks has been owned since 1926 by William Reade, the Aldeburgh builder, and his successors. Bricks bought unsorted were something of a lottery and were sorted as a rule on the building site. Well-burnt bricks of good colour and shape were used for the external facings

A view in Leiston brick-works in the first decade of this century.
J. S. Waddell

of a house. Overburnt bricks of reasonable shape went into the foundations or internal walls and chimneys. Underburnt bricks that were sound and true in shape, usually known as "grizzles", were used up in internal walls in situations where there were no great compressive loads placed upon them. This left the "place" bricks, weak underburnt bricks, perhaps with stones or cracks in them. Regrettably these were all too often worked in with the grizzles, particularly when the building under construction was a cottage property being built at a cut price.

When the bricks were sorted at the brickyard these place bricks often stayed behind, to be used in building the next clamp. Bricks not completely burnt in one burning might come out as sound bricks after being built in a second time. Burning bricks in clamps was on the whole wasteful, but it had the advantage that it involved little capital outlay.

To set up a clamp yard in business once the land had been bought or leased did not cost much. There was the cost of labour in stripping off sufficient topsoil and overburden, collectively known as "callow", to enable the brickearth to be reached. Beyond this there was the levelling, draining and paving of the clamp site, the paving of a weathering area for the clay, the provision of benches, moulds, pallets, barrows and probably a rough shelter for the moulders, but very little besides. A brickmaker would have to finance clay-digging and weathering for one winter before he saw any return, but half a year's wages for a gang of six men was probably not more than a hundred and fifty pounds at the turn of the century, so that the capital tied up in the preparatory works was not great.

Despite this, one must always remember the old saying that "there is nothing to be got out of a brickyard but hard work". The brickmaker at any of the yards on the coast would have been lucky in 1900 to have averaged a pound a thousand all through for his bricks as they lay in the yard. The owners, almost without exception, had other occupations. Thomas Riggs and his son Walter, who successively were lessees of the Aldeburgh brickworks for many years, were barge-owners and also grocers, with a shop in Aldeburgh and a branch for some time in Leiston. James Olding, at one time the Snape brickmaker, was a farmer. Edward Rope at Orford carried on business in succession to his father and uncle as a maltster, corn, seed, coal, wine, spirit, ale and porter merchant, brewer, seller of chemical manures and agent for the Suffolk Alliance Fire & Life Office as well as brickmaker. John Thurlow of Benhall brickyard, who actually lived in Saxmundham, was a stonemason there as well as a brickmaker, while Will and Talbot Carr, who had succeeded the Garretts at Leiston brickworks, were also coal merchants. Talbot Carr rejoiced in the nickname of "Rungy", though for what reason I do not know. John Thurlow was the son of Tom Thurlow, one time school-mate and lifetime friend of Newson Garrett, and a pioneer photographer.

The fact of the Carrs being coal merchants dovetailed in conveniently with the trade of brickyard owner. Brickmaking was a trade of the summer season and coal selling peaked during the winter. Employers like the Carrs who tried to keep their men on the payroll all the year round were helped to do so by this convenient interlocking of labour demand. There were other advantages. Most household coal and coke was supplied forked or riddled, ie without smalls, breeze and dust. The brick clamp or kiln was a convenient way of using up these riddlings. Since brickyard workers were noted for their heavy consumption of beer, Edward Rope, who sold both coal and beer as well as bricks, might be said to have had the best of both worlds.

The brickearth of the coastal brickyards was known as the Chillesford Clay, suggesting that the yard at Chillesford was early on the brickmaking scene. In the area of the pit being worked at Aldeburgh in the eighties this stratum was about fifteen feet thick at its greatest, tapering to four feet, with an overburden of callow about three feet thick. Below the clay is a bed of sandy loam and below that the crag.

At the time of writing the accessible brickearth at Aldeburgh has been worked out and the material currently used in production is brought in by lorry from the old pit at Chillesford, giving a brick very similar in its characteristics to the Aldeburgh bed in its prime, though the earth itself has slightly different characteristics in handling and working, being stickier to handle and leaving a film on tools; moreover, it requires more sand to make it leave the moulds cleanly. The sand used at Aldeburgh comes from a small sandpit owned by the company at Hazlewood.

Though the earth was latterly extracted at Aldeburgh by an excavator, formerly digging was done by hand by the hazardous process of "undermining". The face of the clay exposed in the pit was undercut with spades and picks to a depth of two or three feet. At each end of the undercut a vertical cut was made to provide a line of fracture. The line of cut was then drawn out on the top surface of the clay and wooden wedges were driven in along the line so marked until the selected area of clay was split off and fell to the floor of the pit. The quantity removed each time varied from as little as five or ten tons up to a hundred or even two hundred tons. The wedges used were hardwood—usually oak, ash or chestnut —perhaps three feet long and five or six inches in diameter, banded with an iron ferrule at the top to discourage splitting and sharpened to an easy chisel point. The driving tool was the countryman's applewood beetle.

Brickearth was dug from the pit during the autumn and early winter. In a clamp burning yard, making common bricks, the clay was wheeled to the weathering platform, where it was spread in layers, each layer being sprinkled with breeze before the succeeding layer was placed upon it. The action of the rain and wind combined with the frosts of the winter to weather the clay, breaking down the clods. Stones and shale found in the digging of the clay would have been thrown aside by the diggers, but the weathering process frequently revealed others which would be rejected in the succeeding process of tempering.

In some yards chalk or lime was added to the weathering clay to act as a flux in the subsequent burning, but this was not done at Aldeburgh, where the only additive was about 20% by volume of the underlying sandy loam; nor is it known to have been done in the other coastal brickyards in the past. Once a heap reached its finished height it was left to weather. Digging and stacking might finish about Christmas time and the tempering, the next active step, did not begin till serious frosts were past, so the clay had some three months of weathering. The practice in stacking varied from brickmaker to brickmaker. While some never built above about two feet, a single layer, others stacked in two or even three layers, but it was unusual to go higher than six feet or three layers.

With the return of milder weather the cutting out and tempering of the brickearth would begin. Cutting out was done vertically, using a croom, working from the edge of the stack inwards so as to make sure that the clay in the heap was mingled as much as possible. To make certain of this it was turned over two or three times on the weathering floor, during which operation any stones and rubbish found were picked out. The clay removed from the heap was subjected to tempering to make it sufficiently plastic for the moulder. Sometimes water had to be added to make the clay soft enough for moulding, but this was avoided wherever possible since all the water put into the clay had to be dried out again before burning.

At Aldeburgh and Leiston, perhaps elsewhere as well, tempering was done mechanically by the use of a pugmill, a strong wooden or iron barrel placed vertically, with a vertical shaft in the centre on which were keyed cutting knives. The clay was tipped into the barrel while the shaft and its knives were revolved either by a horse walking in a circular path or by gearing, belts and shafting from a fixed or portable steam engine. As the knives cut into the loose brickearth it was kneaded and pushed through the mill, emerging as pug, a plastic material suitable for throwing.

At Aldeburgh four moulders worked round the pugmill under rough shelters, taking the clay as it emerged from the barrel,

The decaying pug mill and moulder's shelter at Aldeburgh brickworks.

roughly shaping it in their hands into the warp, flinging the warp in turn down into the wetted and sanded mould, and finally striking off the clay flush with the top of the mould, using a strickel. The mould was lifted from its base and given a tap, which caused the green brick to drop out on to a wooden pallet. The moulder had a boy or a learner in attendance whose job it was to pick up the brick with a second pallet and stack it, still held between the two pallets, on the running-off barrow. When loaded the barrows were run to the hacks, where the bricks were dried.

A moulder would produce a green brick about every half-minute, and the cycle of wetting, sanding, moulding, throwing and stacking went on ceaselessly and relentlessly hour after hour. A moulder needed great stamina and incredible resistance to boredom. Since most had reduced the working process to a series of reflex actions, their minds and attention were left free for talking.

Moulders were paid by piecework, frequently by the thousand. Since it was a summer occupation nineteenth-century hours of work were often very long, from soon after first light, say about half past four, until eight in the evening, with only a half-hour break about 3 pm when the pugmill was stopped. Aldeburgh brickmakers, from the time William Reade took over, worked from 6 am to 6 pm stopping for half an hour for breakfast and for an hour at midday.

The village clamp-burning yards produced mainly plain bricks, with a few splayed headers or stretchers for plinths or cills. Leiston was more ambitious and essayed flower pots and chimney pots, which needed a kiln for burning. For many years a man named Swallow was the potmaker at Leiston. In his spare time and with his wife's help he managed to run a small fruit and vegetable shop in Cheapside (Sizewell Road), Leiston, and by prodigious thrift accumulated the funds to build a row of cottages further out along the Sizewell Road, to which he looked to provide an income for his old age. Aldeburgh yard, also using more developed methods than most of its neighbours, acquired a name for intricate "specials", in the making of which more sophisticated techniques were required than in making commons.

A common brick, green from the moulder's hand, was taken by the runner to the hacks, where it was picked from the barrow, holding it between the pallets, and stacked on edge, criss-cross or herringbone, allowing the pallets to be withdrawn and returned to the moulding bench. The hack was an open-sided wooden structure with a boarded, thatched, felted or corrugated iron pitched roof, shoulder high or less, and some two feet across. The loaded hacks were protected at the sides against driving rain or hot sun by bathings, light movable panels of wooden wattle, or wooden

*Placing the bricks to dry
in the hacks.* SPS;
photo by W. J. Brunell

frames covered with hessian or, in the case of most of the coastal
yards, with marsh reed or straw.

Bricks stood in the hacks for as long as it took them to lose
enough moisture to fit them for burning. This period depended
upon the judgement of the brickmaker. Two weeks was probably
the least period, but in long spells of humid, windless weather up to
a month might be needed. To assist even drying the green bricks

were *rallied*, that is to say restacked so as to vary the areas in contact and alter the exposure to the prevailing wind. Judging the drying required discernment.

Once deemed dry enough, the green bricks were drawn from the hacks on to crowding barrows and wheeled to the clamp or kiln. Building a clamp was not a job for a wet day. One torrential summer storm on unprotected bricks could undo three weeks in the hacks. Bricks being loaded into a kiln were more protected than those in a half-built clamp. In every way other than capital outlay a kiln, even the crude updraught kilns of the Suffolk coastal yards, was superior to a clamp. A kiln was a very substantial structure. At Aldeburgh, where the kilns were set into the ground for half their height, the walls were 7 feet 6 inches thick at their base, tapering as they rose but still three bricks (2 feet 3 inches) thick at the top, 20 feet above the base. Kilns had the advantage over clamps that, once built, the enclosing structure and the firing holes and chambers withstood many firings. Aldeburgh used three kilns, the biggest of which could hold 65,000 bricks, the others 55,000 and 35,000 respectively.

Loading was done through arched openings known as wickets about half way up the sides of the kiln, entered from general ground level. The fireholes were in the ends, approached from a large pit, the part nearest the kiln roofed in corrugated iron. The contents of the kiln were built up, as Alfred Rouse described it, "five on two". That is to say, all the green bricks were laid on edge. Each bolt of bricks consisted of two rows laid end on to each other, succeeded by a following course laid five deep at right angles to the first row, and so on until the desired height was reached. A circulating space was created round the perimeter of the kiln, filled with diagonally placed bricks widely spaced. The object of this was to allow the hot flue gases to rise freely up the sides of the kiln to keep the mass of bricks evenly heated; at the same time the diagonal placing of the bricks allowed them to take up the expansion of the mass of bricks in the centre of the kiln.

The kiln was topped off with a platting of wasters from previous burnings and then protected with a temporary pitched roof of boards, removed as the kiln hotted up. Firing took six days or more, correctly, five and a half days, as the fires were allowed to go out at midday on Saturday. For the first three days of firing the kiln was warmed only slowly to tan the green bricks, ie to drive off the residual moisture from them, but from Thursday to Saturday the fires were built up fully. The Chillesford clays were best fired at temperatures in the range 1100° to 1200°F, but in the absence of any means of measuring the temperature the actual heat of the kiln depended upon the judgement and experience of the burners.

The wickets were sealed up against entry of cold air firstly with

A view down into the stoking area of the kiln at Aldeburgh brickworks.

a dry wall of scrap bricks, then a cavity and finally an outer skin of scrap bricks laid in pug, the cavity being filled with sand as the outer skin rose. The fireholes were fitted with pendulum dampers to regulate the supply of air to the fires. The fires were kindled, as in a clamp, with faggots of furze or brushwood and lit with straw. Latterly at Aldeburgh waste timber from the owners' joinery shop and building operations was used to start up the kiln, but the main firing was with coal. Once lit, the fires had to be attended round the clock. The burners worked in two shifts, checking and making up the fires four or five times an hour, according to the state of the wind.

Peter Howard, who worked at one time as a burner, recalled the glories of June nights, with a full moon reflected from the waters of the Alde and the soothing summer scent of mown grass. Life was best on night shift during the three days of tanning, when perhaps no more than 30 to 35 hundredweights of coal might need to be fed into the fires, but when the fires were full on the big kiln needed up to three tons in a twelve-hour shift. Because its fireholes were very long considerable effort was involved in reaching the back of the grates. The burners had a rough couch to rest on.

In pre-war days when bricks still went away by barge from the brickworks jetty there was always the possibility of a bargeman, returning from the Railway or the Albert, dropping in for a few minutes' talk, or a crony might walk up from the town to while away half an hour or so of the evening. The small hours were the silent lonely ones, punctuated by the feet of the rabbits on the roof, the hoot of a hunting owl and the bark of a fox, their ending marked by the splendours of the dawn chorus and the incipient dawn. There were, of course, the chilly, misty dawns when the vapours rolled in off the estuary and the fires were very comforting until the strengthening heat of the sun burned off the mists.

At the peak of barge traffic from the works two or three barges would be alongside the jetty at the same time. Eastwoods, the London builders' merchants, were consistent purchasers of Aldeburgh bricks, shipped in their own or in other barges to upriver wharves and banks of the Thames at Vauxhall, Chelsea Creek, Putney or Chiswick or to the docks at Brentford, southern terminus of the Grand Union Canal. Many of the red quoins, bands and arches that adorn Edwardian developments in Chiswick or Ealing originated on the banks of the Alde.

The night watchman and stoker at Leiston brickworks in its closing years was an old man known as "Chocolate" Ford. Ted Dunn remembers how as a boy he used to come out of the Scout hut after dark and see the glow of the kiln being fired, and how the old man welcomed Ted or his mates in for a chat, probably a pleasant shortening of the lonely hours of the night.

In the nineteen-twenties the making of commons in the coastal brickyards, undercut by factory-made bricks, especially flettons from Peterborough, became uneconomic, though the demand for red facings held up rather better and there was a brief flush of work after the war, up to about 1922. The achievement of a satisfactory success rate with red facings involved burning in a kiln, and one after another the clamp yards dropped out. The last yard thought to have worked with clamps was at Carlton, and there the practice had ceased before 1914.

Leiston brickworks came to an end about 1921 and Snape's a few years later, leaving only Aldeburgh and Cove Bottom at work. One of the casualties of this final slump in village brickmaking was the fortunes of the Newson family, who had had a long involvement in brickmaking in the district both as owners or lessees of yards and as practical brickmakers. In 1879 George Newson was noted by Kelly as having a brick and tile yard at Holly Tree Farm, Yoxford, and another at Benhall. By 1888 he was also noted as working at Snape and Tunstall, and four years later some of the yards were listed as belonging to George Newson and Son, the son being Samuel, who seems to have had charge of the Benhall yard by then. Samuel Newson and Son thereafter appear as brickmakers and farmers at Benhall, Carlton and Snape, where they also traded as coal merchants. None of these enterprises survived beyond the brief period of high demand after the 1914–18 war; by 1922 all were gone. When William Reade wished to reopen the disused Aldeburgh works in 1926 Bill Newson Senior, son of Samuel Newson, and his two sons, Billy Junior and Sam, came to work for him. Old Billy became the leading man in the yard and the maker of "specials".

Billy Newson Senior and young Bill were both makers; Sam was the expert at loading and drawing the kiln. Billy Junior followed his father as moulder of "specials" and taught Arnold Drew the art of making them. Thus there is a direct line of experience at Aldeburgh extending back more than a hundred years. Another brickmaker at Aldeburgh was Albert Paternoster, who worked at one time in the Leiston yard, and yet another employee was Jimmy Cracknell, now retired to East Bergholt.

Aldeburgh hit back at the mass-produced brick by going in for wirecuts, which involved a further degree of mechanization. A wirecut is made by extruding the tempered clay through a die, the cross-section of which is to the dimensions on plan of an unburnt brick. By the operation of a cam the ribbon of clay is extruded intermittently; at each stroke, while the ribbon is still, parallel taut steel wires are drawn down through it, in the manner of a cheese wire, to produce frog-less bricks, which are then removed, hacked and burned in the manner already described. The Aldeburgh wirecuts were sound bricks, but of uninteresting appearance and hence of use only for inside or colour-washed work.

By the early nineteen-sixties the yard was no longer profitable and soon began to lose money. A decision had to be taken, therefore, whether to close down or to modernize. The strength of the yard lay in the attractiveness of its facing bricks and its ability to produce matching "specials". A visual demonstration of this is the facade of the Post Office in Aldeburgh, completed in 1949 by William Reade, using bricks from his own brickyard. Its weakness was the high and increasing expense of making the bricks by hand and burning them in coal-fired kilns. Not only was the coal very expensive but the use of such a fuel was also labour intensive, requiring the constant attendance of a stoker.

The first step in modernization was the building of a 180-foot drying tunnel, in which green bricks were dried in a current of hot air, cutting out the labour of hacking and rallying. The bricks are set out on trucks which are drawn a little way up the tunnel each day, taking ten days to pass through. Three new oil-fired kilns were built, each holding 35,000 bricks. These kilns were wholly above ground, a feature which proved a mixed blessing. It made easier the handling of the bricks during the charging and discharging of the kiln but increased the amount of repairs required in stopping cracks in the walls between successive firings. Oil has its shortcomings as a fuel; it was found to increase the amount of sulphur compounds deposited in the bricks and hence the formation of white efflorescence on the faces of walls built from them.

"Kellie" (kilnman) Dan Whitman "drawing the kiln" at Tuddenham. SPS; photo by W. J. Brunell.

105

Mechanization of the moulding process was to follow, firstly with the introduction of a secondhand Berry hydraulic press capable of producing about a thousand bricks an hour. Under the new regime brickearth was taken from the pit by a mechanical excavator, taken by lorry to the tempering pad and thence by a tractor shovel to the hopper of the brickmaking machine. Moulding by machine saves some time and fuel in drying, as the machine works with clay substantially drier than is possible with hand moulding.

One of the virtues of the yard has always been its ability to produce "specials". For many years Arnold Drew was the sole remaining hand moulder. The restoration of the Moot Hall at Aldeburgh used bricks moulded by him, though the making of bricks for the rebuilding of the Tudor chimneys of Wingfield Castle, Lincolnshire, was a project that attracted rather more attention. In 1976–77 the company was asked to undertake the manufacture of all the "specials" required for the construction of reproduction Tudor chimneys on a building in Buffalo, New York State, intended for use as a restaurant; this involved about three thousand bricks of all kinds, the making, crating and shipping of which was a considerable undertaking.

What made Arnold a compelling man too was his thorough interest in what he did and in the problems that had to be tackled in making the more elaborate examples of his work. Moulds were kept in a store against possible future use, a kind of library of "specials". Arnold was quite happy to talk to anyone who entered his workshop. Indeed conversation at intervals probably helped to counteract monotony, but he never stopped working; all the time he was talking his hands would go on with the routine of moulding.

Originally the works site was part of the land of Aldeburgh Hall Farm, but as the town grew plots of land along the road to Saxmundham were sold off for building; the remaining inaccessible area of brickearth is under the gardens of the houses built on these plots. Aldeburgh Hall Farm was owned for many years by Joseph Flintham, who had the Albert Brewery, but it seems probable that the brickworks was always worked by a lessee. The name of the brickmaker in Kelly's directory for 1855 was John Emeney, whom White had listed in 1844 as a bricklayer. In 1885 and for many years thereafter the lessee of the yard was Thomas Adamson Riggs, who was succeeded by his son Walter. Other names mentioned in connection with the yard are the partnership of Page and Kingsley and Captain the Honourable C. S. M. Bateman Hanbury, who ran it from 1918 to 1921, when he became insolvent, a fate which overtook many operators of brickyards. William Reade took it over in 1926; as far as is known it was unused from 1921 to 1926.

Opposite, top: *The remains of the Aldeburgh Brickworks jetty into the River Alde, spring 1988.*

Opposite, bottom: *Moulder's shelter at Tuddenham Brickworks, a little south of our territory, in the first decade of this century.* SPS; photo by W. J. Brunell

The martello tower at Slaughden, finished in 1812, is built of London stock bricks that have characteristics consistent with an origin in the brickfields of the Thames or Medway estuaries and brought round by sea. On the face of it this appears to suggest that local brickmaking was on too limited a scale to provide the seven hundred thousand or so bricks required for a tower; on the other hand it might be that the strength of the London stocks was preferred to the lesser strengths of local bricks.

The tradition is that the bricks were brought by barges which were run on to the beach at high tide, unloaded between tides and floated off again by the next tide. Though it might be objected that the use of barges on this stretch of coast belongs to the second rather than to the first half of the last century, it is a fact that the *Industrious Anne*, a swimhead spritsail barge built at Crown Quay, Sittingbourne, in 1799, was registered at Aldeburgh in 1800; she was a pioneer in a coastal trade which was to remain for half a century to come, mainly in the hands of brigs and schooners.

It is very likely that in earlier days bricks from Snape and Tunstall were shipped from Snape Bridge, and it is quite possible that bricks left Rope's yard at Orford by ship or barge. In the days when Iken Cliff was still a port bricks may have been sent from there; a small brickyard at Iken was owned by Frances Keer at least until 1879, and as late as 1892 George Chambers was still making pipes and tiles there for land drainage.

Many small yards were insubstantial and transitory. Though clays are widespread, the properties that make a good brickearth are not so common. A depression in a meadow and a few bricks below the surface often mark an old brickyard and the grave of someone's hopes.

Even within the confines of a district as small as that which we are considering there were appreciable differences in the colouration of the finished bricks. At Aldeburgh the bricks are a medium deep uniform red. Benhall, by contrast, made a brick with a pronounced yellow colour, tending towards the bricks of West Suffolk, while at Snape, striking an average between the two, the colour was a medium red tending to orange. Firing influenced the colour of the bricks: the hotter the firing, the darker the bricks tended to be. Where a kiln was wood fired, bricks close to the flame path had a tendency to become bluer, and selected blued headers were often built into patterns in faced work to give variety.

The type of brick kiln used at Aldeburgh and elsewhere in the district, like a city built on a hill, could not be hidden. After dark the glow from its firing could be seen from the air for miles, and this led to the closing in the Second World War of many small works in areas where the flames from the kiln might have been used as beacons by enemy aircraft.

Ships and Barges 9

THE FORTUNES of brickmakers and shipowners were closely linked, and those of both were changed conclusively by the arrival of the railway—brickmaking by the rise of the rail-borne traffic in machine-made bricks from the Midlands and Peterborough, and coastal shipping by the direct competition of the railway for traffic.

The Eastern Counties Railway was promoted with the objective of serving the area by a main line from London to Norwich by way of Colchester, but as narrated elsewhere its financial troubles diverted it from its objective and it fell eventually to the lot of the Eastern Union Railway to build the line to Woodbridge, opened in 1859. From there the East Suffolk Railway continued through Saxmundham and Halesworth to Lowestoft, with a branch to serve Leiston and Aldeburgh. It was the arrival of this branch in Aldeburgh in April, 1860, that broke the dependence of the district upon transport by sea.

Up to that time the coal used had been carried in schooners and brigs, mainly from the ports of the North East of England, though possibly interspersed with cargoes from the South Wales coalfields. With the establishment of coal as a fuel for malting a demand arose for high carbon coals effectively free from traces of contaminating elements, notably arsenic, and this stabilized the seaborne trade with South Wales.

Trading between Snape and the small port of Saundersfoot in Pembrokeshire for such coal was carried on by Newson Garrett during his period of ownership at Snape (1840 to 1893) and was perpetuated by his successors. Coal was brought to the staithe at Saundersfoot by a railway of the unusual gauge of 4 feet 0¾ inch, wider than most narrow gauge lines but less than standard gauge (4 feet 8½ inches), worked by an equally nonconformist stud of locomotives built or altered to suit the restricted dimensions of a tunnel on the line. The passage from Saundersfoot to Snape took, on average, about ten days.

Because of the restricted draught in the Alde above Slaughden the river was navigable only by vessels drawing 10 feet of water or less, barring it to, or at least making it exceedingly difficult for, the old collier brigs. Rope's *Coaster* (106 tons) was still trading to Iken Cliff for them in the eighteen-fifties, but the handier schooners had mainly taken the place of brigs by that time both with the Ropes, in business from the previous century, and with the more recently arrived Garretts, Newson and Richard. Rope's schooners included the *Clementina*, 89 tons, built for them at William Bayley's St Clement's yard at Ipswich in 1834, the second-hand *Queen Adelaide*, the *Plough*, the *Sophia* and the *Dorothea*. Another schooner, George Disbrey's *English Rose*, drawing 13 feet, penetrated as far as Orford.

Newson Garrett owned the 86-ton *Salamander*, but lost her by fire in February, 1858, replacing her with the *Maria*, 56 tons, registered with him on 9th August, 1858, and stated to be "built abroad". The sloop *Deben*, 57 tons, built in Holland in 1846, came into his ownership in 1859 but was deprived of her gear and made into a lighter in 1863. At the end of October the same year he lost the *Maria* off Cromer. His much older *Hope*, 50 tons, also a sloop, was built as early as 1837 at Knottingley, Yorkshire, though she did not come into his hands until September, 1859. The *Hope* survived to be transferred to his son George in 1898, but only just, as she was broken up the next year. The name *Salamander* was transferred to an 84-ton schooner, of unrecorded origin, bought by Newson Garrett in the summer of 1859; this vessel remained with him until 1873, when she was sold to Thomas Davis and William Bate of Hayle, displaced by barges. The last schooner commissioned by him was the *Kate* (83 tons), completed at Groningen, Holland, in 1858 but lost in the North Sea in December, 1864.

By this time he had become attracted to the greater flexibility of barges in the matter of draught and economy of crewing. His first venture into barging was undertaken jointly with Joseph Wood of the Artillery Brewery, Westminster, when the *Bengal*, 65 tons, was registered in their joint names on 10th December, 1857. This first barge was followed the next year by the wholly owned *Argo*, 51 tons, actually built on his premises at Snape, possibly by John Felgate, who was certainly responsible for the *Percy* (95 tons), launched there in 1860. The original registration of the *Percy* was as a "schooner with standing bowsprit", but this was later amended to "barge", after rebuilding and alteration in 1878. It was changed again in 1898 to "ketch", at which it remained until the vessel was removed from the register in 1904 after being stranded and broken up. I take it that she was of the type described by Frank Carr as "a flat-bottomed schooner" or, in the expressive words of a shipbuilder quoted by him, "a schooner with the bottom cut off".

Two years later Newson Garrett acquired ten of the traditional sixty-four shares in the smack *Two Brothers*, originally built in 1822 and noted as being of 25 tons. Upon being bought this vessel was lengthened, supposedly at Snape. Tradition has it that she was intended for use as a pilot cutter. Two years prior Newson had taken over his brother Richard's quarter share of the 35-ton cutter-rigged *Pilot*, built in 1843 at Aldeburgh and enlarged in 1860.

A laden brick barge from Aldeburgh brickyard jetty, on its way to London in the twenties.
Arthur Welford

Newson's brother Richard was the third head of the Leiston engineering firm to bear that name. By 1860 the arrival of the East Suffolk Railway branch to Leiston had decreased Richard's interest in transport by sea, though the schooner *Jane*, the last to be owned by the Leiston partners, was not sold until 1869. Richard had, however, been much earlier in owning ships than his brother, beginning in 1826 with the *Richard & Sarah*, named after his parents.

Though the part played by Newson Garrett in the coasting trade of East Anglia is relatively well known, that of his father, Richard, and his brothers of Leiston is well known.

In 1825 or 1826 Richard II, doubtless pressed by his precocious son, took the decision to commission the building of a ship of his own, the *Richard & Sarah*, built at Woodbridge in 1826 and registered on 22nd June that year. The ship is noted in the register as 57 32/94 tons. The dimensions were correspondingly modest, a length of 49 feet 6 inches, a beam of 16 feet 6 inches and a depth in the hold of 8 feet 1 inch. As to rigging, she was noted as

111

sloop rigged with a running bowsprit, though this was shortlived as by 1830 she was schooner rigged with standing bowsprit.

Her master when newly registered was Philip Fisk. Others recorded were Benjamin Fisk (March, 1827), William Waters (September, 1827), Solomon Rust (September, 1828), and Richard Murch (July, 1831). Murch was appointed at Sunderland, thereby giving at least some clue to the extent of the *Richard & Sarah's* voyaging—she was probably there for coal. Murch appears to have been appointed in an emergency, for the same month he was succeeded by Nicholas Munt, followed in turn by Edmund Jewell (October, 1832), Richard Stevens (October, 1833) and John Howsagoe or Houseagoe (May, 1834). On the death of Richard II the vessel was sold by his personal representatives, Robert Cann, the Woodbridge auctioneer, Robert Appleton, of Broomfield, and Henry Read, of Worlingham, to Richard III.

In the decade between 1830 and 1840 the trade of Leiston Works developed remarkably, and under Richard III the firm became nationally known for seed drills, threshing machines and field implements and began building up an export market in these items. This expansion led Richard III to order from William Hunt of Aldeburgh the rather larger *Jane*, 35 tons, and he subsequently bought also the *Margaret*, 35 tons. With the advent of these vessels Richard sold the *Richard & Sarah* to Thomas Capon of Dennington, and thereafter she had no further links with Leiston Works. After having five further owners, the *Richard & Sarah* disappeared from the register in 1875 with the note "sold to foreigners".

John Houseagoe, the last master of the *Richard & Sarah* under Garrett ownership, was appointed to command the *Jane* when she was registered on 5th November, 1840. She was a two-masted schooner with a standing bowsprit, 58 feet long and 9 feet 8 inches in beam, carvel built with a square stern and a figurehead of "a female bust". Doubtless she was a much more handsome vessel than the rather squat *Richard & Sarah*. Houseagoe seems to have had her for some years, as apart from a very brief period in April, 1846, when Thomas Lord was her master he continued in command until September, 1853, when William Osborne took over the ship.

About the same time as the *Jane* was commissioned Richard Garrett III became the owner of the *Margaret*, another William Hunt vessel, built the previous year for Richard Fennel of Snape, who died soon afterwards. Sold on 31st October, 1840, by Fennel's personal representatives to Richard Garrett, she was carvel built and square sterned, like the *Jane*. She was, however, single masted and, though 45 feet 8 inches long, only 7 feet 4 inches in the beam, with one deck, and rigged as a sloop with a running bowsprit. Richard Garrett placed her under the command of James Barker.

During the 1851 Great Exhibition, of which he was one of the guarantors and at which he shewed a considerable array of his products, including portable steam engines, Richard Garrett resolved to take a three hundred strong contingent of his workmen and their wives to London. For this purpose he had the *Jane* and the *Margaret* cleaned and fitted as living accommodation. They were towed to the Thames by the steam tug *Joseph Soames* and moored at Horseferry Wharf, Millbank, where they served for a week as floating lodgings from which their occupants marched daily to the Exhibition in Hyde Park behind a brass band.

When I was compiling notes on the Garrett ships I talked to "Jumbo" Ward, whose grandfather, "Ducker" Ward, sailed in the *Margaret*. "Jumbo" recalled that she had on occasion sailed to Hamburg. On one voyage from London to the Alde they encountered the Newson Garrett barge *Bengal* capsized on the Buxsey sand; all hands were lost.

The only picture known to portray ships owned by the Leiston Garretts, showing Garrett's workmen and their wives disembarking at Horseferry Road on their way to the Great Exhibition, 1851.
Illustrated London News

113

Richard and his brother Newson Garrett were the joint owners of the brig *Breadalbane*, which they bought on 15th March, 1848. The dimensions of the vessel—80 feet 3 inches in length and 23 feet 1 inch across the beam, with a depth into the hold of 16 feet—were considerably greater than anything previously owned by the Garretts, as was her tonnage of 196. Already a quarter of a century old and obsolete when they had her, having been built in Canada at St Mary's near Montreal in 1823, she was probably a far from sound ship, as well as being far less handy in the Alde than the *Margaret* and the *Jane*, which were themselves inferior in this respect to the increasing number of barges. For the first three months of their ownership she was captained by Charles Pallant, then for eleven months by William Mills and for the rest of her short Garrett career by Edward Catmole. Early in January, 1852, she was broken up at Aldeburgh.

Coastal shipping catered well for only a small proportion of the Leiston Garretts' trade. By the eighteen-forties Richard III was looking with envy at those factories connected to the expanding railway network. When in the railway mania of the mid-eighteen-forties bills were deposited in Parliament for the Ipswich, Norwich and Yarmouth Railway and the Halesworth and Norwich Railway —both ultimately unsuccessful—he was one of the eminent witnesses who gave evidence in their favour before one of the Parliamentary committees on Railway Bills. What he said was investigated a few years ago by Dr Lucy Adrian; it provides an interesting commentary on the scale of his business, even though he probably heightened some of the figures to suit his purpose. According to his evidence between 4,600 and 4,800 tons of material and fuel went into his works annually, of which 1,200 tons of English timber formed the largest item, followed by 850 tons of coal and coke, 800 tons of pig iron, 100 tons of scrap iron, 700 tons of manufactured iron, 300 tons of ironmongery and 70 tons of "oils and colours". These produced about 3,600 tons of finished goods and machines. Of this latter tonnage, he said, "nothing like a half" was sent by sea from Aldeburgh. Notwithstanding his evidence, the promoters failed with their Bills and the railway did not reach Leiston until 1859, when the branch of the East Suffolk entered the village and continued to Aldeburgh.

Contrary to what might have been expected from Richard Garrett's earlier Parliamentary evidence, this did not result in the end of his interest in coastal ships. The *Jane* had been rebuilt and lengthened the year before, and the ownership had on 1st July, 1858, become joint between himself and two of his sons, Richard IV and John. When he died in 1866 the vessel became the property of the two sons. John had by that time become estranged from his family and brothers and was described as "of Magdeburg in the

An Aldeburgh codder lying at anchor in the River Alde, mid 1870s.
Burns Collection

Kingdom of Prussia". In 1860 the *Jane* was valued in a Leiston Works inventory at £1,170 4s 2½d. After some three years of ownership by the uneasy partnership the ship was sold on 25th May, 1869, to William Holroyd of Lowestoft. The *Margaret* became a wreck in 1884.

From the eighteen-sixties onward barges became increasingly prominent in the trade to the Alde, to which they were better adapted than the schooners. Shipbuilding on the Alde declined with the schooners, partly as a direct result of their eclipse and partly because of the demise of the cod smacks for which the Aldeburgh shipbuilders had been noted. William Gardner Hunt, the last owner of Hunts' yard, ceased work in the early eighteen-eighties, about the same time as Castle's neighbouring yard stopped building.

In 1844 about forty vessels were registered at Aldeburgh, but with the coming of the railway the number went down and in 1861 there were only twenty-nine ships at Aldeburgh, which for registration purposes included Orford.

Slaughden Quay itself was under a trust "held of the manor of Aldeburgh under the gift of the Earl of Strafford". The quay estate was let to a wharfinger at £50 a year; the estate included the quay, together with coal yards, saltings and the various buildings and sheds. White, in his *History, Gazetteer and Directory of Suffolk*, 1844, gave Richard Garrett & Sons as the leaseholders, while a Leiston Works inventory of 1860 included "The jetty, crane, railway and rail trucks at Aldbro", valued at £852 16s 9d, of which one half was owned by Richard Garrett & Sons and the other by Newson Garrett. By 1870 the owners of Leiston works had lost interest in coastwise shipping, for with rail sidings direct into their works they were able to handle both inward and outward traffic with an ease that would have been denied them had they continued to make extended use of Aldeburgh. Despite Bruff's subsequent efforts to create a more effective port at Slaughden and to extend the branch railway from Aldeburgh station to the quay, trade on the Alde, except for the grain trade to Snape, continued to decline.

Newson Garrett and his two successors had four screw steamers, the *Dawn*, originally a yacht, the *Eaglet*, the *Katherine*, 71 tons, and the *Gladys*, 47 tons. The *Gladys*, built in 1899, had compound inverted engines by the Vauxhall Ironworks, later to build Vauxhall cars. The hull was by R. & H. Green, Blackwall; the boilers, working at 110 pounds per square inch, were by S. Hodge & Son of Millwall. Her length overall was 78 feet. She was the last of the steamers to work in the service of the malting and was sold back to her builders, by then R. & H. Green & Silley Weir Limited, in 1918; they found her a fresh life in the hands of a Cornish owner until she was broken up in 1951.

At least one boiler for a Newson Garrett steamer was built at Leiston Works by Richard Garrett & Sons; possibly the remainder of the machinery was built there also, but no record survives. This, so far as is known, was the only deliberate incursion by the works into maritime manufacture, though one of their portable engines is said to have been installed in a Murray River steamer in Australia.

The little steamers were handier in the river than the sailing barges and were sometimes used to tow a sailing barge, just as in later years barges were towed up from time to time by Brinkley's motor boat from Orford.

After Newson Garrett died in 1894 his son George carried on the malting and continued the use of the ships until the twenties, when the malting was sold to S. Swonnell & Sons Limited, a company in which George Garrett was a major shareholder, a board member and chairman. All the vessels were old and the remaining traffic was handed over to G. F. Sully, who used both his own and chartered barges. Barge freights ceased with the war, and though commercial traffic on the river has resumed since it has been with auxiliary and fully powered motor craft.

The ferry bell and the ferryman, looking from the Iken bank of the Alde towards Slaughden, possibly in the twenties. The ferry was for foot passengers only. In the left background is the Ionia *beached. Immediately to the left of the oar is the Mariners.*
SPS

Ferry Bell, Slaughden.

W 1361.

116

Roads and Travellers 10

THE ROADS to Aldeburgh, once "deep sands", according to William White, were improved towards the end of the eighteenth century by turnpiking. The first road so treated was the road from Ipswich to Yarmouth by way of Woodbridge, Benhall and Blythe, managed by a trust established in 1782. It was followed in 1792 by a further trust charged with the management of the roads linking Aldeburgh to the Ipswich to Yarmouth road.

Though the institution of turnpiking resulted in an improvement in the condition and management of the roads so managed, it was also widely resented because of the tolls that the trustees were empowered to levy on traffic using the roads. On the whole trustees found direct collection of tolls an onerous task and preferred the practice of farming, whereby the right to collect tolls at a given gate was let in advance at public auction or by tender to the highest bidder. This method of indirect collection had the advantage of affording to the trustees, who were in the main drawn from the clergy and the minor gentry, a degree of detachment from the sordid extraction of toll money—and from the uncouth or vexatious behaviour of gatekeepers.

Although foot passengers paid no tolls and passed through a side gate, in 1846 there was an upset at Blythburgh gate on the Ipswich to Yarmouth road when Cox, the gatekeeper, refused to open the main gate to a pedestrian with a wheelbarrow too large to pass through the side gate. This wrangle went as far as the Halesworth magistrates sitting in Petty Sessions. Though they found the case against Cox to be established, they had doubts as to how they might be empowered to act. In the end the matter was settled under the *Old Pals' Act*. Frederic Cross, the magistrates' clerk, wrote to the turnpike trustees, whose clerk was Robert Baas, another solicitor. Baas in turn saw to it that Cox was reprimanded and told not to do it again.

The trusts managed to keep their finances on an even keel until their catchment areas became connected to the railway system. Thereafter, with the yield of the roads reduced purely to the tolls paid by local traffic, they went into an irremediable decline. The Ipswich to Yarmouth turnpike trust was wound up in 1872 and its functions transferred to the county authorities, and the Aldeburgh turnpike followed soon after.

As the turnpike trusts were wound up all their realizable assets were sold, including the gates and toll cottages. There were gates at the entrance to the Town Marsh at Aldeburgh, at Middleton, Snape and Sternfield, and on the Ipswich to Yarmouth road at Carlton. In few cases were the bond-holders paid out in full; mostly they accepted a reduced sum in settlement of what was nominally due to them.

The abolition of the tolls was welcomed by the inhabitants at large, as the functions of the trustees were taken over by the counties and the cost of repairs defrayed from the rates. It was less popular with those who were ratepayers.

Until 1888 the county administration was in the hands of the justices of the peace or of various *ad hoc* boards, but the Local Government Act of 1888 created the county councils and brought a great improvement in the management of local affairs. Though the management of the main roads was improved the day-to-day maintenance depended on the lengthman, who laid stone in weak spots and potholes as they arose, leaving the stone to be rolled in by traffic, nearly all of which was on iron-shod wheels.

Conditions changed with the arrival of the bicycle. The new race of cyclists, recruited from the ratepaying middle classes, demanded better roads. One practical step taken by road engineers in the face of this pressure was the introduction of steamrolling, at first in the hands of the road contractors. Early in this century East Suffolk County Council abandoned the use of contractors and set up instead a direct labour force to maintain the county roads, at the same time beginning the use of crushed granite as road surfacing material in place of broken flint.

The roads and lanes which fell to be maintained by other authorities did not fare so well. Even after the creation of district councils by the Local Government Act of 1894 the quality of the roads was extremely poor, many being surfaced only with stones picked from the fields, a few with broken flints and some with sea shingle, which would not bind together. Victor Garrett once remarked to me how difficult it was to cycle from Aldringham to Thorpeness because of the loose shingle on the road.

At first Saxmundham and Leiston came under Blything Rural District Council, but as both had powerful groups advocating the sewering of the towns it was suggested diplomatically by the district council that they should seek incorporation as urban districts to deal with their sewers. Both took the hint. The sewers they sought proved to be fruitful sources of controversy, and the question of street paving also proved difficult. In Leiston in particular developers had built houses and cottages with little consideration to the roads and lanes that provided access to them. Many of these thoroughfares were paved with nothing more than builder's rubbish. The inappropriately named Paradise in Leiston was described by Doctor Robert Cook as "simply a quagmire" in wet weather, as also were Long Row, Prospect Place, Lambert Street and, to a lesser extent, Valley Terrace and Dinsdale Road.

The Private Street Works Act empowered councils to recover the cost of paving from the frontagers in proportion to the length of frontage they owned abutting the street in question. Many of the owners of terraces of cottages were working men who by dint of personal frugality had saved just enough money to build the cottages so as to provide an income for their old age, and these men, or their widows, were not at all in favour of the charges that arose from paving the street outside. Though hard cases notoriously make for bad laws, one cannot fail to feel a certain sympathy for these landlords. In Valley Road, Dinsdale Road and Kitchener Road the houses belonged to Frank Garrett, who grumbled but paid; but to some of the landlords in Long Row and similar thoroughfares the thirty or forty pounds that had to be found proved a destabilizing burden.

With the arrival of motor traffic dust became a serious summer problem on the waterbound roads. Not even the granite road from Aldeburgh to Yoxford was immune to dust or totally free from mud. All kinds of treatments for dust were tried; hot tar proved the winner. At first crude tar straight from the tar well of the local gasworks was used, but this soon gave way to refined tars from which water and excess pitch had been removed. East Suffolk, sad to relate, was not in the forefront of local authorities taking up tar painting of roads. It was not until after the 1914–18 war that the tarring gang, with its pair of tar boilers, or even three, became a familiar summer sight in the coastal district.

They were soon joined or superseded by mechanized sprayers, usually mounted on an old steam lorry, whose boiler provided steam not only for propelling the vehicle but also for warming the tar it carried. The late Alf Dawson of Rushmere near Ipswich owned several such outfits. Another who worked over much of Norfolk and Suffolk was Edward Edwards of Norwich. The road was first swept clean of dust, the hot tar was applied, either by cans or brushes or by a sprayer, and then the surface was coated with sand or grit. Sand fell into unpopularity because of its propensity for causing dry skids by motor vehicles, leaving grit in possession of the field; it was soon found that the result of tarring and gritting was improved by rolling the gritted surface with a steamroller.

Tarring was not a panacea for all the evils that had previously beset the roads. It did not turn bad roads into good roads, but it often made bad roads tolerable and sound roads into good ones, at least by the standard of their time.

The traffic that used the roads in pre-railway days was made up of public conveyances such as the mail coaches, the carriers' carts and the mail carts, the private carriages of residents, the carts

and vans of tradesmen and the traffic of farms and forests. The mail coaches have attracted the most notice and have become invested since their demise with an aura of romance which the reality lacked. Cramped, cold and uncomfortable for inside passengers in cold weather, and stifling in the heat, they exposed outside passengers to such rigours in bad weather that deaths from cold were not unknown. For horses they were what W. J. Reader aptly termed "engines of hell".

From Yoxford, on the Ipswich to Yarmouth turnpike, most of the mail carriages departed from John Barnes' posting house, the Three Tuns. The *Mail* left for London at 8 pm and for Yarmouth at 6 am; the *Shannon* ran to Ipswich at 8.30 each morning and to Halesworth at 7 pm, while the Norwich coach, the *Eclipse*, left at 6 am on Mondays and Wednesdays and 5 am on Saturdays. From the *Griffin*, kept by H. Porter, the *Old Blue* left for Ipswich at 10 am and for Yarmouth at 3.30 pm. In Saxmundham the coach trade was

divided between the Bell and the White Hart. The *Shannon* used the White Hart, the *Mail* and the *Old Blue* left from the Bell.

The mail coaches were limited in accommodation and very dear. As an alternative Saxmundham residents could take the omnibus that left the Angel and the White Hart at 5 am on Mondays, Wednesdays, Thursdays and Fridays to link at Ipswich with steamers for London. Those with time enough could go with H. J. & R. Smith's carrier's waggon, which came through from Yoxford and Yarmouth on Mondays and Thursdays, putting up for a change of horses at the Bell.

Several carriers plied the Ipswich road, Sawyer from the Angel, Free and Rous from the White Hart on Mondays and Fridays. Martin left the Bell for Yarmouth on a Friday. On Tuesdays and Saturdays Rous did a short run to Benhall and Free to Middleton. On his return trip from Ipswich Sawyer ran through to Norwich via Bungay. Having stayed the night at Ipswich he

Carlton Hall, Saxmundham, was kept by Richard Garrett IV for the use of his mother, but this phaeton photographed outside its gates in the 1880s hardly seems the carriage for an old lady. The photograph, probably by Charles Clarke, is a masterpiece for the time and the type of subject.

121

arrived back in Saxmundham on Tuesdays and Saturdays, pausing at the Angel before going on to Norwich. On Mondays and Fridays Robert Hogg also ran from the Bell to Norwich.

This by no means exhausted the carriers' services. There was James Taylor, who went to Leiston, where he lived, and Benjamin Baxter, the Aldeburgh carrier, who did trips to Ipswich, leaving early each Tuesday and Friday morning. James Smith ran a lighter and hence faster van to Ipswich from Aldeburgh three times a week (Monday, Wednesday and Friday).

Quite apart from the public services there were many vehicles in private hands. An inventory of 1860 listed the rolling stock of Leiston Works as follows:

Traveller's gig with lamps	£10 10s 0d
Old gig	£ 5 10s 0d
Long cart	£ 6 0s 0d
Small double beast wagon	£12 0s 0d
Spring luggage cart	£ 8 0s 0d
Barn-work cart	£ 4 0s 0d
Red cart	£ 6 10s 0d
Strong road wagon	£15 0s 0d
2 Timber jims	£13 0s 0d
Large Timber jim	£18 0s 0d
Blue Scotch cart	£ 4 10s 0d
4 Wheel truck	£ 3 0s 0d
Flat bottom dray (2 wheels)	£ 6 10s 0d
2 Timber drags and chains	£18 10s 0d
Low 4 wheel dray	£ 4 10s 0d
Low cart	£ 4 0s 0d
Night soil cart	£ 5 0s 0d
Long 2 wheel truck	£ 2 0s 0d
2 Boiler trucks (2 wheelers)	£ 2 10s 0d

This was a year after the railway was opened. Doubtless in pre-railway days the stock was larger.

The list illustrates the number and variety of vehicles owned by the firm. The double beast wagon was a relatively rare vehicle, used for transporting animals for short distances. Droving was the accepted method, but very difficult with a single animal, or two. Equally, of course, if the cow or bullock being transported was a valuable or prize-winning animal more care would be taken in moving it. The wagon may well have been used for Richard Garrett's prize shorthorns.

Richard Garrett & Sons built traction engines at Leiston; indeed, they were the builders, under licence, of one of the first commercially successful traction engines, to the designs of Thomas Aveling of Rochester. Subsequently they built road engines of their own design, but dropped traction engine building altogether for

over ten years in the late eighties and early nineties of the last century because the recession in farming had depressed engine sales so much.

The best known and longest surviving business owning engines and threshing machines was that of H. Heffer, of Farnham St George, already well established by the seventies and still there under the redoubtable "Harbut" until the end of the commercial use of steam in the early nineteen-fifties. Another owner early in the business was John Marshlain, of East Green, Kelsale, gone by the eighteen-eighties; still on the road to Yarmouth but on the northernmost limits of our area was William Holmes at Darsham. Others in the area were James Barber and John Button at Iken and William Woodbridge at Tunstall.

In this century Leslie Cooper returned to his native Suffolk after an adventurous career in South America and set himself up as a threshing contractor. The engine he bought was a Garrett single cylinder engine with piston valves for controlling the entry of steam to the cylinder, a thoroughly modern engine designed by the firm to be the first of a new generation of traction engines. Unfortunately Leslie's engine remained alone. Instead the trade as a whole soldiered on with what it had until the advent of the combine harvester did away with threshing altogether.

Saxmundham Station, with a gravel road in the foreground, and a Royal Mail van and a dog-cart posed in front of the building. One of the posters refers to the Midland Railway's acquisition of the Northern Counties Railway, placing the date about 1903.
Burns Collection

123

Just as traction engine driving as a trade has gone, saved from extinction only by the preservation movement, the drover's trade has also gone, without the least prospect of revival. Before the arrival of the railway cattle and sheep were regularly travelled to London from East Suffolk, sometimes direct and sometimes to a holding and refattening farm in what are now the suburbs, at Leyton, Walthamstow, Southgate or Tottenham. The practice did not cease with the building of railways, though the numbers of sheep and cattle sent by train rose year by year. Cattle and sheep continued to be driven on the hoof from farm to loading station, however, as well as to and from local markets or to local purchasers.

The professional drovers often worked for auctioneers on market day as part of their general activity. In general they were what would be called today "self-employed", undertaking to deliver beasts or sheep to a given destination for an agreed fee or a customary tariff. Seldom fastidious and almost invariably partial to beer, the drovers were a hard-living crowd; their equipment was a good dog and a big stick. Sometimes when moving sheep a horse and cart would be taken along behind to pick up lame or sick sheep or the corpse of any that might die on the road.

The marshes of the coast were much used during the warmer months of the year for bringing on or fattening store cattle, the grazing being let out for the purpose to graziers. Cattle were bought in usually through dealers such as Forsdyke of Leiston and others more distant. In the years up to 1939 there were many dealers from Ireland or of Irish descent in the cattle trade of East Anglia. The movement of cattle on the hoof to or from the marshes more or less ended with the war of 1939–45, having been in steep decline in the years running up to it.

How was it done? That we learn in the words of Kersey Cooper, agent to the Duke of Grafton at Euston, related by Hermann Biddell in *The Suffolk Horse Stud Book*, Volume 1:

First I met a drove of colts—thirty, forty, fifty, I should think—more than I could count. Then came a hundred beasts—cows, lean bullocks, young things; footsore, tired and hungry as they could be; followed by the biggest flock of sheep I ever met in a road in my life. They were like the flocks of Abraham. At last came old Boon, leading a pony and cart with half a dozen skins and two lame sheep.

Boon was a tall man—six feet one, and stooped a good deal, rather leaned forward and plunged along in a slop down to his shoes like a man with sore feet on flint stones, and always walked with his eyes on his boots.

"Well, my good man, and whose, in the name of goodness, are all these things you've got here?"

Boon pulled up, took his eyes off the ground and said very slowly:
"Well, they belong to my marstar."

"But who is your master?"

"My marstar, sar? Why, the gentleman that own all these couts and ship and things!"

"Well, where are you going with these 'ship and things'?"

"I'm a-going arter some feed my marstar ha' bowt for 'em."

"And where are you going tonight—you can't lie on the road, can you?"

"Oh dear, no sar—there's too many on 'em to lay i' the rud—I can't lodge 'em i' the rud."

"Well, well shepherd, as long as they are not going to mine I don't know that I've any business with it—good night."

"Good night sar—but I was just a-going to say pra-ay could you tell me where Mistar Karsay Cooper live somewhere in these parts? I was to go to him for a night's lodging."

The most abject apology followed, and profuse were the explanations that he "hadn't the la-est idea who I was a-speaking tu, but you know, sar, my marstar al'ays tell me not to know nothing when anybody ax me about my business. He said he thowt you had a little middar close to the house that 'ud du nicely." And in the "little middar" the mixed multitude lodged, and little was left but the soil when they passed on the next day for another stage.

Another figure to be seen on the roads was the stallion-leader, walking his charge on a circuit of farms to provide its services to the mares from which their owners desired to breed. This was not perhaps the practice with breed champions but was certainly the case with more workaday sircs.

Also associated with horses was the itinerant horse-singer, walking a round of public house stables and endeavouring to be in a town on market day so as to attend to the tidying of horses' coats. Like many such men of passage whose business took them into public houses, they tended all to suffer from the same complaint, over-partiality for beer.

Gipsies and horses are closely associated, and there were generally a few gipsy families to be found in the district. Knodishall Common or Cold fair Green was a favourite stopping point, as also was the piece of common by Snape Church. There was another favoured spot on Blaxhall Common, still known as Gipsies' Pit. Though they were seldom welcome, there were some places at which they were more tolerated than at others. Police constables on the whole looked askance at all travellers, rating them all as thieves and no-goods.

The district did not provide any of the seasonal work which attracted the gipsies to other parts of the country such as hop and fruit picking to Kent and Herefordshire or pea and bean picking to the Fens. Nevertheless, there were some gipsy families who were to be seen there in the old days at regular intervals. One such was the Loveridge family, members of which can still be encountered from time to time. Other gipsies known to have travelled it in the opening decade of this century were the Boswells, the Buttons, the Taylors and the ever-present Lees and Smiths. The old Cold Fair on Knodishall Common was a gathering point for gipsies; after it died out there was no other such focal point.

There were also hawkers and knife grinders. Packmen were broadly in two varieties, the regular and the once-only. According to what they sold the regular men would cover their circle of villages at intervals varying from once a week to once or twice a year. A typical packman might sell needles, thread, buttons, darning wool, shoe laces and the like, and was welcomed.

In the second category came the "bug fat" man. When no one had a refrigerator flies were a constant problem, and a hot market day might find him selling his fly repellent. On his table he would have, side by side, two fairly ripe meat bones. One would be covered in flies; the other, having on it a cube of bug-fat, had not a fly near it. The onlookers would pay good money for this magic product, but all were doomed to disappointment, as the cubes had been made the night before by the vendor from a few melted candle ends and a little dye. The secret? The bone without flies had been dipped in paraffin oil.

The practitioners of these dubious arts were not gipsies. While principle might not have barred gipsy men from relieving gullible *gaujos* of a few coppers, experience had taught them that the public were very wary of them in such situations. There were, however, trusted traders among these occasional men, and Romanies to boot. These were the brushers, sellers of brooms and brushes for domestic use and perhaps of baskets as well. The brusher lived in a wagon of a somewhat different design from those of other travellers, the entrance being at the rear instead of over the front lock as in most wagons. Brushes were hung around it and also carried in a rack on the roof.

The population of the roads included also a large number of tramps, in the words of the Elizabethan Poor Law "poor, indigent and impotent persons", eking out a precarious living by begging, poaching, casual work and, it must be admitted, petty theft. During the warmer months it was, perhaps, not beyond possibility to maintain life by these means, but in the winter months it was much harder for a roader to stay alive by his own efforts. Many abandoned the attempt and applied for admission to a Poor Law Institution—to wit a workhouse—there to stay until the next spring released their pent-up urge to wander. The "Beloved Coast" fell within the Plomesgate Union, the workhouse of which was at Wickham Market. Built in 1836–37, it had room for 370 inhabitants, though it was seldom full. At the January peak it would house 275–300, but in the middle of the year, about July, probably not more than a hundred. The next to the north was that of the Blything Union, at Bulcamp.

Before the 1914–18 war a well-known tramp was "Weary Willie", who spent each summer on the move through the villages of the area. There was another venerable old gentleman, bearded,

The present B1122 road at Theberton as it appeared in the first decade of this century.
J. S. Waddell

well spoken and gentlemanly in his better moments, who appeared in Leiston about three times a summer to sleep on one of the seats in the Recreation Ground. Rumour had it that he had once been a university professor. Unfeeling small boys would tantalize him until he drove them off with an exhibition of bad language that was very far from gentlemanly.

Another man of the roads still remembered was Montgomery, the blind organ grinder, a married man first seen in the district in about the eighteen-nineties. He and his wife, who had five or six children of their own and had adopted others, lived frugally but decently in a flint cottage in Mill Road, Westleton, with a little shed at the side in which the barrel organ was kept. At first he used to pull the barrel organ himself, accompanied by one of the children as a guide. Later well-wishers, of whom there was no lack, bought him a donkey to draw the organ. Montgomery used to ride on a little footboard at the side, holding the reins but probably relying upon the donkey to guide him past obstacles, if one of the children was not there. He appeared at intervals in the villages around Westleton, occasionally venturing, some say, as far as Aldeburgh. Eventually he moved away to Halesworth during the 1914–18 war.

Arthur Greenway (by the rear wheel of the tractor) filling the water tanks of his Fowler steam tractor (works number 14412) from a roadside brook on his way to Aldeburgh regatta, August 1936. The Jollity Farm *ride which it was hauling was a type of ark and took its name from a recently popular song.*
R. G. Pratt

Trains and Buses 11

THERE IS little doubt that the Eastern Counties Railway was not a good one. Railway promoters were not noted for their chivalry, nor were the companies, once the lines were built and opened, given to considerate behaviour one toward another, but the ECR plumbed the depths on both counts.

It was precarious in its finances on both capital and revenue accounts, the former largely as a result of extortionate sums exacted by way of payment from the company by landowners through whose land or near to whose land the line ran. On the revenue side the company was to a considerable extent a victim of its original optimism. Because of the capital troubles it had been unable to carry out all its original plans and traffic had consequently failed to develop as predicted, though in part, it must be said, this was the consequence of the forecasting of traffic having been very optimistic in the first place.

As to the actual operation of the railway, the record was also poor. Trains were slow and unreliable, carriages uncomfortable, and the safety record was not good. The company suffered major accidents at Brentwood on 19th August, 1840 (four deaths) and Tottenham on 20th February, 1860 (seven deaths), as well as numerous minor ones, the leisurely speed of the trains often mitigating the consequences of those that did occur. The *Railway Record* of August, 1845, contains the following gem:

> It appears that two miles below Romford a spare engine is kept in readiness for the purpose of propelling such trains as, owing to the wretched inefficiency of the plant, may appear to be in need of assistance up the incline to Brentwood. And further it seems that the driver is allowed to run his assistant engine on to the train while it is in motion. On Friday last the collision was sufficiently violent to floor the passengers in the whole train and snap the coupling irons attaching the last carriage to the other three, leaving this single carriage jumping by itself on the top of a high embankment, and us, who were in it, in the certain conviction that we were going over. Many passengers were injured ... Having lost my ticket in the mêlée I was required at Chelmsford to pay a second fare from London; thus I rode twenty-six miles and paid for sixty; I suppose the luxury of the concussion was reckoned equal to the other thirty-four.

The railway was often a target of *Punch's* barbs:

On Wednesday last a respectably dressed young man was seen to go to the Shoreditch terminus of the Eastern Counties Railway and deliberately take a ticket for Cambridge. He has not since been heard of. No motive has been assigned for his rash act.

The Eastern Counties succeeded in building its line from London to Colchester with great difficulty, measured by the facts that despite the company having been incorporated in 1836 it did not open to Colchester until 7th March, 1843. Money was squandered on building the line to a track gauge of 5 feet (compared with the standard 4 feet 8½ inches, a piffling difference) with provision in the earthworks, bridges and tunnels for widening to 7 feet 0¼ inch if this was subsequently found to be required. The line this far, just over fifty miles, had taken up £2½ million in capital, which in the original estimates had been deemed sufficient to build the railway right through to Great Yarmouth. The ECR decided to terminate at Colchester and to leave railway construction in untrodden Suffolk to others. However, over the years it grew by taking in the Northern and Eastern, giving access to Cambridge, and the Norfolk Railway, which took it into Norwich.

Hopes of the extension of railway facilities into East Suffolk were revived by the promotion in 1843 of the Eastern Union Railway, which was authorized in 1847 to construct, *inter alia,* a line from Ipswich to Woodbridge, though it proved impossible to finance and was not built. Seven years later in a renewed burst of railway building activity in the area the Ipswich–Woodbridge proposal was revived and Parliamentary approval was obtained to a renewal of its legal powers to build.

Meanwhile there had been activity to the north of the district. The Norfolk Railway, formed by an amalgamation of the Yarmouth & Norwich Railway and the Norwich & Brandon Railway in 1845, had obtained control of the Reedham Junction to Lowestoft line of the Lowestoft Railway & Harbour Company in 1846. In 1851 a local line was incorporated to run from Halesworth via Beccles to a junction with the Reedham–Lowestoft line at Haddiscoe. This was completed and opened in December, 1854, the working being undertaken by the Eastern Counties Railway, which had by that time assumed control of the Norfolk Railway.

During 1854 the Eastern Union had obtained an extension of its Parliamentary powers to build to Woodbridge, while the former Halesworth, Beccles and Haddiscoe Railway changed its name to the more grandiose title of East Suffolk Railway and came forward with a scheme to drive southward to an end-on junction at Woodbridge with the Eastern Union Railway, with branches to Leiston, for Garrett's works, to Snape, for traffic to the maltings, and to Framlingham. The promotion of this line owed much to Sir Samuel Morton Peto, who at that time was intensely interested in

The Aveling & Porter geared steam locomotive that provided the motive power on Richard Garrett & Sons' private tramway from Leiston Station to the Town Works.
B. J. Finch

British Railways' 0-6-0 tender engine No 65447, one of a class built by the former Great Eastern Railway between 1883 and 1913, picks its way across the Alde bridge at Snape. Dr Ian C. Allen

the development of the town of Lowestoft. Peto, in the face of the opposition of the Norfolk Railway and its successor, wished to obtain more direct access by rail from Lowestoft to London. It was in pursuance of this intention that he had inspired the promotion of that seemingly innocuous branch line to link Halesworth to Haddiscoe.

In 1854 the Halesworth, Beccles & Haddiscoe, by then the East Suffolk, sought, and obtained after a fairly perfunctory examination of its traffic prospects by the Parliamentary Committee, an Act for the extension of its railway from Halesworth southward by way of Darsham and Saxmundham to the Eastern Union Railway at Woodbridge.

In the promotion of this expansion of the East Suffolk Railway Peto was joined by the Ipswich brewer and banker John Chevallier Cobbold. To some extent Peto's interest arose directly from his instincts as a railway speculator, but much more from the secondary financial consideration that the building of the railway was calculated both to enhance the development of the town and port of Lowestoft, in the furtherance of which he had direct financial interests, and also to bring work to the contracting partnership of Peto, Brassey & Betts, who were to build the new line. Superficially at least the involvement of Cobbold was solely that of a spectator. Neither man was especially altruistic or sentimental, but even so it is doubtful if a bald summary of the financial advantages to them represented the sum of their motives. In each there probably burned a small flame of belief that the railway would advance the interests of East Suffolk, to which Cobbold belonged by birth and Peto by adoption.

Peto had already succeeded in enlisting the support of Richard Garrett in the Great Exhibition of 1851 and had led him to enroll as a guarantor. He now brought both Richard and Newson into the orbit of the East Suffolk Railway, on the board of which Richard was accorded a seat. Each of the Garrett brothers had very strong commercial motives for wishing the railway to be constructed and for seeing that branches were provided to serve the sites of their respective places of business.

Dr Lucy Adrian (Lady Adrian), of Cambridge University, spent some time in 1983 and 1984 investigating Richard Garrett's evidence to the Parliamentary Committee in 1846 on the Bills promoting the Ipswich, Norwich and Yarmouth Railway and the Halesworth & Norwich Railway. Both Bills were lost, but Garrett's evidence was that an annual tonnage of between 4,600 and 4,800 tons of fuel and raw materials entered his works, and finished goods totalling 3,600 to 3,800 tons left it. Without doubt the tonnages would have risen considerably—probably to more than twice the 1846 figures—by the mid-fifties. In the same period the number of men employed by Richard Garrett had gone up from a little over two hundred to over five hundred, so the acquisition of a railway branch was of more pressing importance to him than a mere matter of prestige or even ownership of shares in the railway.

The East Suffolk, including the Leiston branch, was finally opened on 1st June, 1859, at which date the Eastern Union line from Woodbridge to Ipswich began operation, but the branch was not extended to Aldeburgh until 12th April, 1860. A station of considerable charm was built at Aldeburgh, with fully roofed platform and full height wall to protect it from the winter winds off the North Sea. It was sited well out of the town on the road to Saxmundham, convenient for the new estate of middle-class homes which Newson Garrett had in contemplation, and well placed to enable the line to be extended round the back of the town to Slaughden Quay, but not otherwise well situated.

The branch served Aldeburgh for a hundred years, carrying goods until 1959 and conveying passengers until 1966. After the withdrawal of the passenger service the line was cut back from Aldeburgh to the old coal and sugar beet siding on the south side of the level crossing over the Sizewell Road at Leiston, where improvements had been carried out and a heavy gantry installed to enable flasks of nuclear waste from Sizewell power station to be loaded on to rail wagons. This is now the sole traffic of the branch.

Newson's branch to Snape was a less elaborate affair, for goods only, extending only 1 mile 32 chains from Snape Junction on the main line. It was worked on the "one engine in steam" principle, very much as a long siding would have been worked, the locomotive pushing incoming trucks down ahead of it and drawing the returns back. A small yard and a presentable office and house were provided at Snape on the west side of the road. A line crossed over the road into the malting, which provided much of the traffic. Incoming traffic, besides that to the malting, was made up of coal, building materials for the builder's merchant who had a store in the station yard, and the general requirements of an agricultural district. As to outgoings, at one time the branch originated the largest tonnage of sugar beet handled by any goods station in East Anglia.

Latterly the traffic declined to a mere shadow, leaving the station master, Jock Campbell, with much time on his hands. By a curious economy that station was not connected to the signal telephone network and he never knew exactly when the train was on the way. Jock loved bathing. There were few days when he went without his dip. He once described to Dr Ian Allen how he had been disconcerted while swimming under the bridge to find the train crossing it above him. It was probably the first time the yard had been shunted by a shunter clad only in wet bathing trunks.

The maximum speed of trains was limited to 15 mph throughout the life of the branch, which ceased operation as from 7th March, 1960. Because of weight restrictions the locomotives used had to be light of foot. Latterly the ex-Great Eastern Railway maids-of-all-work, the J15 class 0-6-0 tender engines, provided the motive power. The course of the line was mostly at or near level except for the approach to Snape Junction which was made up a gradient of 1 in 53, the same, incidentally, as that off the main line on to the Aldeburgh branch. The practice of the regular enginemen was to rush it. Those who through unfamiliarity or inborn caution balked at making a rush were prone to find that their steed had jibbed before the climb had been completed, which meant either setting back and taking another run or, in extreme cases, sending for assistance.

Snape was run by the Great Eastern Railway and by its successor, the London & North Eastern Railway, as a properly manned goods station, with station master and uniformed staff, though it declined somewhat in its terminal years under British Railways. The house still stands and is lived in, but little else remains.

All the railways in the area were joined together as from 7th August, 1862, in the Great Eastern Railway. It took several years of the life of the new company to divest it of the bad management and general malpractices of its predecessor and to put its financial affairs in good order, but by about 1870 it had done so. It went on to become a model of what a pre-grouping railway should have

No 67230 2-4-2 tank engine of Class F6 mounting the 1 in 53 bank of the Aldeburgh branch as it left the main line at Saxmundham in December 1955.
Dr Ian C. Allen

been, continuing until taken into the London & North Eastern Railway in 1923.

The Aldeburgh branch had little hope of generating worthwhile traffic beyond Leiston. The town of Aldeburgh developed only slowly. The beach fishermen benefited from the facilities provided by the railway for getting catches to more profitable markets than existed locally, but almost everything else depended upon the growth of the town as a holiday resort and summer home for the well-to-do. An attempt begun in the eighteen-seventies to convert twenty-five acres of land on the hill overlooking the marshes west of the town into an estate of "gentlemen's houses" had a very slow start. New Town, as it was briefly called, absorbed the promoter's capital in landscaping and tree planting, the beneficial results of which can be seen today, but the "gentlemen" at whom it was aimed as a residential area remained coy. It was given fresh life when Newson Garrett took it over from the outside company, dotting the grounds with large, comfortable but rather whimsical houses which he bestowed upon his children and their spouses.

The gasworks (1855/56), at the Slaughden end of the town, handily situated for supplying gas to the new estate, had been launched as the result of an earlier initiative by Newson Garrett involving the use of seaborne coal. It continued to receive coal by sea long after the arrival of the railway, and it was only in comparatively recent years that it took its supplies by rail. In 1870 Newson also played a leading role in the construction of a waterworks and water tower, tapping supplies in a much deeper and therefore safer stratum than the shallow surface wells from which supplies had earlier been drawn or pumped.

The proprietors of the town's hotels arranged for small horse-drawn buses to meet all trains arriving at Aldeburgh Station. In Leiston the Garrods kept a similar small bus and also, on request, provided a horse cab to meet trains at the station. In the nineteen-twenties motors took over and Harry J. Beaton of the White Lion, G. C. Pritt of the Wentworth and Robert Constable of the East Suffolk advertized that they met all trains, as did C. A. Ward, proprietor of the motor garage near the Cottage Hospital. In addition to his buses to meet the trains Ward ran a bus daily to Thorpe and to the golf course.

The twenties saw the arrival in Aldeburgh of Richard A. Moore, who began a garage on the old Albert Brewery site in Victoria Road, a few hundred yards down from the station, providing cars and buses for hire as well as catering for the needs of the private motorist. Calling his buses *The Speedwell Saloons* (though some local people nicknamed them *Bluebirds* from the bird in flight which he chose as an emblem), he instituted a through

Wards' bus from Aldeburgh to Thorpeness, c1920. The vehicle is an early Model T Ford, with a Baico conversion which has made it longer. Originally the wheels were fitted where the sprocket wheel of the chain drive can be seen, but the chassis has been extended and the wheels moved back onto a new dead axle where they are driven by roller chain from the original live axle. Burns Collection

service from Aldeburgh to Ipswich, by way of Aldringham and Leiston, very soon to be followed by the newly-formed Eastern Counties Road Car Company, who took over the whole service in December, 1925. Moore's fleet at the time consisted of three fourteen-seaters, two on Ford Model T chassis and the other on a one-ton Morris chassis. None of them entered the passenger-carrying fleet of the Eastern Counties company though the Morris, which was nearly new, saw some three years' service as a van.

In Leiston Freddy Garrod equipped himself with a Ford Model T taxicab and a fourteen-seater bus named the *Sans Pareil*, also on a Model T chassis. He never launched into stage-carriage work but contented himself with transporting private parties and the local sports teams. The taxicab still survives in the small private museum at Theberton set up by the late Pat Keeble. Nearly all the older inhabitants of Leiston have memories of *Sans Pareil* and its driver, Ted Morley. Soon after it arrived Ted Dunn's father, George, hired it to take his family for a day's outing to Lowestoft. Mrs Dunn took a picnic lunch for the smaller children but Ted, at eleven the eldest, was taken off with his father into town to lunch on twelve oysters, three for Ted and the rest for his father.

When first I came to the Aldeburgh branch it was worked by former Great Eastern Railway 2-4-2 tank engines of the F6 class, tired and worn old hacks newly displaced from the London (Liverpool Street) suburban services by the advance of electrification. The Aldeburgh branch was not easy to work; it curved sharply off the junction with the main line north of Saxmundham Station up a slope of 1 in 53, through a cutting where the rails were often moist, and beneath trees which in autumn added fallen leaves to the other problems of the locomotives in maintaining adhesion on this difficult stretch. Jack Runnacles, driver-in-charge on the branch at this period, a cautious character, compounded the already serious problems the locomotives had by the timidity of his driving, often causing a stall by refusing to get on as great a rush as possible at the slope. All other matters apart, however, the two F6s were quite awful old engines, even with the two-coach trains customary on the branch. The usual engine on the line was No 67239 but was sometimes replaced by No 67230, otherwise to be found on the Framlingham branch.

Later they were replaced by a British Railways standard 2-6-2 tank engine, a very sound machine and master of the work, while the passenger working latterly passed to diesel railcars. The last time I rode on the branch the driver was George Rowse, a West Yorkshireman who had transferred to Ipswich after years at Barnsley. The contrast between the placid life he led as the chauffeur of the Aldeburgh diesel set and the work at Barnsley was total. At Barnsley he had taken turns in driving the huge six-cylinder 2-8-8-2 Garratt (no direct connection with the Leiston firm) on mineral traffic over the Pennines. Tiresome though the bank up out of Saxmundham had been to the old F6s, it was a pimple compared with the 1 in 40 gradient of Worsborough Bank on the Garratt run.

Leiston Works was served by a private tramway, which made an end-on connection to a siding on the south side of the station, crossed Station Road by a private crossing and then curved away downhill in a southerly direction till it crossed Main Street and entered the original works. The crossing over Main Street was controlled by the uniformed constable who manned Garrett's gatehouse, in earlier days it was gated, which was just as well in view of the way the tramway was worked. The system used was that the works horses drew the incoming wagons across the Station Road crossing as far as the head of the incline. There the wagons were stopped on their brakes and the horses detached. When the Main Street crossing was closed the brakes were released and the wagons ran by gravity down the slope, over the crossing and up the slope into the old works yard until brought to a standstill by the gradient, whereupon the brakes were again pinned down.

The practice came to an end in the mid-twenties after a loaded wagon left the rails on the curve and embedded itself in the wall of an adjoining cottage. After that the firm bought themselves a locomotive. The engine they bought was as remarkable in its way as had been their earlier method of working. Built by Aveling &

Porter Ltd of Rochester, it was essentially a large traction engine mounted upon railway wheels, the cylinders and engine work mounted on top of the boiler as in an engine intended for use on the road. It had been built originally for use at the gypsum mines at Mountfield, Sussex, and carried at Leiston the name *Sirapite*, which had been bestowed upon it at Mountfield. *Sirapite* was the brand name of a patented gypsum plaster manufactured at Mountfield, said to have the advantages of plaster of Paris without its disadvantages. For this reason the publicity department had intended to call it *Parisite* until someone pointed out the possibly unfortunate connotations, whereupon they reversed the spelling of Paris.

Whether the story is true or not—and it deserves to be—*Sirapite* served the works there for nearly forty years and is now preserved by Mr William McAlpine. While it was at Leiston it was one of the sights of the Aldeburgh branch; small boys and others used to scan the scene at Leiston Station eagerly for a sight of it. Percy Newstead, who drove it, kept it very clean and polished the brass regularly. Despite its unconventional outline it was a useful worker. Because its drive was through gears, like a traction engine, rather than direct, as in a rail locomotive, the engine turned over several times during a single revolution of the wheels on the track. In consequence the sound of it pushing loaded wagons up the gradient at the old works was like the *Flying Scotsman* ascending out of King's Cross. By contrast the elderly battery electric locomotive which superseded it in the nineteen-sixties made hardly a sound beyond a rumble and was, on the whole, ignored.

An Eastern Counties Tilling Stevens bus in Aldeburgh High Street c1930. SPS

Considered by itself the Aldeburgh line was a lost cause. At the time of the closure of the line Aldeburgh's resident population was only about three thousand, though possibly double that on peak days during the summer. By that time, however, the overall statistics of summer visitors had little relevance to the railway, as most visitors arrived in their own cars. In 1965, the last full year of working before closure, only a little over 16,000 tickets were collected at Aldeburgh. This terminal decline apart, it is doubtful if the line had ever been viable in terms of pure accountancy at any time in its life. The whole of the East Suffolk line, not only its branches, had been conceived in the atmosphere of the Railway Mania and of unrealizable hopes. Nevertheless, in its heyday the Great Eastern Railway had treated unremunerative branches as part of the price that had to be paid to achieve a credible image as the principal source of transport within its area. Without the branch the town of Aldeburgh would not have been able to develop as a holiday resort, while the Garrett works at Leiston would certainly not have achieved its peak—at which it employed some 2,000 people—had it remained detached from the railway system.

Leisure and Amusements

12

SUMMER VISITORS came to Aldeburgh and the coast in search of quietness and relaxation. For children there was the beach, which in the last century was wider and flatter than today; much erosion has since occurred. Adults who wished to bathe could do so by stepping decorously from bathing machines into the water. The earliest reference I have found to bathing machines at Aldeburgh is in Crabbe in 1810, though he does not record whom they belonged to.

Three proprietors latterly divided the bathing machine rights between them, the Pallants by the Moot Hall, the Collis's by the lifeboat (his yard was in Marsh Lane), and Robert Cable, who died in 1938, at the Fort Green end. Others involved were Charles Harling, and members of the Ward family: Thomas, known as Whispering Tom from his stentorian voice, and George. While the bathing machine was high on the beach, bathers entered, fully clad, by the rear door, disrobed and put on their bathing dress in the privacy of the cabin; this was then hauled into the water by the attendant and his horse, enabling the occupant to slip unobserved out of the front door and down the steps into water deep enough to cover him or her at once.

The bathing machine proprietors kept diving rafts moored off their stations and a boatman was in attendance in case of accidents.

Bathing machines were used by the well-off locals, but the sons and daughters of the fishermen and other working people of the town went in from the beach, perhaps less inhibited by decorum. Except for a few dedicated swimmers and life-savers, once the town children became adults they spent less time in the water, and by middle age and after, few went into the sea at all. Many of the Aldeburgh cod fishermen, who sailed to arctic or sub-arctic waters, are said to have refused to learn to swim on the grounds that once in the water they would have had no hope, and that swimming would only have prolonged the agony.

There were generally donkey rides to be had along the beach or the Crag Path. John Waddell recalled that a visit to Aldeburgh as a small child was not complete without a ride on one of the group of donkeys that plied for hire under the charge of local boys, mostly young sons of the beach families. For a very young child the

An inseparable part, for many, of a visit to Aldeburgh—donkey rides on the beach. Here, in front of the Brudenell Hotel, the boys in charge of the donkeys are Charles Strowger and Gordon Kemp.
Burns Collection

pace would be most sedate, with a hand extended to help him or her keep a seat, but with older children a brisk trot was the order.

Aldeburgh was considered a staid watering place. This is not to say, however, that it was necessarily boring to those who lived there. For many of the younger men cricket provided the amusement of summer evenings and Saturday afternoons, while bowls was more widely played then than today. In Leiston, for instance, there was a good bowling green behind the White Horse. Early this century, other greens were constructed at the Constitutional Club and the Leiston Works Athletic Club. Whereas the two former greens tended to be used by the tradesmen of the town and the foremen and office staff of the works, the Athletic Club was open to any employed by Garretts and drew many devotees into the game.

At the White Horse two or three small boys used to attend to return the woods to the players, each of whom contributed a penny to a kitty, duly divided amongst the boys. Ted Dunn was often there and might have carried away a shilling for his evening's work. He related to me how his mother invariably held out her hand for the money as soon as he entered the door on his return home. He commented, "I used to manage to hold on to a penny or so but she had the rest. It was just plain greediness, she wasn't even hard up.

140

My father was still alive and running the barber's shop and he had his war pension besides."

Tennis was another popular game and clubs flourished in both Aldeburgh and Leiston. If anything, it has increased over the years despite other distractions. Many men with large families but in small cottages used the public house as a social club in order to get away, perhaps unfairly, from the clamour at home. Dominoes was a popular pub game, closely followed by various games of cards, pontoon and nap being favourites.

Pubs were also associated with both indoor and also outdoor, or steel, quoits (not played any more). The district was organized into the Saxmundham District Quoits League based at the White Hart at Saxmundham. Saxmundham gave its name to at least one other local league, the Saxmundham Bowls League, and was well provided with sports clubs. Besides, predictably, a tennis club, it had a hockey club and a miniature rifle club, which had a range at Brook Farm by the North Entrance. There was also a rifle club in Aldeburgh. Their range at the Cragg Pit on Leiston Road was opened on 20th October, 1907, by Mrs Money Coutts.

A Victorian and Edwardian attraction on the beach at Aldeburgh was the *camera obscura*, situated on the site of the house now known as Jubilee Villa, facing the Crag Path, flanked by

Joe Challis, the butcher, being presented with the challenge cup of the White Horse Bowling Club, Leiston. Behind the garden wall can be seen the Works Institute. The date is believed to be 1910. J. S. Waddell

141

Leiston Tennis Club, 1908, with Frank Walker's bright young man from the works well represented. In the front row, third from left, is Doug Lewin, fourth from left on the second row is Piet Roll, four to his right is Frank Heading and on his right is Sid Mawer. The man in the dark suit with the buttonhole was the son of one of Garrett's German agents, Henninger of Darmstadt. Third from the left in the fourth row is Jack Simpson.
J. S. Waddell

Mizpah, which carried the date of 1877, and Edinburgh House. A *camera obscura* was a system of lenses and prisms set up on the roof of the building; it was powered by the attendant and commentator turning a handwheel. The image was projected onto a white bowl placed in the centre of the viewing floor, round which the customers stood. For a penny or so the little group could watch the panorama of the coast from about The Haven in the north to the martello in the south. As the lenses moved round, so the image in the bowl followed and the little audience subconsciously moved round too. The attendant, meanwhile, drew the attention of his watchers to the salient features of the scene. Many seaside resorts had a *camera obscura;* the one in Aldeburgh is believed to have been dismantled in the 1914–18 war.

Gardening provided an absorbing hobby for many, as well as useful assistance in feeding the household. Village cottages, on the whole, had sizeable gardens, but those in the old town at Aldeburgh and in the village centre at Leiston were on very small plots. The allotment movement helped out in these instances; there were cases where a householder not only cultivated a large garden at home but also ran two or three rods of allotment. A little tool and potting shed went with many allotments, and an old chair in the shed offered the opportunity for relaxation.

On the sandy soils of the coastal strip, keeping the land moist was a perennial problem. Waste water from the kitchen or backhouse was saved for the garden, and the water from the house roof and outhouses was diverted into water butts. Outside the areas served by piped water—broadly Aldeburgh, Leiston and Saxmundham—water from the water butts was used also for washing clothes and floors, and not infrequently the members of the household too.

The garden received the daily offerings of the slop pail and the periodical cleansings of the midden. Household budgets were too tight, on the whole, to permit the purchase of fertilizers. Kitchen compost, leaf mould, slops, and horse and cattle droppings gathered from the road had to nourish the soil. Keeping chickens or bantams provided the family with eggs and helped the garden with manure; a pig yielded even more.

Horticultural societies proliferated in the middle years of the last century. That at Leiston, for example, was set up in 1865 with Sir William Rose (of Leiston Abbey) as president and Henry Garrett as his vice president. Though the average society liked to enlist the membership of the well-to-do for monetary and moral support, the management and judging of the shows was mainly in the hands of practical gardeners. The head gardeners of the large country estates provided an immense fund of experience, freely drawn upon by the artisan gardening societies. The annual show provided the opportunity for keen gardeners from diverse villages to meet exchange ideas, seeds, cuttings and views upon the merits or demerits of the varieties under cultivation.

Until this century cycling was mainly a middle-class mode of transport. The old ordinary or penny farthing was an awkward machine to travel any distance on; a market in second-hand machines and a progressive reduction in the prices of new ones in the first decade of this century made many workmen into cyclists. The road surfaces were a deterrent— plentiful mud and slush in the wetter months and liberal quantities of dust in the summer—sharp flints were a menace to the tyres. With the advent of tarred surfaces in the twenties, however, cycling became more widely indulged in as a pastime.

Organized entertainment, on an amateur basis and away from public houses, gathered momentum with the rise of the temperance movement in the middle years of the last century. Drinking to excess had been a long-standing social evil, held to encourage petty crime. Low pubs too frequently provided the means of disposing of the spoils of theft, under the eyes of the publican. The temperance reformers, some secular but the majority associated with the free churches, attempted to combat this situation. Direct onslaughts were subjected to ribaldry, barracking or even physical violence, sometimes invited by the extreme language used by reformers. Dissent in religion had a strong and growing base in East Anglia, but even so direct appeals to temperance had only muted success. James Larner, a noted chapel man in Framlingham, was a powerful speaker against strong drink but despite his local connections drew only meagre audiences.

Alternative entertainments were a more hopeful antidote to the heavy drinkers. In Aldeburgh Mr Bowles, accompanied on the piano by his daughter, was in demand as a concert singer and violinist. Other local musical attractions were the Cremona Musical Union and Mr Sydney Herberte, and several brass bands of the Volunteers were often in requisition. Leiston Works boasted a brass band, and in addition the Peskett Family String Band, managed by Robert Peskett, was in demand for dances and like functions in Leiston. The Corn Exchange at Saxmundham provided an early and convenient gathering point for public functions. Rather later, in 1861, the Garretts built a Works Institute in Leiston in which was incorporated a meeting hall; in 1888, in honour of Queen Victoria's Golden Jubilee, Aldeburgh was presented with the Jubilee Hall by a band of subscribers headed by Newson Garrett.

The last century saw off the legal disabilities imposed upon dissenters, and a positive flood of free churches and chapels arose, often financed by their own, largely working class, congregations. The rejection of this mortal but certain life for the promise of the life immortal is a view certainly in decline today, but was, in the eighteen-sixties and seventies, a powerful reforming influence, making the chapels into centres of a flourishing social life. The missionary tours of the American evangelists Ira D. Sankey and Dwight Lyman Moody in 1873, 1881, 1883 and 1899 drew in many to these chapel congregations and left them with a legacy of new and emotional hymns and choruses.

The churches of the area and most of the chapels ran Sunday schools. Originally begun in the eighteenth century to give the elements of education to children who spent their weekdays at work, the Sunday school became transformed in the last century into a means of imparting religion to the young. The Sunday schools also provided companionship, and physical warmth and shelter in the colder months of the year; also the chance of taking part in the annual outing and tea. It was not uncommon for boys and girls to belong to two such schools, and thus to be Church of England in the morning but Nonconformist in the afternoon.

There were also itinerant entertainers. At the humblest level there was the organ grinder, moving his instrument by horse or donkey or even pushing it himself, sleeping in sheds or barns or in the open in mild weather, and in the cheapest hostels when it was cold. Of these the best remembered is Hoppy Charlie, an Italian with only one leg who travelled East Anglia with his monkey. Eventually amidst lamentation the monkey died. Some while later Charlie found himself a wife and was duly married by the late Canon Wintle, who had claims to being the patron saint of barrel organ men. Charlie's wife took the cup round for coppers as once the monkey had done. After a while she asked him "Won't you be getting another monkey, Charlie?", to which Charlie, evidently not without a streak of sardonic humour, replied "I not want a new monkey, gotta you now."

A rare event was a visit by a travelling menagerie. *The East Anglian Daily Times* reported on 13th August, 1875:

> Mr John Day's collection of wild beasts visited Leiston on Wednesday last and was well patronised. An exhibition of this kind has not visited us for about a quarter of a century. The splendid band of the establishment played a capital selection of music during the afternoon and evening.

Dancing bears, brown bears tamed and muzzled, taught to stand upright and shuffle a few steps, were once common, led round by their leader. Changes in public attitudes and the introduction of legislation eventually caused the disappearance of these bears. More sweeping changes were taking place in the travelling fairs that visited the district. These fairs had long roots extending back to mediaeval times or before, and also involved the sale of animals and the hiring of servants, particularly farm servants. Such a fair was held annually on 11th and 12th December at Cold Fair Green, Knodishall. Pigot, writing in 1839, stated that fairs were held in Aldeburgh on 1st March and 3rd May each year. In earlier years the fairs were in the centre of the town in Oakley Square, but disorderly behaviour on the part of their visitors caused them to be moved to Fort Green. By about the middle of the last century most of these fairs had shed all their commercial functions, and retained only that of entertainment. These pleasure fairs were made up almost entirely of what a modern showman would term "side-stuff", that is to say hooplas and other games of skill or chance, freak shows, boxing booths, food and sweetmeat stalls, jugglers and the like.

Fairs were increased in popularity by the invention of the steam-driven roundabout by Soames of Marsham (Norfolk), a invention taken up and improved upon by Frederick Savage of King's Lynn, by Tidmans of Norwich and by Walkers of Tewkesbury, who between them went on to design a galaxy of fairground riding machines all powered by steam. These new riding machines required capital for their purchase and called into being a new class of master showman; such a capital outlay needed more to sustain it

An Aldeburgh regatta fair on Fort Green, early 1920s. Burns Collection

could be provided by a bleak common in deep country a couple of weeks before Christmas, and fairs such as the Knodishall Cold Fair faded out; the end came with the 1914–18 war.

A fair originally held in Oakley Square and later on Fort Green accompanied the Aldeburgh Regatta, normally held on the last Monday in August. The regatta included sailing, rowing and sculling events and the town was *en fête* for it. The public houses opened all day and partisanship not infrequently led to arguments and fisticuffs. Walking between the Moot Hall and Fort Green, Ted Dunn once saw upwards of a dozen fights in progress. The component units of a fair are not all in the same ownership, but it is an assembly of independent proprietors. At one time the allocation of pitches was a free-for-all. A Punch and Judy man, carrying the whole outfit on his back or on a barrow, could generally get on to the ground somewhere, but if the owner of a big machine made the journey only to find his ground gone, he was at a serious loss.

To overcome this problem the Showmen's Guild was formed in 1910 to regulate the management of fairgrounds. As the system is now operated one showman, the lessee, undertakes to obtain the ground and to pay the rent to the landlord. He is responsible for measuring out the pitches required by the other showmen, his tenants, from whom he collects proportionate rents, reserving sufficient ground for his own machines. Tenants who have been regular attenders acquire rights to their grounds which they can sell or depute to another. The lessee sees to it also that there are not too many machines of one type on a fairground. At a small fair one of each is usually enough, though a big fair, such as Nottingham Goose Fair, can accommodate more.

Showmen's children, on the whole, tend to marry into other fairground families, and in consequence the owners of machines at the ground are often related. Thus at a fair in Leiston or Aldeburgh in the thirties one might have expected to find Bert and Sid Stocks (brothers), together with Billy Barker and Johnny Barker (in-laws to Bert Stocks—Charlotte Stocks was a Miss Barker before she married Bert). Others who appeared at pre-war fairs on the coast were the Underwood family, the Abbotts, the Greenaways and Fred Harris.

The fairground was also responsible for introducing the cinema to the coast. The first moving pictures to be seen publicly in East Anglia were shown on Monday 11th January, 1897, at the Agricultural Hall, Norwich, as an added attraction to George Gilbert's circus, appearing there for the Christmas season. This was closely followed by Randall Williams, the East Anglian showman, who bought an outfit and on 15th February, 1897, took it to Lynn Mart, the opening fair of the travelling season, held in the Tuesday Market at King's Lynn. Savage of Lynn, the noted maker of fairground machines, had introduced a new model of velocipede riding machine (patented by Collins and Savage in 1896) on which the punters rode on safety-cycles (two identical wheels), instead of on horses or animals. This had been intended to be the great novelty at the fair. In the event and to the chagrin of Savage and of the showman who had bought the ride, Randall Williams' moving pictures became the star attraction instead. Not only did he have the pictures, he also had electric light, which drew almost as much attention.

Savage was a realist. Sizing up the situation he set in hand the designing and building of a transportable cinematograph show, which he completed before the year was out. This included a sixty foot by forty foot auditorium tent with a boarded floor. Patrons generally were expected to stand, but there were seats at the front for forty, the twelve "best" seats being equipped with arms, backs and cushions in Utrecht velvet. Neither makers nor purchasers had grasped the fact that the best viewing position in a cinema auditorium was at the back rather than at the front, as in a live theatre, and consequently, for some time, shows were built with the most elaborate seating at the front. The front of the show tent was elaborate with imaginative murals and a gilded pay box approached by steps; this set the pattern for many similar outfits. The show was hauled by a six nominal horse power steam traction engine with a dynamo capable of providing light for the show.

The proliferation of moving picture shows on fairgrounds was rapid. Randall Williams himself did not live to see his own venture beyond infancy, as he died in November, 1898, but the business was carried on by his son, Randall Williams Junior. Another noted traveller early in the moving picture business in East Anglia was James Crighton, soon to be followed by Charles Thurston of Norwich. The technical development of the apparatus used was rapid, and the pace-setters in the business, with a round of big fairs capable of providing capacity audiences, kept their projection equipment and films abreast of the latest improvements. The earlier and less advanced equipment discarded by the pioneers percolated down through the strata of fairground society, until finally it was used on village greens and waste ground.

The patrons of such performances were liable to see jerky movements, badly lit and made almost illegible by the scratches sustained by the film through repeated use; however, so great was the novelty that it was still deemed worthwhile.

Early projectors had as a light source either limelight or an electric carbon arc lamp. Limelight was produced by burning bottled hydrogen gas with oxygen and playing the flame into a cone of lime, producing a brilliant white light. The arc lamp struck an electric arc between two carbon electrodes. Both types of light source generated much heat, the conjunction of which, with inflammable cellulose nitrate film created a considerable fire risk, made worse by inexpert handling of the film itself, which unwound from the projector onto the floor or into a sack until it could be rewound. During this time it was vulnerable to the carelessly dropped match or discarded cigarette butt.

Though East Anglia escaped disastrous cinema fires they did occur elsewhere on a scale that led to public concern, culminating in the Cinematograph Act 1906. One of the provisions of the Act limited the length of any one reel of film to a thousand feet. Another made it obligatory to separate the projector from the audience space by means of a non-combustible enclosure, of brick or blockwork in a fixed cinema, or metal in a tented show.

The first fixed cinema in East Anglia was the Gem at Great Yarmouth, which opened in 1906, but Leiston and Aldeburgh, offering fewer attractions to promoters, had to continue to rely for several more years upon travelling cinemas.

By about 1910 the district was served by the show owned by Tommy Cottrell, whose permanent address was in Droitwich. Cottrell's appears to have been the first moving picture show seen in Leiston on a regular basis. His shows took place either in a "fit-up" pitched variously on a paddock in Valley Road, or on land opposite the White Horse, or in the rented hall of the Constitutional Club, built in 1909. Cottrell used electricity to light his show, generated by the Garrett-built showman's steam tractor East Lynne. Tommy Cottrell described his undertaking as "Cottrell's Dramatic Picture Co.".

It had a very brief sway, however, for the potential of the cinema had been recognized by Frank E. Walker, one of the senior staff of Richard Garrett & Sons Ltd. He was a cultivated man, a keen motorist and able to fly aircraft. Walker came to the conclusion in 1913 that the sizes of the audiences Cottrell was attracting were sufficient to make a fixed cinema profitable. He discussed his ideas with Emerich Schmach, the chief draughtsman at Garretts, with J. B. Harrison, Frank Garrett Senior's personal assistant, and with an outside friend, Captain E. B. B. Levett-Scrivener, of Sibton Abbey, Yoxford, a retired naval officer.

Together they purchased from William Catling a small paddock next to his butcher's shop in Aldeburgh Road, here, the following year, they had a cinema built to the designs of the firm of W. H. Heath Ltd of Manchester. The contractors were Humphreys Ltd of Knightsbridge, London. Described somewhat ambiguously as capable of seating "six to seven hundred", it was arranged on one raked floor and titled the Picture House. Electricity was provided by a gas engine and dynamo at the rear, and two small dressing rooms and a stage made it possible for live shows to be put on. The front was taken up by two lock-up shops with the cinema entrance between. The office and projection room were over the shops, approached by an iron spiral staircase. The only substantial change over the years was the adoption of sound in 1930. The first manager (1914–15) was T. H. Pike, but he resigned in September, 1915, and was succeeded by W. S. Hammick.

Ted Dunn described Hammick as "wearing a stiff collar so high that if he had moved his head sharply he would have cut his ears off". John Waddell, who went to the matinées at the Picture House as a boy, remembered how Hammick attempted to keep the children in order by banging unruly characters on the head with his torch. Pike had combined operation of the projector with his duties as manager, but when Hammick took over a separate operator was appointed, Gilbert Croyle (at £2 per week), with an assistant, Charles Christmas (at five shillings a week). A boy in the Garrett office, Reggie King, was appointed as part-time clerk at three shillings a week. King ended his career, forty-eight years later, as general manager of the Garrett works and a board member. A later projectionist, in the early twenties, was Jack Cross. Jack was totally absorbed in his work and made his own newsreel

Ted Dunn, dressed in his brother's Sea Scout uniform, played the part of a sailor in the amateur film Mystery of the Meare, *made by Jack Cross, the projectionist at the Leiston cinema.*
Mrs E. C. Dunn

films of local events. He also made a fictional film called *The Mystery of the Mere,* in which he used local children as the cast. Ten Dunn had a part as a sailor, and he wore his brother's sea-scout uniform.

By 1926 Albert Free, who had joined as a boy, had taken over as the operator, a post he occupied until he died in 1957, but not before his son Peter had joined him as assistant and understudy. He continued as operator to run the day to day affairs of the cinema.

Schmach had soon vanished from the scene. He was born a citizen of Austria–Hungary, despite over thirty years of working for the Garretts, living in Leiston, marriage to a local woman, and years of service as a chorister had omitted to change his nationality, so, like Ganz (*see* chapter 14), he was sent away from Leiston when war broke out to live in Godalming, Surrey. Death and retirement weeded out the other promoter Grace Walker, Frank's widow, remained a director and was secretary until 1976, when the company decided that they could not continue to operate the cinema. Fortunately the Suffolk Coastal District Council agreed to take it over and it continues under the name of the Film Theatre, the bookings and similar functions being undertaken by the Town Clerk's office. As I write it has been announced that the Central Electricity Generating Board has granted fifty thousand pounds towards its general refurbishment.

Aldeburgh had to wait until after the 1914–18 war for its cinema. The site was originally a shop and house called *The Chestnuts,* going back at least until 1851. These were sold in 1920 to Harry Lander of Great Newport Street, London, who built the cinema incorporating parts of the original buildings. It was sold the following year to Walter Riggs and Sidney Lewer, who traded as Aldeburgh Cinema and Amusements. It is said that George Garrett of Snape provided some of the money for the enterprise.

In 1927 the owning company, tiring of direct participation, let the cinema to Raymond Rayner for "the purpose", as the lease expressed it, of high class cinematograph exhibitions, stage plays and concerts". This was a time when agriculture in the surrounding countryside was doing very badly, and the Garrett engineering works at Leiston had undergone a sharp decline in output (some two thousand people were employed in 1917, but ten years later there was only a quarter of that number). Rayner had the rather different characteristics of the Aldeburgh *clientèle* as a cushion between his venture and the economic deprivation of the surrounding areas. The town had acquired a regular trade amongst holidaymakers who appreciated its quietness and serenity, and the same characteristics had attracted as permanent residents numbers of the well-to-do, many retired from business, the professions or the colonial service.

The minimum charge at Aldeburgh was sixpence (2½p), limited to the front two rows, compared with twopence-halfpenny at Leiston and, as Queenie Dunn recalls, a penny-halfpenny on matinée days at the front. She and a friend used to walk (c1920) about three miles each way from Eastbridge to go to the cinema. Out of her week's earnings from errands and odd jobs she used to spend a penny on a bar of Sharp's toffee. If there was enough money left she would then buy a twopenny-halfpenny ticket. If not it meant the front row for a penny-halfpenny. When Arnold Drew was a lad in Aldeburgh in silent film days he undertook errands and odd jobs to earn enough money to go to the pictures. Sixpence earned would enable him go to the Aldeburgh cinema but for only fourpence he could take a child's day return on the train to Leiston (a penny-halfpenny) and pay to go into the cinema (twopence-halfpenny). Sevenpence in earnings enabled him not only to go to Leiston's Picture House but to go across afterwards to Frank Maorelli's fish and chip shop for a "tuppenny and one"—a twopenny piece of fried fish and a pennyworth of chips, with free salt and vinegar.

The Aldeburgh cinema survived the transition to sound, but by the second half of the thirties it was felt that reconstruction was needed to maintain the standards that had been set. This was carried out under the direction of Ley, Colbeck and Partners of 214 Bishopsgate, London, who have since become internationally famous architects. The cinema after this building was essentially as it remains today.

Very soon after the work was completed the Second World War broke out. There were no more holidaymakers and many of the residents who had used the cinema moved away to live in areas less exposed to enemy attack. By way of compensation, however, many of those who remained found themselves much better off financially, and there were soon soldiers and airmen stationed in the surrounding areas. Bombs destroyed the cottage hospital next to the Aldeburgh cinema, and the landward side of the High Street up to and including the Post Office, but the cinema itself was only superficially damaged.

In 1951 Rayner bought the property, which he had already leased for twenty-four years. In a report to a prospective lender to whom Rayner had submitted a proposal for a capital loan, the London firm of surveyors Cuthbert Lake Ford and Clapham said of him and his cinema:

> One of the attractions of the cinema over its competitors at Leiston and Saxmundham is the fact that the proposed borrower [Rayner] maintains a very high standard of decorative repair and cleanliness and in a rural community, where there is, perhaps, a tendency to vegetate,

the cinema under review stands out as a model of its kind but not in an offensive or ostentatious manner.

By this time the cinema trade, as a whole, was in retreat from the burgeoning of television, and many owners had not found it possible or worthwhile to maintain the standards of their cinemas. Rayner, however, had managed to keep his establishment neat and spruce and for a few years more continued in sole control.

Meanwhile the Aldeburgh Festival had been established and was an outstanding success. Obliquely, the cinema gained some of this. Although getting on in years Raymond Rayner had made a determined effort to live up to what was expected of him, but when he died in 1965 the absence of potential commercial successors made it apparent that running a cinema up to these standards promised little hope of a commensurate return.

The prospect of losing the cinema suddenly made it seem very dear to the townspeople. Spurred by this danger Stephen Reiss, the then manager of the Festival, canvassed the suggestion of its being bought by a consortium of local well-wishers involved in or close to the Festival itself. He secured the backing of Benjamin Britten, Peter Pears, Arthur Harrison, the Honourable Hugh Gathorne-Hardy, Grace Agate and Charles and Laetitia Gifford. The first two require no introduction. Arthur Harrison, who lived at Snape, was a retired preparatory school master, Hugh Gathorne-Hardy was a chartered accountant, Grace Agate was Mayor of Aldeburgh, Charles Gifford was an economist and Treasurer of the Festival.

The eighth member of the syndicate was Ted Bostock, whose family had been in the travelling circus business since 1660, and was the owner of a small chain of cinemas based in Dovercourt. Ted alone had had previous experience of cinema management, and knew whom to turn to for supplies and renewals and how to cope with the minor emergencies. When he retired he sold his shares to Adnams, the Southwold brewers; they are represented on the present board by Mrs Prudence Loftus.

The syndicate's offer was successful and for a decade the cinema was run by Stephen Reiss, more or less as an adjunct of the Festival. When he left in 1975 the consortium, from whom the board of directors was constituted, faced another crisis. As Mrs Gifford put it: "The Board had to face up to the fact that one of them would have to provide the management or we would have to sell the Cinema. I took it on and have been the managing director ever since."

At the time of writing, after, in Mrs Gifford's words, "considerable ups and downs", Aldeburgh Cinema Ltd, is reasonably prosperous and working closely with the local community, who back it up through a supporters' club with a membership of over five hundred.

In Saxmundham at about the end of the First World War the Kinema was opened in High Street by C. R. Punchard, superseding various temporary shows held in the Corn Exchange and elsewhere.

Later came the Playhouse, opened in 1934 in Church Street. As at the Leiston Picture House it was mostly on one raked floor, but with a small gallery as well. The promoter, owner and manager was Captain G. L. Atkinson. After years of makeshift picture shows Saxmundham felt justified in making a big occasion of the inauguration of its cinema, the newest and arguably the best in the area, and the opening ceremony was performed by Lord Cranbrook. It had one feature much appreciated by courting couples, namly a proportion of double seats, and only one serious drawback, the vibration of heavy traffic on the A12 road through the main street of the town two hundred yards away. Indeed the reverberations of trains on the railway at twice the distance away could be felt.

The cinema paid well from the beginning, and as at Leiston and Aldeburgh the war brought plenty of custom from the neighbouring camps and aerodromes, but in 1945 Captain Atkinson died, leaving his widow to carry on the business with the help of Mrs A. Foster, who acted as manageress. When her husband, Henry, was demobilized from the Navy he took over as manager. At that time Mrs Atkinson turned it into a limited company with herself and Mrs Foster as directors, together with a Mr Smith. Under this management it ran until 1960, by which time the day of the small country cinema was nearly over. The venture soon became insolvent and in the following year was closed and became a car showroom. Harry Archer, chief projectionist from 1946 until the closure, still lives in Samundham, as do Mr and Mrs Henry Foster. The cinema still lingers on in the memories of numerous middle-aged couples who did their courting in those cosy and accommodating double seats.

The horse races at Snape, over a course of seven miles (compared with the one and a half miles of the Derby) were probably the only major races in the area. The course was set in the sandy area between the turnpike road past Snape church, on the north side, and the River Alde to the south, forming the bowl of a frying pan the handle of which was the avenue of trees extending north toward Friston Hall. The races began in 1727 but declined in the first half of the next century, finally guttering out in 1842. However, while in their prime they were "much frequented by the London jockeys". Subsequently the coast saw no horse racing on the flat, and in the absence of fox hunting no point-to-point racing either. East Suffolk as a whole was given over to the preservation of game to the exclusion of fox hunting, but in the coast of our definition this was never carried to the extravagant and obsessive lengths practised at, for instance, Elveden Hall. Nevertheless local landowners shot over their estates with their guests and, from time to time, their tenants. The Ogilvies of Sizewell Hall, with something in excess of six thousand acres at their disposal, had considerable scope in planning their shoots. Shooting was not a poor man's pastime, and if a working man's family ate game it was usually obtained by poaching, the traditional method of the countryman. Rabbits abounded in the Sandlings and there was no shortage of hares.

Fishing, however, whether from the shore or a boat, was a widely appreciated pastime. That the sea had a compelling influence upon the men of the coast cannot be doubted. It has declined somewhat today. "Russian Bob" Cable of Aldeburgh went to sea as a boy of twelve and his family heard no more of him till he reappeared at home at the age of twenty-seven. Lewis Chandler, the clerk responsible for many years for the staff registers at Leiston Works, noted time and time again against the names of those coming onto or leaving the works such remarks as "has been

The Sunday school treat of Leiston UMF Church, 5th July, 1913.
Curiously there seem to be more adults than children.
J. S. Waddell

fishing", "left to go fishing", or, more telling, "left to go back to the fishing". Aside from following fishing as a living, many practised it as a pastime. It was possible to catch whiting and cod from the beach, and occasionally bass. Sprats and herring were landed from boats, and shrimps and prawns could be netted.

The ability to salt and smoke fish at home appealed to many, and those with space set up small smokehouses. Herring for smoking might be bought locally, or at Lowestoft or Southwold, or even caught by the curer. The results varied according to his skill in the smokehouse. A salted, lightly wind-dried bloater, eaten at once, had a succulent perfection rarely approached today. On the other hand a herring might be saturated in salt and smoked to the texture of cardboard. Some part-time curers smoked solely for domestic purposes. Others hawked their wares to neighbours or in public houses. A salt herring spiked on a toasting fork or poker and given a token grilling at the bar fire stimulated the thirst of the eater in a way that was good for publicans' sales.

Then, of course, there were eels, found in season in the watercourses of the Aldeburgh, Lantern and Thorpe marshes or the Minsmere Levels. After the Leiston brickworks closed, Queenie Dunn's father, Will Lumpkin, who then lived at Eastbridge, worked at bottomfying the dykes there. Section by section the watercourses were dammed off, when the flow was low, by boards driven vertically into the bottom, supported from bank to bank by cross poling boards. The length was drained or pumped as free of water as possible, prior to the marshmen cleaning the weed and sludge away. As they worked the bottomfyers found numerous eels. Eel pie and stewed eels were prominent items on the domestic menus of the men cleaning the dykes; freshwater coarse fish were also found occasionally, but as in any area with access to newly-caught sea fish, freshwater fish were thought to taste unacceptably insipid.

He also recalled how he and Queenie, in their courting days, used to go eel-babbing. This was done after dark, which also appealed to a young couple. The preparation, however, had to be done during the day. Twenty or thirty big earthworms were dug up and impaled end to end on a coarse thread. This was the bab. It was used on a rod and line and suspended so that the lowest worm was just off the dyke bottom. When an eel took the lowest worm the thread caught in its mouth. The knack was to twitch the eel out sharply onto the bank, where the catcher (Queenie) pounced on it: if the eel got away in the grass it was very hard to catch. Once caught the eels were kept alive by tying them together with a length of twine, each held just below the head. One end of the string was tied to a weight stone and the other to an improvised float, usually a willow stick, the whole thing being dropped back into the dyke.

Scout rally at Leiston,
17th July, 1920.
J. S. Waddell

Walking the beaches between tides could produce much of interest and profit to those able to interpret what they saw. Amber was to be found, as well as citrines and jet, washed down by the longshore drift from Whitby. Driftwood kept many families in firewood and provided raw material for sheds or fences. In addition there were sometimes objects washed from ships. The action of the sea, culminating in the storm and flood of 1953, has altered the configuration of the beaches, but in the twenties Sizewell beach was wider and sandier than now. For a spell this led to motor cyclists congregating on the beach, and even holding organized races. This came to an end after a motor cyclist collided with and killed a child during practice. Grass track racing was also held at Benhall.

*   *   *

In those days there was a small and remote group of houses at Minsmere Sluice, comprising a row of cottages, in one of which lived the Booty family; there was also the Black House, the Red House and a tea house known as the Pavilion.

157

William Booty, the doyen of the Minsmere cottagers and patriarch of the clan, had been a boiler-maker apprentice on Leiston Works from 1852 to 1859 but left when his time was out. He was on the works again from 1867 to 1871, when he left after the failure of the 1871 strike at the works. He went back again for sixteen months in 1872 and 1873, then had an absence of some six years before returning for the last time in 1879, whereafter he never again left the works until he died, still working as a boiler-maker, at seventy-five in January, 1914. Booty must have been a most proficient workman, for in the twelve months up to the time of his leaving in 1873 he had earned no less than £110.

There was no made road to the settlement. Tradesmen went along a track at the top of the bank from Sizewell or, by permission, over the Lower Abbey farm road. The Red House and Black House were used only as holiday houses, but the cottages were lived in all the year round. There were, naturally, no sewers to the buildings and the customers at the Pavilion were provided with an earth closet at the end of the garden, approached through a bower of rambling roses. The houses and cottages ceased to be used when the coast defences were erected in the Second World War, and the last remains were destroyed by the 1953 flooding, but for years the rambling roses that had once shrouded the Pavilion loos continued in chaotic defiance.

The original thatched club-house of the Aldeburgh Golf Club.
SPS

158

The Long Shop   13

FOR THE FIRST three-quarters of this century the centre of
Leiston, the square of property bounded by Main Street,
Haylings Road, Cross Street and High Street, was solidly Garrett-
owned, except for the enclaves formed by the Black Horse, the
Royal Standard and the short row of shops in the High Street
which included Titlow's ironmongery shop.

The obsolescence of the buildings and the changes in the
firm's products during the nineteen-sixties meant that production
was progressively transferred to the Station Works, or the "Top"
works as it was often called, until on 10th April, 1978, all work at
the Town Works ceased and thenceforth everything was transferred to the Station Works. The year 1978 marked the bicentenary of Leiston Works in the hands of the Garretts and their
successors. Sadly the following year saw the closing of the whole
enterprise. The business, which had begun as a blacksmith's forge,
already a going concern when the first Richard Garrett took over in
1778, had blossomed into a large manufactory of seed drills,
threshing machines, horse hoes and other agricultural implements,
and had gone on to make traction engines and other types of
engines in considerable variety. It later made electric lorries, trolley
buses, specialized tractors, guns and intricate machinery for the
box-making and plastics industry. Its luck had at last run out.

By 1978 many of the buildings on the old site had been taken
down, some for reuse at the Station Works. These clearances and
the further demolitions that have taken place since have thrown
into prominence the remarkable building known to generations of
Leiston Works people as the Long Shop. Though not the oldest
building on the site, it had grounds for being considered the most
interesting. Possibly the oldest parts were the flint-walled buildings
forming the scullery annex to the Works House and parts of the
Drawing Office store. I am of the opinion, without positive proof,
that the scullery annex could well have been the original house at
the time when the forge employed only a handful of men and the
grindstones were powered by a horse walking in a circle.

The Long Shop was conceived and built when the third
Richard Garrett was head of the firm, and it was he who altered the
status of the firm from that of a group of village tradesmen to that
of internationally-known manufacturers. Born in 1807, he was a
man of trifling education but immense intelligence and ability. At
the age of fourteen, such education as he received already behind

him, he was at work in the business, which then employed about sixty men. Five years later he took control of its finances, and seven years on again his father gave up his share of the management to become a full-time farmer, leaving his ambitious son in total control at twenty-six.

By 1837 Richard Garrett's improvements to the design of threshing machines and seed drills had raised him to such a level of eminence that he was one of those consulted by the Duke of Richmond and Mr William Shaw when they took in hand the formation of the Royal Agricultural Society. In 1848, sensing the strides steam power could make in farming, he began constructing portable steam engines for farm use. Within three years the trade in these engines had increased to such an extent that he had to contemplate the building of an entirely new workshop for them. The building that resulted was the Long Shop.

By this time the workforce had increased to three hundred. By 1857 it was to reach five hundred, and by 1862 six hundred. Though his eldest son Richard and youngest son Frank carried on the business successfully after his death and, indeed, built it up by the time of Frank's death to a point where some two thousand people were employed, it was never again the glorious zestful adventure that it had been under his control; this spirit of enterprise reached its height in 1851.

Temperamentally unable to tackle anything with less than total commitment, he had been drawn into the orbit of the Great Exhibition of 1851 by being persuaded to become one of its guarantors. The man who had done the persuading was Samuel Peto, whom he knew through the major part Peto had played in the building of railways, particularly the East Suffolk Railway, and the development of Lowestoft. Richard was soon caught up in the excitement of the exhibition: he had a stand there, and designed and built a new and, as it turned out, not particularly successful design of portable steam engine to be shown there. He visited the exhibition repeatedly, and persuaded many friends to go; he also sent a large number of his workmen and their wives to view it.

Richard was attentive to what he saw on the stands of other exhibitors. He was particularly interested in the guns of Samuel Colt, the American maker which were turned out with precision, good finish and at low cost by what approximated to assembly-line methods. Colt revolvers were assembled on flow-line principles by semi-skilled labour, from standardized components manufactured to rigidly defined limits. This eliminated the hours of laborious hand-fitting that went into weapons made by traditional gunsmith's methods.

Guns interested Richard, partly, no doubt, because he enjoyed a day's game shooting, but also because he was interested in the

nascent Volunteer Movement. Moreover, certain of his forebears had been gunsmiths at Wickham Market.

Garrett took home ideas from the Great Exhibition, that no doubt contributed to the construction of his new building, expressly for the manufacture of portable steam engines on a logical work-flow. For some years he bought the boilers for these engines from London boiler-makers who could deliver by sea to Slaughden, thus eliminating boiler-making facilities, but he had his own foundry and smith's shop to feed in raw castings and forgings to the new production department, and he set about organizing machine work and fitting.

The new building was of impressive dimensions, about 80 feet by 36 feet on plan internally, and some 25 feet to the eaves. On the ground floor he arranged an erection bay down the centre of the shop with the heavy machining and assembly areas round the periphery. The central erecting bay was open up to the roof, but the remaining area of the ground floor was covered by a gallery on

The interior of the Long Shop when it was ten years old, from Measom's Guide to the Great Eastern Railway, 1863.

161

which were housed some of the lighter machine tools, and the fitters doing sub-assemblies. The open area of the shop was served by an overhead travelling crane.

The construction of the shop was interesting. The enclosing structure was of local red bricks, 22½ inches thick at ground level; the firm had its own brick kiln in 1852, so it is likely that this was the source of the bricks. The best bricks seem to have been used for external facings and the place bricks for the interior face. Yellow gault bricks were used for external quoins. Internally the whole gallery, the columns and beams which served the dual purpose of carrying it and the crane rails were formed of heavy pine timbers, stiffened with cast-iron knees and braces instead of the internal structure of cast-iron columns and beams and brick jack-arches adopted for comparable contemporary structures elsewhere. Richard Garrett III may have adopted this rather dated structure because all the castings used in it were within the capacity of his own foundry, and the timbers could be worked in his own carpenter's shop; otherwise he would have had to buy it elsewhere, and have it shipped to Slaughden. The smallness of the crane on the quay there would have made unloading diffucult, and transport between Slaughen and Leiston was not good. Rail transport did not reach Leiston for another ten years and then only by a branch of the East Suffolk Railway of which Richard was a director.

The deal floor of the gallery was formed of a double skin of tongued and grooved boarding; a wooden staircase gave access from the ground floor, though the original has since been replaced. The pitched roof was constructed of timber and covered with local red pantiles, with three glass-topped louvred ventilators and a central area of glazing over the erecting bay. There is no doubt that originally this was putty-glazed in wooden bars as in many other parts of the old works, but in latter years the original glazing in the Long Shop was replaced by wired glass in lead-clothed bars. Internally the tiled roof slopes were lined with lime plaster on a ground of reed. At the eaves the rainwater was probably collected into cast-iron moulded gutters (which were, in modern times, replaced by asbestos) carried on a dog-tooth course of brickwork and discharging into iron downpipes. Originally there were large double doors in each end wall, but those at the west end were subsequently altered when a later workshop was added. Over each set of doors was a semi-circular headed window and the north elevation had segmented windows on each floor. Other, older buildings abutted the south wall, thus only a few windows could be tucked in that side to light the gallery.

The shop was lit by coal gas from the Garrett gas works, which had been set up during the preceding two years on a piece of land just to the west of the Long Shop site (facing the road to Snape). It was thus known for several generations as Gas Hill. The gas was burned in batswing burners, many of which were in use within the memory of men still living when I first became involved in recording the history of Garrett's but heating seems to have been of the most vestigial character, probably by stoves or braziers. Of plumbing or sanitary facilities the building was entirely innocent.

That Richard put a great deal of pride and care into his new workshop is evident from the elevational design. To crown it he erected a handsome clock turret at the east end, surmounted by a weather vane carrying a silhouette of the portable engine and threshing machine entered in the Great Exhibition. The weather vane was transferred to the new administration block at the Station Works but has now been returned to the Long Shop and re-erected in its original position—sadly the clock mechanism is lost.

Ten to fifteen years was probably the longest that the new workshop could have contained the whole of the portable engine work, as trade in portable engines escalated rapidly. The building was soon absorbed into the general activities of the works, the ground floor as a machine shop and the gallery as a fitting shop.

By the opening years of this century the south-east corner of

A detailed view of one of the cast iron stiffeners, with Richard Garrett's initials and the date of building. B. J. Finch

the gallery housed a few very old lathes on which apprentices did simple and repetitive turning of such items as block bolts (the bolts used to bolt the crank shaft saddles of portables to the boilers), but was mainly given over to fitting benches where gangs of fitters, expert and seemingly oblivious to monotony, fitted up sub-assemblies.

During its last twenty years of commercial use the Long Shop was merely a store for unused machinery and plant, unimportant stores and old drawings.

When I became involved with the works as a kind of unofficial archivist and historian the company was a wholly owned subsidiary of Beyer Peacock and Co. of Manchester, widely and justly famed as builders of railway locomotives. The fame of the parent company had become centred upon their building of the Beyer-Garratt articulated steam locomotive, using a system which enabled very large and powerful locomotives to run upon relatively lightly constructed and sharply curved railways; this was of great interest to the former Commonwealth and Empire countries. That it should have borne the name Garratt was a coincidence. The inventor of the system was a locomotive engineer called Garratt, working on the New South Wales Government Railways; unable to get his ideas taken up there, he was forced to hawk them around the major locomotive builders of the world until he came to Beyer Peacock. The resemblance between his patronym and that of the founding family of the works at Leiston, which was later to become a Beyer Peacock subsidiary, was coincidental: the names were spelt differently.

By the nineteen-fifties this forward-looking vision at Beyer Peacock had run out. The board could not bring itself to believe, in spite of advice to the contrary, that the fact that their order books for steam locomotives were full did not mean that steam had a long-term commercial future. James Hadfield, who had spent years at the head of their drawing office and some years as a director, forecast fairly accurately how events would go but he was simply not believed. In consequence the day arrived when having embarked upon the building of diesel locomotives too late and with too little commitment Beyer Peacock found itself unable to continue in business.

Subsequently, under a new chairman, Eric V. Robinson, the Beyer Peacock works at Gorton was closed and demolished, the site sold and a capital repayment made to shareholders. This left Richard Garrett Engineering Works Limited (later renamed Richard Garrett Engineering Limited) as the principal revenue earner of the group. Had it not been making a profit it would probably have shared the fate of some other non-earning subsidiaries, such as Anti-attrition Metals Limited, and been woundup.

In the year that followed, James Hadfield's son Reginald was appointed managing director with two long-standing Leiston men as his co-directors, Reginald Clarke in secretarial and accountancy matters and Ernest Cuthbert in engineering. The task they were set was to modernize the Leiston operation without the injection of capital from outside the company. The strategy that evolved was the modernization of the Station Works and the clearing by stages of the Town Works, enabling the site value to be realized.

In 1967 Garrett's appointed H. T. Cadbury-Brown and Partners as architects, to prepare an outline scheme for the redevelopment of the town site for a combination of housing, commerce and public amenities. No one at that time attached very much importance to the buildings that stood on the site.

When Cadbury-Brown & Partners put forward a revised plan, in March 1969, proposing to retain the office block "because it was thought to be of historical interest", the Highways and Buildings Committee of Leiston Urban District Council scarcely took the suggestion seriously. One member laughed outright. The dilemma of the Garrett board of directors was that while they were personally not against preservation, every one of the old buildings that might be left standing would diminish the commercial prospects of the remainder of the site, hence denying some of capital needed to modernize the Station Works.

These development prospects were much overestimated. No developer came forward to make an offer for the land in terms acceptable to the firm. The company did not want industry there because it would have competed with its own demands for the available labour; housing had been largely blighted by the proximity of Sizewell A and the possibility of Sizewell B, while the big multiple traders, whom it had been hoped would have been attracted, were put off by the smallness of the population within the catchment area.

By 1972 the official local government outlook had changed significantly. On 27th July, 1972, Mr Alan Way, the County Planning Officer, reported to the Committee "the site . . . contains two buildings which should be retained, if at all possible. These are the Works House, one of Leiston's very few Grade II listed buildings . . . and an engine shed of industrial archaeological interest near the centre of the site". The Leiston UDC was sceptical, but two months later Councillor Leslie Farrow, sometime-head of the Works Drawing Office, made the remark that while the (Works) House and Engine House would not fit in with a modern scheme, the Engine House if retained could be turned into a museum. This, as far as I know, is the first public reference to the Long Shop (for such was the "engine shed" and "engine house") having a future as a museum.

The Leiston UDC still remained lukewarm, and some members actively hostile, to any preservation attempts until it lost its identity in the Suffolk Coastal District Council, but the County Council later became increasingly aware of the historical value of the buildings.

Within the company, changes had modified attitudes. Robinson, dissatisfied with the Heath government's attitude to industry, had announced his intention to retire from the chair of the parent company and to sell his holding. The new chairman, Colonel John Barstow, had neither the time nor inclination to be his own group managing director as Robinson had done, and in 1974 appointed Christopher Bland to fill the post. For business and personal reasons this led to the resignation of Reginald Hadfield. Michael Hilton was appointed to the management of Leiston works and soon afterwards to the boards of the subsidiary and the group. Both Bland and Hilton, new to the scene, were in favour of the retention of a group of the old buildings.

Some while before, I had been able to persuade Reginald Hadfield and his co-directors to lodge the historical records of the firm with the County Archivist, W. R. Serjeant, at County Hall, Ipswich, who later became actively interested in the preservation of the buildings. At about the same time the Suffolk Preservation Society became aware of the peril in which the old buildings stood and actively concerned for their retention. Cecil Lightfoot, CBE, the recently retired former Clerk to the old East Suffolk County Council, also became interested. On 21st July, 1976, Bill (W.) Serjeant was successful in convening a meeting in the Garrett boardroom, at which those interested in furthering the preservation of the group of buildings centred on the Works House and Long Shop sat round the table with company representatives and several potential contributors to the work. The minutes of this meeting are attached as an appendix.

Things soon got in motion from here. Cecil Lightfoot agreed to take the chair of a working committee. On 14th October, 1978, the Long Shop became a Grade II listed building and a week later Mr Cadbury-Brown carried out an inspection in preparation for a detailed report and feasibility study. On the company side Christopher Bland became so interested in the Long Shop that he invited his friend Michael Thomas of the Avoncraft Museum of Buildings, Stoke Heath, Bromsgrove, Worcestershire, to inspect it.

Mr Thomas stressed the importance of its preservation; the intensity of his interest reinforced Christopher Bland's resolve to do his utmost to ensure the survival of the building. On 22nd May, 1978, the working party was told by Michael Hilton, as managing director of Richard Garrett Engineering, that the company was prepared to give them the Long Shop and an associated piece of

The interior of the Long Shop a hundred years on. B. J. Finch

land. In the interim the listing of the building had been lifted from Grade II to Grade II*, and the Cadbury-Brown report was delivered in September 1977, making it clear that from the constructional and architectural standpoint the museum proposals were feasible.

The work of the committee became intensified. Cecil Lightfoot decided to relinquish the chair for health reasons and was succeeded by Lord Medway, soon to become Earl of Cranbrook. The bicentenary of the firm was celebrated on 17th June, 1978, marked by local celebrations and by the publication of my book, *Garrett 200*. Sadly however, things were far from well within the company and, unknown to most of the committee, it was in grave financial peril.

Essentially the Committee had no funds beyond those given by its own members and by the project's band of well-wishers. The

Manpower Services Commission seemed the most appropriate body to approach for help and they agreed to finance the salary and expenses of a Project Officer for a year, as a result of which Keith Pittman was appointed. Garretts found him an office and a store room, where he began to collect suitable artefacts for exhibition. Despite its problems the company adhered to its promise to give the Long Shop to the committee. For this purpose an independent trust of four members was set up with the Earl of Cranbrook in the chair. Other members were Michael Hilton, Frank Barker and Trevor Hawkings, the two latter both councillors, at county and district respectively.

In April, 1980, repairs began on the roof, which were completed by the end of June. Garretts told the committee at the end of June that though they would still give them the Long Shop, straitened finances made it necessary to sell the ancillary buildings, for which an offer of £15,000 had been made. After discussion the committee decided to match that offer but within a week the company had called in the receiver and negotiations had to begin afresh with him. Regretfully the committee had to give Keith Pittman notice, and he left on 5th September, 1980. Early 1981 was a period of many anxieties but by the latter end of the summer success was clearly in sight and the conveyance was completed early in September. The Trust Deed itself bears the date 4th September.

The trustees were now faced with the task of transforming their asset into the museum which they had in mind. They had already obtained a certain amount of help in cleaning and painting the remains of the old boiler house, the building which now forms the Loggia, from a Manpower Services Commission Scheme.

It was to the Commission that the trustees turned again. The logic of this was clear. The amount of restoration work required to the buildings, despite the work already done to the roof of the Long Shop, was certainly beyond the powers of the volunteer help available. Lack of finance prevented its being placed in the hands of professional contractors. The Commission, therefore, seemed by far the most promising source of assistance. In addition to the building work, there was also the problem of preparing the artefacts, of which there were a large number, for showing to the public.

In November, 1982, after preliminary talks with the Manpower Services Commission (MSC) Regional Office at Ipswich had given encouraging signs, a formal proposal was approved. This enabled a full-time project manager to be appointed. The choice fell upon A. J. (Tony) Errington, a mechanical engineer with experience of works management. His initial brief was to make the whole site safe and to commence the work of adapting the buildings into a museum. For a while the old Welfare Office remained in the hands of a tenant, a firm of light engineers, but once they had gone it was turned into a temporary office. The Old Despatch Department next to it was also cleared and made watertight for use as a workshop in which exhibits could be prepared. For a while work on larger pieces was carried out on the ground floor of the Long Shop, but its usefulness was circumscribed by the poor state of the floor, a mixture of end grain wood blocks, concrete and stone slabs.

Before the Long Shop could be opened to the public this floor had to be renewed. Whilst it was the aim to keep some of the floor's original character, there was no hope of re-laying the whole area with wood block for financial reasons alone. The plan was adopted, therefore, of re-laying the floor of the central area with those of the original wood blocks that were capable of reuse, with sections at each end in granite setts found on the site. The two side aisles were relaid in reinforced concrete. While the floor was being renewed the opportunity was taken to tie together the brick plinths, on which the timber columns were founded by reinforced concrete beams. The gallery was structurally sound but the boarded floor was in bad condition: for the time being the idea of restoring it was left in abeyance.

The winter's work included stripping off a century and a quarter's coating of whitewash from the walls of the ground floor; the stripped brickwork was given a coat of stabilizing solution and two coats of white Sandtex, which gave a fair representation of the original whitewash without its tendency to flake and powder.

During this period the Trustees were given by the Central Electricity Generating Board a considerable amount of material and equipment from redundant power stations. Much of the machinery and equipment of the workshop was acquired this way, together with furniture for the office. The closure of the historic Deptford Power Station yielded two lorry-loads of condemned scaffold boarding, out of which was to come enough sound material to renew the floor of the gallery.

Meanwhile, in the workshop an Aveling Barford diesel road roller was put into working trim, and the Garrett steam roller repatriated from Spain was given cosmetic treatment for static display. During this period the Trust received the Garrett no 4 compound tractor *Princess Marina*, together with a Garrett portable engine and compound condensing semi-stationery engine from Brace's sawmill at Ongar, Essex.

On 28th April, 1984, the museum was opened ceremonially by Sir Joshua Rowley, Lord Lieutenant of Suffolk. Several local owners brought their preserved engines to the opening, and the British Legion Band played on the Parade Ground on the site of the old Engine Turnery at the Haylings Road end of the site.

Throughout that summer, until the end of September, the museum opened on each weekday, staffed by the MSC from Monday to Friday and by volunteers each Saturday. Work on the buildings and exhibited items continued so far as was compatible with the presence of the public.

Once the season had ended, work began on the task of stripping up the old floor of the gallery. Where the old surface had worn into hollows under foot traffic, these had been levelled with foundry sand and a new layer of boards laid over the top. In some cases there were four layers of board, all of which had to be removed. The floor joists were then repaired, or renewed where necessary, and the floor was re laid with the Deptford scaffold boards, which had, in the meantime, been planed.

During the same winter the workshop roof was repaired and the rooflights reglazed, using the services of a building contractor.

More apparent to the public was the decision to fit toughened glass sliding doors to the front of the old Boiler House facing Main Street down the yard; this now serves as a shop window for the museum.

On completion of the new floor to the gallery in March, 1985, a start was made on re-roofing the South Workshop, since renamed the Richard Garrett Hall.

When the museum reopened on 1st April, 1985, the Trustees felt that the tremendous advances made during the winter justified a charge being made for admission, fixed at 60p for adults and 30p for children and other concessionary visitors. A pair of very fine doors obtained that summer from Ipswich Power Station were used in the west end of the Long Shop. It was from Ipswich that Leiston had taken its power when electricity was first brought to the town by the East Suffolk Electricity Distribution Co. in 1928, so the doors had at least a tenuous connection with the town's history.

Opening of the Gallery to the public was necessarily deferred until a satisfactory fire escape could be provided. Tony Errington had the good fortune to be able to purchase a large quantity of spiral staircase material, used but in near mint condition, which yielded enough components to build the necessary fire escape from the Gallery, as well as a second staircase. This was built in the winter of 1986–87 to serve a new first-floor office housed in hitherto wasted space in the roof over the archway between the Tally House and the Exhibition Hall.

That year the Ford Motor Company celebrated seventy-five years of trading in Great Britain by a series of grants to conservation projects. John Waddell of Ford was present when the award to the Long Shop was announced. With its aid the west gable, defaced by the later construction of further buildings, since demolished, was renovated and a large sign, *Long Shop Museum*, was erected.

The new offices over the archway were brought into use in May, 1987, enabling the entrance to the Exhibition Hall to be improved and removing the administration entirely from the exhibition area, thus bringing the use of the available space within the buildings to its optimum.

The number and variety of the major exhibits has increased: in early 1986 the front of a Garrett baker's oven was presented to the museum, and was erected in the Richard Garrett Hall. Also recovered and restored for exhibition was a Garrett-built living wagon, which earned the museum the 1987 *Museum of the Year Award for Suffolk*.

For a long time it was believed that the Leiston-built electric trolley bus repatriated from Denmark and owned by the Transport Museum at Carlton Colville was the only example of the make to survive. The museum administration was, therefore, excited by the news that another, albeit 'very dilapidated', existed on a piece of ground above the car park of the Butt & Oyster pub at Pin Mill, Ipswich. While they were considering how this might be recovered, another was found on a small holding at Saxmundham. Eventually both were recovered with the help of the 45th Field Regiment from Colchester Garrison. Both buses were in very poor shape but it is hoped that material from both will combine to make one exhibit. As I am writing the restoration work is just beginning. Also completed in the winter of 1987–88 was the work on the Garrett threshing machine, all except for the renewal of the sieves because of difficulty in obtaining suitable perforated metal sheet for them.

The Long Shop has also been reunited with its weather vane. In 1986 S. & S. Engineering, which had taken over the Top Works from the Receiver of Richard Garrett Engineering Ltd, itself went into receivership and the trustees were allowed to have the weather vane back.

The Museum has recently grown and expanded into the life of the district. In the summers of 1986 and 1987 it was the scene of a reunion of retired Garrett employees. It was also used in 1986 to house an exhibition of model engineering, to which it gave an appropriate backdrop. It has formed a useful addition to the places available to local schools for school visits. Out of the success of these visits came the annual Schools' Living History Project, first held in 1986, in which, for a week, schools took over the museum. Professional stage people were employed to play the parts of Mr and Mrs Richard Garrett and figures in the management of the works, while children took the parts of employees and apprentices. The costume adopted was roughly that for the period immediately before the First World War, though the presence of Mr and Mrs Richard Garrett as characters in the tableau would have placed the actual date about fifty years earlier. Other completed exhibits include an extensive display of the story of Snape village, and participation in the reunion of the 357th Fighter Group, which was based at Leiston Airfield during the Second World War.

The whole concept and execution of the project is an example of what can be done with very limited capital resources and a low annual budget. The part of the Manpower Services Commission personnel and the volunteers has been vital to this success, and it must be said that the commitment of both to the work has been total. It was, therefore, a source of great satisfaction to all those involved in the project, paid staff, volunteers, management, friends and committee when the Chairman was able to announce at the opening, on 19th April, of the 1988 summer season that the museum had been nominated to receive the Premier Prize in the 1988 Steam Heritage Awards of British Coal.

Editors Extraordinary 14

THE *Aldeburgh Times* was printed on pink newsprint, and appeared each Friday. Though it came to an end before the outbreak of the First World War, it is still remembered in the district, perhaps because of the extraordinary character, Charles Ganz, who was its editor.

Charles was German, although he had lived on the East Coast for some time. When war came, the fact that he had neglected to change his nationality meant that his presence was no longer acceptable on the country's eastern seaboard, and he was sent away to some non-strategic area inland. He eventually became a British citizen and ended his life residing at Bexhill.

William Whitling was the publisher of the paper, which appeared from 1900–1912. His main occupation was the ownership of a stationer's shop in High Street, Aldeburgh, now the Cragg Sisters' tea room. Ganz, who lived at 1 Leveson Villas, Aldeburgh, certainly acted as editor, although in its latter years he may have owned it as well. Notwithstanding the grandiose tones of its full official title, for most of its short life *The Aldeburgh, Leiston and Saxmundham Times* (retitled for a brief spell in 1909–1910 *The Suffolk Sea Coast Times*) was, in reality, an unpretentious journal, rarely extending to more than eight pages and retailing at a halfpenny a copy. The economics were precarious; its downfall appears to have come about after Ganz became deeply involved in the strike and lock-out at the nearby works of Richard Garrett & Sons Limited in Leiston in April 1912 but while the *Aldeburgh Times* lasted, its name and that of Charles Ganz were all but synonymous in the eyes of its readership.

Possessing no printing machinery of his own, Ganz had the paper printed by Powells of Lowestoft. As he was the sole staff of the paper, he had to do his own news gathering, spending his days foraging for it in the local area: Saxmundham in the west, Westleton to the north, Snape and Tunstall to the south were the limits of the paper's circulation.

Small boys were welcome informants, paid in kind out of a packet of bull's-eyes carried in his coat pocket. Wednesday was his day to call in Leiston, with the first stop usually at the Police Station. The bulk of his copy was sent to Powells by post. Friday was the day the paper went to press; that day Ganz would catch the first train out of Aldeburgh at 6.57 am, change at Saxmundham and arrive in Lowestoft at 9 am. With him he took his late news, which would be set that morning. In the afternoon it was printed, to be finished and handed to him at about 7 pm.

He then set off home carrying his bundles of newspapers. While changing trains at Saxmundham he just had time to deliver to Crisp's, the newsagents, after which he would join the branch train for three miles to Leiston, where again he made deliveries. There were no more trains that night and he walked the last four miles home, usually heralding his approach with fine, powerful song. He carried with him the copies for Aldringham. With his Teutonic reverence for method Charles was usually on time to the minute. Years later an old resident recalled to Frank Waddell, "You could set your watch by him."

His musical talents did not stop at singing, for he was a noted violinist and seldom travelled far, except on Fridays, without his violin. This made him a popular visitor when reporting the village concerts or entertainments, for he could often be coaxed into providing an *impromptu* extra turn.

Times were very hard at the beginning of this century among the fishermen of Aldeburgh. The cod-smacks for which the town was noted had been displaced by steam vessels sailing from Lowestoft or the ports to the north, so only inshore fishing was left to them. Charles was a great campaigner on behalf of the fishermen and of the lifeboat which they crewed. He was interested in the work-songs that had been sung by the cod fishermen on their voyages to the Norwegian coast or to Iceland and he learned their words and tunes.

The lifeboat was launched off the beach, and hauled up again on its return, by a very large capstan in the centre of a paved circle at the head of the beach. With three men on each capstan spar, they would tramp round and round for up to half an hour to pull it up the beach. Despite the hard work, places at the capstan and the tickets for payment that went with them were keenly contested, sometimes with fists. When the maroon was fired to summon the crew there would be a rush to the beach; Ganz, complete with violin, was as fast as any. His mission was not to wind but to play the songs he had collected and learned, soothing frayed tempers while waiting for the lifeboat to return, and lightening the labour of winding. He was never deterred by the weather. On one memorable occasion he is said to have arrived at the capstan clad in his nightshirt and a bowler hat, but still with his violin. One of the songs of the cod fishermen had words roughly as follows:

> When we come to Harwich Pier
> The folks all flock from far and near
> To see us heave our cod on deck
> And smack 'em on the head with a bloody great stick.

Winding in the lifeboat by tramping round the capstan; but no sign of Charles Ganz and his fiddle to liven the proceedings. SPS

This refers to the fact that before the days of block ice or of refrigerated holds the fish were transported live in wet wells in the smack and killed before being landed at Harwich by being knocked on the head, either on deck with the stick referred to in the song or against the coaming.

Also sung was the bargeman's "stormy-weather" song, one of the more respectable verses of which went:

> Up came a mermaid all covered in muck
> So we took her down below and had a good time*
> Stormy weather boys, stormy weather boys,
> When the wind blows our barges'll go.

Alternative versions were sung.

Ganz would stand in the centre of the capstan, playing as the winding went on, and then would dash home to write up the story. What happened if the lifeboat went to sea on a Friday is not recorded.

Despite his unconventional behaviour, Ganz was respected as a serious musician and served several years as conductor of the Aldeburgh Choral Society. Besides this he had a keen interest in the two Aldeburgh poets, Crabbe and Edward Fitzgerald. Ganz, indeed, was the leading organizer of the celebrations arranged to mark the Crabbe centenary in 1904.

He also had a prominent hand in the running of the Aldeburgh Sprat Dinner, held annually from 1903. This combined his liking for song with his love of a frolic and his championing of the longshore fishermen. It was designed, at least nominally, by the better-off burghers to promote the enjoyment of sprats and, it was hoped, to promote their sales. The menu was made up of sprats, fried, boiled or savoury, followed by what was called "olde English fare" and concluded with plum pudding. The tickets for the early dinners were "humorously and appropriately" designed by R. André, while later tickets—certainly those for 1912 and 1913—were designed by Cecil Lay. Though the participants did not know it, the 1913 dinner was to be the last. Charles Ganz sang *The Spratters' Song*, written by Cecil Lay and set to his own music by H. H. Weltch. (The song probably sounded better after a drink or two.) It went:

> To sea, to sea, the storm is o'er
> Haul out the nets, unship the oar
> Now dolphins leap, and mermaid's song
> Comes lisping with the winds along
> . . . with the winds along
> The stout sails fill, our bark swings free
> Heave ho, yo ho, to sea, to sea.

With its *art nouveau* flavour, this song was a marked contrast to the capstan songs.

Like many provincial newsmen Ganz acted as local reporter for a London daily, in his case the *Daily News*. In politics Ganz was a Liberal, and he found himself up against the Garretts of Leiston Works, who were heavily Conservative. Though he never lost a chance of lampooning them, his great opportunity arose from the firm's standing antipathy towards unions. Many of the tradesmen on the works were members of trade unions, but until 1904 no union branch existed nearer to Leiston than Ipswich. Moves to establish local branches had been consistently blocked by the survivors of the disastrous strike of 1871, who desired no repetition of the events of that year.

By 1911 their numbers were much reduced. The boiler-makers had quietly set an example by forming a branch in Leiston in 1904. A secret Saturday meeting early in 1912, called to consider extending union activity, was discussed indiscreetly and was reported to Frank Garrett Junior. There was also a proposal to form a branch of the Gasworkers' & General Labourers' Union, and doubtless there were others less reported.

These events took place against the sombre backdrop of the long strike of the coal miners in the opening months of 1912, a strike suspected of having an undercurrent of revolution. As a consequence of the coal strike, Leiston Works took the precaution of placing all employment on a day-to-day basis as from 29th February and, beginning on March 6th instituted short-time working by delaying the opening of the works until 9 am from Monday to Friday, closing altogether each Saturday. The loss of earnings resulting from these restrictions of hours led to further anti-Garrett feeling and some rather wild threats about what the unions would do, given sufficient backing. Certainly the political and industrial atmosphere in the town was tense, and public opinion was polarized. Frank Garrett Junior's reaction to this union trouble was to discharge about eighty men of known or suspected radical or Socialist beliefs, justifying his action by reference to shortages of materials occasioned by the coal strike. The action was ill advised as well as unjust, with serious consequences. Charles Ganz sent off a lengthy despatch to the *Daily News*, which induced that Liberal newspaper to devote the better part of a column to a report, bitterly derisory, of an interview with Frank Garrett. It opened with the following three paragraphs, and was reprinted in full by the *Aldeburgh Times* on 13th March, 1912, under the biggest headlines the town had seen:

WE KNOW NO POLITICS

STRANGE STORY OF DISMISSALS

SUFFOLK EMPLOYER'S ACTION

"DUE NOT TO POLITICS BUT TO STRIKE"

(From Our Special Correspondent)
LEISTON SUFFOLK Friday

There can be no more distressing event in the history of a prosperous firm than the arrival of a day when it is thought necessary to discharge large bodies of men who have served the firm faithfully. One may assume, I think, that this necessity becomes the more distressing to a firm whose strenuously political members make a point of knowing no politics in their business when it is discovered that nearly every one of the men belongs to a political party of which the members of the firm, in their private capacity, do not approve. Such a conjunction of circumstances tends to make the unfortunate men think they are suffering on account of their political convictions.

This is what has happened in the little manufacturing town of Leiston where the engineering works of Messrs. Richard Garrett & Sons Limited employing 1,400 hands, strike an unexpected note of brisk activity on the rural countryside between Saxmundham and Aldeburgh. Leiston is in the Eye Division of Suffolk and members of the Garrett family have been conspicuous in the unsuccessful fights which have been made to return a Tariff Reformer to Parliament in the place of the Hon. Harold Pearson. But, as Mr Frank Garrett assured me today, this has had nothing to do with the selection of the discharged men.

In giving notice that certain employees would only be retained from day to day in consequence of the coal strike Messrs. Garretts were only taking the reasonable precautions adopted by other firms. When this was followed by the discharge of some 40 men, on the Wednesday of last week, nobody was very much surprised. Then came other discharges, until the total yesterday was between 80 and 90. The most curious feature of it all, however, was that, with one or two minor exceptions, all the men who were turned adrift were known Radicals or Socialists, some of them occupying prominent positions in local political associations and Nonconformist chapels.

Not only, continued the report, had he discharged many sound workmen on the strength of gossip but he had gone so far as to sack Ishmael Girling, the foreman of the threshing machine shop, a man of irreproachable character and loyalty, merely for protesting at the method of selecting the men for discharge.

Tempers had been short before the *Daily News* report. Furious at having been made to look a total fool in the pages of a national paper, Frank Garrett resolved to have a final settlement with unionism and the radical element on the works. Still ostensibly because of the coal strike he ordered a lock-out from finishing time on 4th April, 1912, in terms as follows:

NOTICE

Owing to the coal strike the works will be closed down on Thursday April 4th at 5.30 p.m. and wages will be paid in full up to that time on Saturday the 6th at 12 noon.

The works will be reopened as soon as possible and every workman will be informed individually if and when he can be re-engaged. All those going from home should leave their addressess with their respective foremen. This necessary notice is given with extreme regret.

Frank Garrett Junior

April 1st, 1912

Seldom can the date of notice have been so appropriate to the deed. During the bitter days that followed the walls of the new "White City"* were daubed in whitewash, "Mr Garrett—God doesn't pay his debts in money". In the short term the men were total losers. The absolute lock-out was short and selected men began to be taken back the next week. In three weeks the incident was largely over, and all except those it was desired to exclude were back at work.

---

*This was the nickname of the new tool room and turnery on the corner of Main Street and Haylings Road, and referred to the contemporary Franco-British Exhibition.

If Frank Garrett hoped that he had stamped out unionism and socialist aspirations in Leiston, he was grievously in error. He had, it is true, turned away those whose voices had been heard louder than others but many more remained, and in some cases their reaction was a sharp turn to the left.

Ganz also had his triumphs, against lesser opponents. The bombastic and self-important were his particular targets. In this he was helped by his sense of humour. It was customary to give very full and sometimes *verbatim* coverage to meetings of the Aldeburgh Borough Council, of which he was a member. Usually he paid speakers the courtesy of tidying up any lapses of grammar or syntax. With an opponent or someone he disliked, he would dispense with this service. Many a speaker winced to find himself reported on the following lines:

> Smith: "I don't agree. That there wall ain't in nobody's way, so I say let that be."

He also loved to start controversies, particularly when real news was scarce, by a provocative editorial, or by the old device of a letter to the editor, written either by him or by a friend at his behest.

One of the boys he rewarded periodically with a bull's-eye for the gathering of a news item was Frank Waddell, in whom he won an ally. The Waddell family, as noted elsewhere, were Liberals and Frank received no parental discouragement from imparting juicy items to Ganz. Not long before the incident of the lock-out, in the winter of 1911–12, Colonel Frank Garrett's car, a Gladiator, skidded and mounted the pavement. No damage or injury resulted but it was duly reported and paid for with a sweet. Not long after, Frank actually saw an attempt by rowdies to overturn the car being used by the Liberal candidate. An eyewitness account earned the eleven-year-old reporter a penny, his first object lesson that there was actual coin of the realm to be had working for the press.

The departure of Ganz and the outbreak of war temporarily deprived Frank of his news money, but another opportunity came when the Zeppelin was brought down at Theberton on 17th June, 1917. Frank was on the scene about a quarter of an hour after it came down, soon enough in fact to speak to a dying member of the crew, trapped in the wreckage of the gondola, whom he was powerless to help but whose words and predicament haunted him, "So hot, so hot. All bones broken." He was dead before he could be got out. By that afternoon the reporters of the London dailies were on the scene. On his way back to the Zeppelin after a combined breakfast and lunch Frank was given a lift in the car of the *Daily Mirror* reporter. His eyewitness account and services as a guide earned him a shilling.

The remains of Zeppelin L48 at Theberton.

Soon afterwards he joined the Army. Demobilised in 1919, he had a short time on the dole before being given a job in Garrett's drawing office. (The war had blunted Colonel Garrett's political prejudices and heightened his sympathy for his fellow townsmen.) Two years later Frank became Leiston football correspondent for the Ipswich-based East Anglian Daily Times group. For five shillings a week he had to watch the senior club's Saturday match, send a 120-word telegram covering the first half and sixty words covering the second half, writing an account for that evening's *Football Star* and a summary for the Monday daily. Within a month or two he was promoted to the status of local correspondent at seven and sixpence a week, soon increased to ten shillings. On the strength of this he equipped himself with a 2¼ hp Connaught motor cycle, an airman's helmet, goggles, waterproof and leggings. As Frank himself put it, "I was all set. How could I go wrong?"

However, go wrong he did: when Frank was away from home, which was not often, he had an arrangement with a former part-time reporter to cover any assignments expected. On the weekend of the mishap Frank intended to go to Bury St Edmunds to visit his fiancée, Madge Fysh. Only one thing had to be reported, a British

Legion Fête at Dunwich, and when Frank opened his voucher copy of the daily on his return on the Monday morning he was startled to find the report headed "Successful British Legion Fêtes at Dunwich and Leiston". Under it, he read of how successful the Dunwich affair had been and also how grateful the Knodishall branch of the Legion were to Mr and Mrs A. Cooper for the use of their grounds at Leiston for a second gathering, reported with great fluency.

His satisfaction was short-lived. An hour later, as he was working at thresher details, the gateman phoned through to say that Stanley Cockrell, secretary of Knodishall British Legion, was at the gate to see him. Expecting thanks, Frank went down to meet an unexpectedly unsmiling visitor. "Report all right?" he asked, perhaps smugly. "Report's alright. The fête isn't till next week," snapped back Stanley.

Enquiries revealed the truth. Returning from Dunwich his stand-in, perhaps over-full of the joys of life, had seen the Knodishall poster in a shop window and not noticing the date had imagined Frank had forgotten about it. Loyally he had "written round the bill". Even the ebullient Frank was silenced for some days. He suffered a letter of rebuke from the news editor, much ribbing from his mates and from the town weekly, the *Leiston Observer,* which had filled the gap left by the death of the *Aldeburgh Times,* and the humiliation of a discreet paragraph of apology in the Friday edition.

Under all the ribbing, however, the editor of the *Leiston Observer* had taken note of his generally acute powers of observation, and when the laughter had died dowwn Frank received an offer, worth another seven shillings and sixpence a week, to report for the Observer as well.

Not long after this he attended and reported upon the inquest into the death of a child knocked down and killed by a car driven by a local lady of some social distinction in the area. Two days after his report had appeared in the county paper, he found it more or less *verbatim* in the *Daily Mail.* Highly indignant, he wrote to the editor of the *Daily Mail* protesting that, as he had been the only reporter present, his copyright had been infringed, for which he demanded compensation. Nothing happened and he wrote again, this time threatening legal action. In reply he was sent twelve shillings and sixpence.

Frank now had the idea of becoming local correspondent for the *Daily Mail* on a retainer basis. To his surprise the proposal was accepted. As he remarked, "It was a great day when the first batch of yellow press passes arrived". It should be explained that news was sent in by reporters by way of special rate telegrams to which the press pass was attached, the cost being debited to the bulk

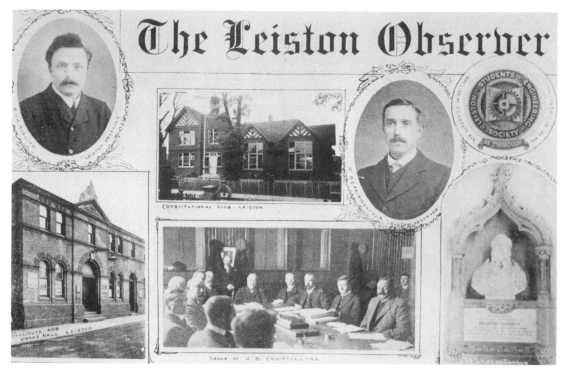

A montage done by the late J. S. Waddell to advertise the Leiston Observer. *The centrepiece is a group of Leiston Urban District councillors. Left facing the camera is W. J. Marshall, of Garrett's, and right foreground is Colonel Frank Garrett whilst in the chair is Percy Barrett.*

account of the newspaper. With his customary effrontery Frank then wrote offering his services to all the London dailies as well as to the Press Association and Exchange Telegraph, eventually getting himself retained by all of them.

When the Press Association passes arrived, they were often accompanied by a set of instructions. One, in particular, was memorable. He was told never to write "When the police arrived life was found to be extinct", but rather "the man was dead". The pass system had great advantages for correspondents with multiple agencies. All they had to do was to write out one telegram, attach it to the appropriate press passes, and it was automatically sent to all the newspapers included.

Early in 1932 Garretts closed, and Frank was out of a job; his only income was his earnings from freelance journalism. By this time he and Madge were married and had a son, John. Thirty years later Frank observed to me, "The one thing I didn't lack was cheek." He wrote to the editor of the *East Anglian Daily Times* proposing that he should equip himself with a car which would enable him to cover a much wider district for the paper; for this he would get an enhanced weekly stipend. After an interview with the editor, who was, perhaps, impressed by his nerve, he was engaged.

He bought a second-hand Austin Seven for thirty-five pounds, of which five were paid at once and the rest in deferred payments, and became a full-time journalist. The salary he had negotiated was a basic two pounds a week plus three farthings a line for anything printed, meeting his own expenses. The East Anglian group comprised the twenty-page daily, an evening paper and a good weekly. In addition to all this he also reported on occasions for the Norwich-based *Eastern Daily Press*.

By July, 1938, he was well off enough to move from his council house in St Margarets Crescent to a new house in Victory Road, Leiston. Almost at once his son, John, caught scarlet fever. Madge did all Frank's typing, looked after the telephone and nursed their son. At 6.30 am on the Saturday of the August Bank Holiday, Frank had a 'phone call from PC Bird of Southwold, one of his many friends in the police. Two teenagers from Pinner, Middlesex, had borrowed their father's car for a trip to the seaside and, nearing Southwold, had crashed through a bridge parapet and fallen twenty feet down into the River Blyth. The car floated, they scrambled onto the roof and drifted downstream, their shouts for help unheard, until the car touched the bank enabling them to get ashore. Bird had found them, soaked, dazed, bloody and covered in mud. The story, with Frank's own pictures, made the London evening papers that night.

Later the same day he was back there to cover the opening of the annual camp on Southwold Common, which was founded by King George VI while he was still Duke of York. Frank was resigned to reporting how many hundredweights of potatoes and sides of bacon would be eaten by the four hundred campers in the ensuing week when he saw one boy, wearing a public school blazer, heavily bandaged and wheeling a damaged bicycle. The next day the Sunday papers had his report:

> Three hundred and ninety nine boys had travelled from London and other places by train and bus to the Duke of York's Camp on Southwold Common last night. One who had cycled the one hundred miles from his home was knocked down by a bus within sight of the camp.

Meanwhile, the wretched car from Pinner, abandoned in the River Blyth, had freed itself from the bank and floated on downstream, to jam under a bridge, where it caused a back-up of water that flooded an area of marsh and endangered cattle.

This Bank Holiday brought the usual crop of sports and galas, but Southwold again provided an incident for the dailies. A boy from the Scout camp by the harbour went sleep-walking and fell into the harbour. In grave danger of being swept out to sea he was rescued, with considerable courage and great acumen, by two fellow campers who had fortunately heard his shouts.

At the end of the day he went back to Southwold. There was consternation at the Duke of York's camp. The King himself was due to land from the Royal Yacht the following Wednesday for a visit to the camp. It had just been discovered that a stray horse had eaten most of the leaves and some of the bark on a tree he had planted on a previous visit. The Mayor and Corporation were assembled, endeavouring to devise camouflage. Concealment was made impossible by Frank's story and pictures, carried in national and local papers, with headlines of "The Horse that Ate the King's Tree". The next day a retired military officer living in Southwold offered his services as keeper of the King's tree, giving another paragraph.

Meanwhile, a girl had rescued a drowning man at Sizewell on the Monday and another on the Tuesday, but her story of personal gallantry was largely missed; Frank went back to view the venerable royal yacht at Southwold. Suddenly, morse code was seen flashing from the ship. A retired coastguard was hastily summoned to read it but his Morse had rusted with retirement and there was some delay in understanding the message. Eventually it was sorted out. There was no catastrophe aboard; the King merely wanted Captain Patterson, the camp commander, to go out to him to discuss arrangements. The Heath Robinson air of the episode earned a few more shillings from Fleet Street. The sea became rougher during the night, preventing the use of the pinnace from the yacht, and the King was brought ashore by two fishermen who rowed out from the beach, a circumstance that seemed not to worry his Majesty but caused some anxious faces amongst his entourage.

As the national papers had arranged to send reporters from London to cover the King's day at Southwold, Frank expected the Wednesday to be easy. It was not. An early morning call from a friendly policeman took him out to the road from Snape to Orford, where a car had overturned into a pond during the night suffocating two of the four occupants. By 8.30 am he had his story and pictures on their way to London. The rest of the day he spent at Southwold covering the Royal visit for his local papers. On his way home he found the Retreat House at Leiston Abbey on fire and stayed to report that.

On the Thursday there was a tragic drowning at Thorpeness when the wife of an officer on leave from India died while trying to save her son, who was in difficulties off the beach. He was rescued by someone else but she was lost. Besides all this there was the inquest on the car victims, the grounding of a yacht, the collapse and death of a visitor to Aldeburgh golf course and an accident in the harvest field, besides the routines of weddings, funerals and sports events.

During the Second World War, when Leiston became part of

the defence area, censorship and the absence of summer visitors cut down his scope as a freelance reporter, but he took on the wartime job of Fuel Overseer and Inspector.

In 1944 the editor of the *Leiston Observer* died and Frank was offered the part-time position, at three pounds a week. Because of newsprint restrictions it was down to four pages, consisting mainly of advertising, but he had his own paper at last. All his efforts were put into plans to improve it, but the only way to gain more space was to increase it by another four pages, which had to wait on the relaxation of newsprint rationing. Meanwhile, the *Observer* jogged on with its four pages but the works did a fair amount of general printing, and financially the situation was not too bad.

In the summer of 1945 the paper and its editor were very intimately involved in a dreadful tragedy. On the afternoon of 9th July, a beautiful summer Sunday, Daphne Bacon, the fifteen-year-old daughter of Frank's print-shop foreman, Harry Bacon, was found with head wounds in a rye field near Aldringham Church and died the same night in Ipswich Hospital. All she was able to say was "British soldier hit me with stick."

That day Madge was on a visit to her parents at Bury St Edmunds, and Frank went to a picnic with friends. He went straight to bed on his return, and drove to the office the next morning seeing no one on the way. By the time he walked into the office at 9 o'clock he was probably the only adult in Leiston who did not know of the murder. After a quick look at the post, he went through to speak to Harry in the works. Receiving no response to his greeting he made a remark that he would subsequently have given much not to have said. "Come on, Harry, let's start the week with a smile." Harry was reading some copy. Looking up he said in leaden tones, "Did you know my daughter was murdered yesterday?"

Life moved very fast for Frank after that. After a "flash" message to his London, Ipswich and Norwich papers and an SOS to Madge to come home he took himself, almost at a sprint, to the Police Station, which he hardly left for a fortnight. When Madge got back on Tuesday she found the house full of reporters. Detective Inspector Ted Greeno and Detective Sergeant Frank Hodge of Scotland Yard were called in to take charge of the case and soon found Frank a useful source of local information. There were not many goings-on that he did not hear about in the town, and local people, shy of going direct to the police, used him as a go-between.

Besides writing for his own paper, he provided, once the London reporters had left, continuous copy to the three London evening papers (the *Evening News*, *Evening Standard* and *Star*), seven dailies, three agencies and the Sunday papers. At about 1 am on the morning of 23rd July Detective Sergeant George Reade, of the East Suffolk police, phoned to say that Gunner Dennis Eric Bailey of the Royal Artillery had been charged with the murder. To get the news to their ten London and East Anglian dailies in time for the morning edition, Madge sent five messages from their private telephone and Frank sent the rest from the office. The *Daily Mirror* cleared and reset the front page with the news on the strength of his call.

Fate had not finished with Harry Bacon, however. After Bailey had been charged, but before the trial, he went to Sizewell beach on a Sunday afternoon in August with his brother Percy, Daphne's twin sister Brenda and his eldest daughter, Monica. Percy picked up an object on the beach, later suspected of being a detonator. Not liking the look of it he threw it away, whereupon it exploded, riddling his lower body and blowing off three fingers, while Monica was shocked and wounded.

After the war Frank went on happily with the *Observer* and his freelancing for the London papers, but technologically the paper was running on a shoe-string. All typesetting was done by hand, and the actual printing was done on a hand-fed Wharfedale machine, of great antiquity when installed over thirty years before. The thumping and groaning that emanated from it as it laboured through the weekly edition could be heard in the street outside. One day an unannounced visitor walked into the shop and asked to see the Wharfedale. Asked how she had known it was there she replied that she had recognized the sound. It turned out that her father had been the designer of the machine and that, so far as she knew, the Leiston example was the last to be left at work. Keeping it going, however, had become difficult almost to the point of impossibility. Factory parts were no longer made and the race of jobbing engineers who could make bespoken spares at a day or two's notice had also all but vanished. The old machine's fate was nearly sealed by the breakage of a link in the overhead delivery chain. Frantic enquiries all over the country had failed to produce a spare, but someone had the idea of going to see "Harbut" (H. H. Heffer—see chapter 5). He managed to find a suitable link on a discarded self-binder.

By 1954 the *Observer* went over to machine setting, but the Wharfedale went on for another four years until a cylinder failed and it proved impossible to replace it.

The biggest single episode of the fifteen years after the war was the East Coast flooding of 1953, but the most sustained interest was aroused by the establishment of the Aldeburgh Festival under the influence of Benjamin Britten and Peter Pears. (The construction of the atomic power station on the shore at Sizewell overshadowed the festival for a time, along with all other long term considerations.) Frank had become something of a local institution, and was pressed into service in all kind of emergencies. On one occasion he was diverted from decorating his bathroom to take to Aldeburgh Hospital an expectant mother who had gone into labour. They arrived with the child half-born. The boy was christened "Morris", as his birthplace was partly in Frank's Morris car.

Any local paper that is run commercially has to maximize its readership, but when the district served is as thinly populated as that covered by the *Leiston Observer* it has to please everyone, or at least offend none, if it is to remain alive. This resulted in bland reporting pervading the contents of the *Observer*, the style once being described as "tea and buns". As an antidote to this one or two of the town's Communists and more extreme radicals began a rival paper, the *Leiston Leader*, produced on a rotary duplicator and edited by Paxton Chadwick. Paxton was a talented commercial artist and illustrator, and a gifted cartoonist. His cartoons were the scourge of his political opponents, and Frank Waddell from time to time found himself the butt of them. Pax was elected to the urban district council, its first Communist member, and eventually became chairman. He courted the Labour members, on whom he depended for support, but used to flay the Independents, whom he once taunted as "Torypendants".

A husband and wife were elected to the council as Independents and gave a cocktail party to celebrate, to which they invited their fellow Independent councillors and several of the townsfolk of like mind politically, including Frank. Pax was not invited; his next cartoon depicted the occasion, with caricatures of those he thought had been present, correctly, as it turned out, except for one lady who though in the cartoon was not at the party. Half of Frank was shown, holding half a glass, and the caption was "Half the press were there."

Paxton paid little heed to the law of libel, though no one sued him, despite some seemingly having cause. He was widely liked, even by some of the victims of his satire. His readiness to help with deserving causes, collective or individual, may well have been the underlying reason for his popularity, but others simply took to his engaging personality and forgave his political venom. His early death in 1961 was generally regretted, not least by Frank Waddell, who had suffered a lot from his attacks. In his editorial in the *Leiston Observer* he wrote, "The town may never again see such a personality." To date it seems he has been right.

On 1st January, 1960, the *Observer* was taken over from its local owners by the East Anglian Daily Times group, whom Frank had served as a freelance for about thirty-five years. His time as an active journalist was running out and on 27th December, 1960, he suffered a serious heart attack. Though he recovered with great determination he was never really able to go back to work and he eventually had to take early retirement. His interest in the paper never waned. Madge continued to contribute a column to it and Frank's successor as editor, his former second-in-command, used often to come up to his house in Victory Road to discuss problems with him. He was particularly pleased that, though he was not a member of any pension scheme, the directors of the group voluntarily paid him a pension in recognition of his many years of service. After his retirement he amused himself with a small antique shop in Cross Street, Leiston, and died of a final devastating heart attack on 28th October, 1973, when he and Madge were living at a bungalow at Fryerning, adjacent to the farmhouse where his son John and daughter-in-law Kitty lived.

Making coffins for the dead crew of the Zeppelin at Jimmy Cutts' builder's yard in Cross Street, Leiston. The man in the background next to the open coffin against the workshop was Arthur Cracknell, the lad in the foreground was Reggie Hubbard. J. S. Waddell

An Aside on Artists   15

IN THE LAST two decades of the nineteenth century the village
schoolmaster at Aldringham was Adolphus Lay, the scion of an
Essex family of seafarers. He is remembered as a patient, kindly
man, absorbed in his leisure hours by the history of the parish he
had adopted. He was, moreover, a man of refinement, well read
and a good draughtsman. In his retirement he took to going for
long walks. Ted Dunn and his brother Dick, as boys, once met him
during one of these. They stopped to talk, and before long found
themselves deep in the history of the parish. Recalling the occasion
seventy years later Ted said, "That must have been interesting, to
have kept us boys listening to him for so long."

Adolphus Lay's wife, Annie, is not remembered with such
affection. She was a farmer's daughter from Kent and harboured
social aspirations. The post of village schoolmaster at that time was
not an exalted one and certainly did not command a large salary.
Mrs Lay is said to have had private means which enabled her to
keep herself a little aloof from village life and to attempt to keep
her son Cecil Howard (1885–1956) away from contact and
friendships with the village boys from the school. This ran contrary
to his own inclinations or at least to the traits he displayed in later
life.

A maternal great uncle is said to have paid for Cecil's
education both at the Queen Elizabeth School at Ipswich and as an
architectural pupil of John Shewell Corder, then at the height of
his career as an East Anglian architect. Cecil was unhappy in
Corder's office. As an imaginative young man he found it difficult
to stomach a commercial practice conducted as what, in his eyes,
was a drawing factory. The habitual use of the same designs, or
trivial variations of them, the repetition of stock details and
standard specification clauses all upset him. Moreover, to Cecil Lay,
torn in his admiration between the neo-Georgian and Art
Nouveau, Corder represented reaction.

Subsequently he moved to the Architectural Association
Schools in London, where he found the atmosphere much more in
line with his own outlook. He followed this with an equally happy
spell in the Low Countries, where, nominally at least, he studied art
and architecture. He then lived in London until 1914, where his
stipend from his great uncle enabled him to live enjoyably in the
aura of the London progressive circle of art and poetry. He
became, for a while, a close friend of Jacob Epstein. In 1912, at the

age of twenty-seven and at the end of his studies, he was elected an Associate of the Royal Institute of British Architects.

At that time he was described as a handsome young man of considerable charm. As to his physique, those who knew him described him as relatively frail, heedless of his bodily requirements and indifferent to regular meals. A friend once described him as having been raised on strong tea. Indeed, a taste for strong tea and plenty of cigarettes lasted for life.

In order to satisfy his mother's ambition to live in the largest house in the village he designed Raidsend for her with Art Nouveau nuances but without total commitment to the style. Though a striking creation, Raidsend, in my opinion, is not to be compared with his later designs for Pantiles and Fen Cottage on Aldringham Common, which are totally at peace with their surroundings.

Though Lay had recoiled from the commercial aspects of architectural life as displayed in Corder's office, nevertheless after his election to the Royal Institute of British Architects, he practised

Neglected and falling into disrepair, Raidsend, the house built for his parents, pictured in October 1987, shows the early work of Cecil Lay.

his profession assiduously and with constancy, despite his predilection for painting and capabilities as a poet. The First World War interrupted his work, though his poor standard of physical fitness barred him from the Army. Instead he worked in munitions as a shell examiner, first at Woolwich and later at Ipswich. After a nervous breakdown in 1921 he returned to Aldringham for good. From then onwards it was the centre of his life.

Aside from Raidsend, his earliest major work in Aldringham was the formal Georgian red-brick Baptist Chapel on Aldringham Common, dating from 1915, noted with approval by Nicholas Pevsner. Sadly it is now in slow decay. When Lay resumed work after 1921, he largely renounced the Georgian idiom; Pantiles was essentially Suffolk vernacular, whilst Fen Cottage was a scaled-down version of a manorial hall.

In the twenties and thirties, Cecil Lay enjoyed a regular succession of professional commissions. In executing one such for Haworthe Chadburn, the painter, at his house at Middleton, he met his client's daughter Joan; they subsequently married in 1932.

Joan's domestic and intellectual backing seems to have given him the atmosphere which he found conducive to work. He published six volumes of poems between 1927 and 1935 (a series broken off by the bankruptcy of his publisher), and also carried out most of his forty paintings in oils. During this time his work was twice accepted by the Royal Academy. His oil on board, *The Warreners*, exhibited at the Academy in 1933, is a true expression of his liking for his surroundings and for the rural pursuits of coastal Suffolk. In its distance there was almost certainly a self portrait, a tall, booted figure in a long raincoat, unbuttoned, the collar partly turned up, the hands tucked into trouser pockets, wearing a fisherman's hat and observing with interest what the rabbit catchers were up to.

This was the last painting he exhibited at the Academy, though he continued to paint in oils and to submit work for consideration each year. Notwithstanding the lack of interest at the Academy, his oils were welcomed in the exhibitions of the Ipswich Art Club and the Sole Bay Group at Walberswick.

Why the Royal Academy set its face against him is not entirely clear, though there are indicators. Fashion in art had turned a little away from the naive style in which his oils were painted and he had turned, for his part, away from the portrayal of the life around him. His painting *The Cricket Match* (1939) depicts town children perched on a high fence, watching the cricket match, while some children are standing on the pavement, having relayed to them what is happening inside the ground. It is as well done technically as anything in his earlier work, but its superficially joky atmosphere and underlying social protest may well have left him at odds with

the selection committee. Social documentaries were not, probably, foremost in their thoughts in 1939.

As he grew older and physically less fit, Lay became more solitary and isolated in his outlook. He ceased to worry much about what was thought of him or of the critics' views of his work. He spent hours on long walks, usually alone, sketched and drew copiously from life, frequently in the open, and painted in watercolours. His sketches changed over the years. His drawing of Markins Mill at Snape, done when he was twenty-three, is a clear and accurate pen and ink perspective of the mill and a useful documentary record. His drawings of twenty years later are vividly alive, economical of line, sparing of subject matter. His sketch of grass-track motor cycle racing at Benhall is full of immediacy, bristling with action. By contrast his drawing of Wickham Market, with the church in the background, though marked by the same thrifty use of line, is of immense tranquillity. Lay could undoubtedly have been a noted cartoonist; as it was he left behind him a treasury of vivid impressions, locked away and seldom seen. He also wrote verses and generally took the stance of local eccentric, voluble both in person and on paper and highly opinionated. Frank Waddell, as Editor of the *Leiston Observer*, was frequently on the receiving end of his correspondence; as he put it, Lay became a "dotty old man", generally liked in the district but dodged by those who did not have plenty of time to spare for a long conversation.

Most of his paintings and drawings passed to his widow on his death, though they were dispersed in 1978 after two exhibitions, in Aldeburgh and London respectively. The selling of the drawings was largely entrusted by Joan Lay to Cecil Fry, who at that time had galleries in both Aldeburgh and London. He remarked to me in 1987 that when first he was introduced to the collection at Aldringham he was astounded at its diversity and the richness of the talent displayed. The oils were mostly sold by Michael Parkin. Many remain in the hands of their original purchasers. The owner of *The Warreners*, to whose kindness I am indebted for permission to reproduce the photograph of it, remains as enthusiastic about his purchase as when he made it.

Sadly none of the paintings was bought for permanent public exhibition. When Lay painted the countryside of the coast he did so as a native, as one who has grown up with it and seen it in all moods and seasons. He even looked part of it, in his well-worn tweed suits, creased and made baggy by careless wearing and even less care when not being worn, his pocket watch tucked into the left pocket of his waistcoat and the well-thumbed strap looping across to a waistcoat button hole. Tucking his left hand into his trousers pocket he would stab away with his right, probably with a cigarette between his fingers as he emphasized the points of his discourse. As Frank said, "If he really got going you never got away in under half-an-hour", but he had a soft spot for him, nevertheless.

Ted Dunn knew him quite well and recalled him as a very kindly and unaffected man. Ted, who started and ended his working life at Garretts' works at Leiston, also spent time as a plasterer, when he worked several times on contracts supervised by Lay. It was far from the custom of those times for architects visiting their contracts to converse with workmen, but Ted, as a lad, had always been polite and interested in his (Lay's) father, and he, in his turn, never failed to have a few words of conversation with Ted.

Lay had had a predecessor on the coast, equally interested in the countryside though perhaps without the full diversity of talent that he displayed.

As the barge and the railway had ousted the brigs and schooners from the River Alde, the Rope family had turned back to their shore activities centred around Orford—the corn, coal and

His son, G. T. Rope (1845–1929), always considered a physical weakling by his family but who, nevertheless, reached the age of eighty-five and met his death in an accident. George T. Rope was a quiet, meditative man, a lifelong bachelor, and an artist with great gifts for portraying horses.
Courtesy W. Rope; photo by B. J. Finch

manure trade, coupled with malting, on a small scale, and brewing. George Rope Senior concentrated upon farming at Blaxhall, but his son, George Thomas (1845–1929), considered of too frail a physique to be a farmer, forsook the traditional family pursuits to study art, finding his subjects in the countryside around him and on the banks of the Alde. In 1877 his painting *The Harvest Mice* was hung at the Royal Academy, and subsequently sold for £26 5s, a considerable sum at a time when few farm workers' earnings reached one pound a week. Perhaps there existed in the shy artist a kind of empathy towards the equally elusive mice. Slight of figure, quiet in speech, George Rope was an acute observer, though his work is not perhaps to contemporary taste; he was much interested in farm horses. Such works as his oil on canvas of the mare *Marigold* in the stable at the Grove are not only acutely observed but superbly executed.

Many of his paintings in oils are of the buildings at the Grove at Blaxhall or of views in the lanes at Blaxhall. Among the collection owned by his great nephew, Richard, is a study of Markin's windmill at Snape painted in 1897, eleven years before Lay's sketch. Though there have been intermittent outbursts of interest in his paintings sustained public acclaim has consistently eluded him and none of his works is known to be on public display.

Like Lay, too, George Rope loved walking the fields and lanes of Blaxhall. The family collection includes sensitively executed pencil drawings of hedgerow subjects—groups of young rabbits, twigs of trees, holly, acorns, tree stumps and fungus. Despite having been deemed too delicate for farming, George lived to the age of eighty-five, and even then, as Richard Rope put it, "it took an accident to kill him". At Langford Bridge near his home the horse pulling his trap, frightened by a motor car, ran away. The wheel of the trap mounted the board walk used by foot passengers in time of flood, George was thrown out and he was carried home to the Grove to die two days later of his injuries.

No other men of the Rope family displayed George's interest in art, but his sister Ellen Mary (1855–1934) was a sculptress, modeller and plaster designer who achieved, at her peak around the turn of the century, rather greater recognition than was accorded her brother. Ellen Rope studied (*c*1878–84) in London at the Slade School, under Alphonse Legros, and at the British Museum. She was first accepted for exhibition at the Royal Academy in 1885 when three of her panels in low relief, *David Playing before Saul*, *Children in Apple Tree* and *Cupid Shooting* were shown. Thereafter, until 1904, her work was on show at twelve of the Summer Exhibitions. She was responsible for four panels, each four feet six inches long, for the Women's Building at the Chicago Exhibition representing *Faith, Hope, Charity* and *Heavenly Wisdom*.

She also designed a great frieze, twenty feet long, for the Council Chamber of Rotherhithe Town Hall, now destroyed. M. H. Spielman, writing about 1910, said of it that it "seems to lack something of her usual qualities of composition and balance". The *Memorial* in Salisbury Cathedral and the *Pied Piper* for Shelley House are probably more worthy of her considerable talent. After about 1896 she worked as a designer for the Della Robbia Pottery at Birkenhead for a decade. She also executed numerous memorials placed in churches besides that mentioned by Spielman, the most distant for Michaelhouse School Chapel near Durban in South Africa. Her panel *Boys with Palms*, dated 1907, is in the Ipswich Museum.

In the succeeding generation talent proliferated yet further. George's brother Arthur Mingay Rope (1850–1946) and his wife Agnes Maud (*née* Aldrich) farmed at Lower Abbey, Leiston. Two of their children, Dorothy Anne (1883–1970) and Margaret Edith (1891–1988), followed the course set by their aunt and uncle.

Dorothy, the sculptress of the pair, became an art teacher. For

G. T. Rope's painting of the Suffolk mare Marigold in a loose-box attached to the stable at The Grove, Blaxhall.
Courtesy W. Rope; photo by B. J. Finch

some years up to her retirement in 1949 she taught at Dame Alice Owen's Girls' School, an endowed school, administered by the Brewers' Company, giving grammar school education to girls in Clerkenwell, London.

Her sister Margaret Edith received her early education from her aunt at Blaxhall, followed by a spell at Wimbledon High School. From there she passed on to the Chelsea School of Art. Her interest in stained glass was aroused by her cousin, Margaret Agnes Rope (1882–1953), daughter of her father's brother, a doctor of medicine who practised in Shrewsbury. Margaret Agnes worked in stained glass, and her work attracted the admiration of her rather younger cousin, who herself took up stained glass at the LCC Central School of Arts & Crafts under Karl Parsons and Alfred J. Drury. Whilst still studying Margaret Edith began work, in 1911, at the Glass House, Fulham, assisting Margaret Agnes in the making of the beautiful Rope family memorial window for Blaxhall Church.

After a pause during the First World War, when she served in the Women's Land Army, she resumed working with her cousin at the studio in the Glass House, where in 1919 she executed her first independent commission, the two-light window *Christ with Children* for Clippesby Church, Norfolk. In 1923, Margaret Agnes, who was a devout Roman Catholic, became a novice nun in the Carmelite order, and although she never lost her love of stained glass it was no longer the central inspiration of her life.

After her cousin's departure, Margaret Edith worked on at the same studio in the Glass House for a while, but subsequently moved to 61 Deodar Road, Putney, and after that to no. 81. The Second World War interrupted her work. After a spell with evacuated children in North Wales she spent most of the war in Storrington, Sussex, but when it was over she returned to Deodar Road. No 81 had been bombed but she set up her studio workshop and kiln at no 89. With the help of her friend and pupil Clare Dawson she embarked upon a very prolific period. The output of those years included the windows of the Carmelite Church at Quidenham, Norfolk, in the design of which she was once again associated with her cousin, Margaret Agnes. Towards the end of her working life she made the magnificent St Luke and St Matthew windows for the north aisle of Leiston Church, the former in 1958 in memory of Dr Herbert M. Sylvester (1870–1927), who was a general practitioner in Leiston, and the second in 1960 in memory of her parents. The St Luke window was commissioned by Dr Sylvester's widow; its companion was her own gift to the church.

Margaret Edith's most viewed work was the lioness emblem for Richard Garrett & Sons Ltd, which was the trademark for the under-type steam wagons built at Leiston Works between 1922 and

Margaret Edith Rope at work in her Putney studio.
Courtesy W. Rope; photo by B. J. Finch

1932 and symbolized strength, silence and speed. The emblem that she created, a lioness crouched in the manner of the ancient Egyptian bas-reliefs, was a forceful and distinctive trademark. It was unfortunately misunderstood by many of the men who drove the wagons, by whom the emblem was known as "the Garrett greyhound".

During her working life Margaret Edith was responsible for over fifty windows, a list of which is set out in Appendix A (although it may not be complete). The wide distribution of her work is striking. Her windows are to be found in Australia, South Africa, Ceylon, Malta and Trinidad.

The acclaim accorded to workers in glass is normally muted; this may be because it is not the norm for stained glass to be

assembled in exhibitions or viewed in galleries, and it does not lend itself readily to adequate representation in books or albums. A stained glass artist in the round, producing complicated windows, must be a skilled artisan as well as an artist. Windows which are part of the envelope of a building must withstand wind and weather, and no matter how they may delight the eye, will fail in their purpose if they are badly made.

In 1986 the William Morris Gallery, in the London Borough of Waltham Forest, led by its curator Peter Cormack, organized an exhibition of stained glass by women artists of the Arts and Crafts Movement, in which were included examples of the work of both Margaret Edith and Margaret Agnes Rope. The catalogue of the exhibition incorporated biographical notes on the artists themselves as well as descriptive material on the exhibits.

The association of the gallery with such an exhibition was not, of course, fortuitous. The name of William Morris has become all but synonymous with the objective of reuniting the functions of artist and artisan. Interest in reviving stained glass dated back to the 1830s, and grew with the demand created by the Victorian obsession for restoring churches, which gathered pace as Gothicism swept through architecture in the middle years of the last century. By the 1860s, stained glass was in production on a scale that could be termed "industrial" by such firms as James Powell & Sons in London and Halls in Bristol, with the artistic and artisan aspects firmly separated. Powells employed Emma Cons as one of their glass painters, but on the whole only a trifling proportion of stained glass design was in the hands of women.

The increasing impatience of young women of the Victorian middle classes with the stifling domesticity within which they were expected by custom to conduct their lives led to their seeking outlets in which their talents or bents could be used. In the case of Elizabeth Garrett, this took the form of an assault upon the male citadel of medicine. Other girls from comparable backgrounds looked to the arts. By about 1880 the numbers of trained artists, men and women, were too great to find careers in the fine arts, a state of affairs that coincided with extensive awareness of William Morris's lucid and vigorous restatement of the importance of applied art. About this time Christopher Whall (1849–1924), encouraged by Britten & Gilson, the Southwark glass makers, abandoned his attempt to be a painter and set about learning the whole craft of stained glass so that he was able to carry out the entire process of design, cutting, painting, firing and leading.

Whall's association with Britten & Gilson involved him in the formative stages of their manufacture of what they called "Early English" glass, first produced at the instance of the architect, Edward S. Prior, who desired a material showing the character and the uneven thickness of early English glass. In Britten & Gilson's process the molten glass was blown in a box-shaped mould, in a shape not unlike a whisky decanter, producing four rectangular slabs from the sides and a square from the base, thinnest at the corners of the box and thick in the centres of the pieces. Chance Brothers of Birmingham followed with their "Norman" glass, which exhibited much the same characteristics. Whall produced the first window to be made from "Early English" glass, and as a result he and it became firmly associated with the Arts and Crafts Movement.

Mary Lowndes (1857–1929) was the first of the rebellious Victorian girls to join Whall in creating windows. After having studied art at the Slade, and as a pupil of Henry Holliday (1839–1927), she taught herself the craft aspects of window making and by the mid 1890s embarked upon making windows at Britten & Gilson's works, where she encountered Whall and became firmly attracted into the Arts and Crafts Movement. In 1897 she went into partnership with Alfred Drury, who had been head glazier to Britten & Gilson, to set up the firm of Lowndes & Drury at 35 Park Walk, Chelsea. In 1906, finding Park Walk too cramped, they moved to the Glass House, Lettice Street, Fulham.

Mary Lowndes was a prominent member of the Women's Suffrage Movement, believing that women were as entitled to a voice in electoral affairs as they were in business or the professions. By helping to create the Arts and Crafts Movement in stained glass

George Rope's painting of the spot, Langford Bridge, where years later he was involved in the accident that brought about his death.
Courtesy W. Rope; photo by B. J. Finch

199

she was founding a field of activity in which men and women worked as individuals of equal status, and in which educated girls from the middle classes, with access to the necessary funds, could carve out satisfying careers for themselves. One of the strengths of the Arts and Crafts Movement was that it helped many artists to become craftsmen and craftswomen. Its weakness was that it did little to promote the cause of artisans who might also have wished to combine the two aspects. Without money they could not become trained as artists nor finance the outlay needed to set themselves up as self-employed professionals. But, as Margaret Rope's St Luke and St Matthew windows at Leiston demonstrate, it did lift English stained glass to a level of beauty and accomplishment such as it had not reached for three centuries.

G. T. Rope's skill as a sketcher. The morning view to the east on the banks of the Alde near Dunningworth Hall.
Courtesy W. Rope; photo by B. J. Finch

Register of stained glass windows by Edith Rope and Margaret Agnes Rope

Compiled by Peter Cormack and his staff at the William Morris Gallery, London Borough of Waltham Forest

MARGARET EDITH ALDRICH ROPE (1891–1988)

Buckinghamshire
Eddlesborough: Parish church	2 lights 1933
Lane End: Parish church	1948

Cornwall
Polperro: St John's church	south 1956 east 1959

Derbyshire
Chesterfield: Parish church	south side 1952

Co. Durham
Roker: St Andrew's church	mural with MacDonald Gill

Essex
Ickleton: Parish church	east window 1929

Hampshire
Hartley Wintney: Parish church	4 lights & mural 1939

Herefordshire
Hereford: All Saints' church	east window 1933

Hertfordshire
Bishop's Stortford: St Michael's church	south porch 1950

Kent
Bromley: Parish church	several 1953–59
Whitstable: All Saints' church	1927

Lancashire
Royton: St Paul's church	3 lights 1928

London
Chelsea: St Mary's Bourne St	circular window 1952
Gladstone Park: St Francis of Assisi church	3 lights 1933–37
Grange Park: St Peter's church	several 1957–65
Haggerston: St Augustine's church	several 1931–47*
Haggerston: St Saviour's Priory	chapel windows 1924

Highgate: St Augustine's church	2 lights
London Docks: St Peter's church	east 1949 south chapel 1954

Middlesex
Northolt Park: St Barnabas' church	east 1954 west 1957

Norfolk
Clippesby. Parish church	2 lights
Quidenham: Carmelite monastery church	1956–57

Somerset
Bicknoller: Parish church	west 1952

Stirlingshire
Falkirk	1 light 1935

Suffolk
Barnby: Parish church	east 1963
Kesgrave: RC church	2 windows 1948, 1958
Little Glemham: Parish church	3 lights 1929
Leiston: Parish church	2 north transept windows 1960
	3 light north 1958

Sussex
Bolney: Parish church	1 light 1947
Chichester: Bishop Otter College	2 lights 1934

Warwickshire
Coventry: St John's church	east 1950

Wiltshire
Lydiard Millicent: Parish church	south transept 1963

Worcestershire
Malvern: Holy Name Convent	cloister window 1963

Yorkshire
Far Headingley: St Chad's Church	east window c1923

Australia
Mullewa: RC church	1 light 1923

South Africa
Capetown: St John's church, Green Pt	4 roundels 1925
Ofcolaco (N. Transvaal):	2 lights 1951

Ceylon
Passara Gonakelle Estate:	2 lights 1953

Malta
Sliema: Holy Trinity church	1 light 1947

Trinidad
Port of Spain:	rose window 1932

continued.,

*Windows from St Augustine's, Haggerston, are now in St Mary Magdalene's church, Munster Square (crypt).

MARGARET AGNES ROPE (1882–1953)

Cheshire
Birkenhead: RC church of the Holy Name — English Martyrs
Carmelite Nuns

Birkenhead: RC church of Our Lady — 1 light Annunciation
Hoylake: Parish church — 1 light St George *c*1920
Latchford: (Nr Warrington): RC church — 2 light More & Fisher
2 light Bl John Finch & Jas Bell 1939

Stockport: RC Church of Our Lady
& the Apostles — 3 light Holy Family

Dorset
Hinton Martel: RC Church(?) — Tempera paintings—Life of Christ

Co. Durham
Ushaw: RC College

Dyfed
Llandovery: RC Church — 1 light Vaughan mem. 1938

Gwent
Llanarth Court: RC Chapel — 2 lights SS Francis & Bernard

Lanarkshire
Lanark: St Mary's RC Church — 2 light Gethsemane & Crucifixion
2 light Prodigal Son

Suffolk
East Bergholt: Convent Chapel — 2 lights David & Isaiah
Kesgrave: RC Church — east 3 light 1932
lancet in south sanctuary
2 light south nave More & Fisher
2 lights in west porch
small panel north extension

Surrey
Oxted: RC Church — 1 light St Hedwig

Italy—Vatican State
Rome: English College — 1 light St Ralph Sherwin 1936

Australia
Geraldton (West Australia): RC cathedral   several windows
Mullewa:

South Africa
Balgowan (Nr Pietermaritzburg):
Michaelhouse School Chapel   several windows
Randfontein· RC Church(?)   1 light Good Samaritan

APPENDIX TWO

NOTE OF A MEETING HELD AT THE OFFICES OF RICHARD GARRETT (ENGINEERING) LTD., LEISTON, TO DISCUSS THE FUTURE OF THE 'LONG SHOP' ON THE OLD WORKS SITE, HELD ON 21st JULY, 1976, AT 2.30 pm.

Present

W. D. Akester	Retired Board Member, Ransomes, Sims and Jefferies Ltd.
D. Cannons P. Clarke }	Richard Garrett (Engineering) Ltd.
G. C. Lightfoot S. C. Mason J. H. Popham }	Suffolk Preservation Society
W. R. Serjeant	Suffolk County Archivist
M. Talbot	Planning Dept., Suffolk Coastal District Council
R. A. Whitehead	Historian of Richard Garrett Ltd.
G. Wilding	Director, Museum of East Anglian Life

Apologies for absence were received from Mr. D. Charman, Archivist to the British Steel Corporation.

1. Papers by Messrs Charman, Serjeant, and Wilding were pre-circulated and formed the basis for discussion.
2. It was generally agreed that the Long Shop, as a distinguished example of mid-19th century engineering workshop design and construction, was an important and probably unique feature of the industrial archaeology of Suffolk and worthy of preservation.
3. It was considered that supposing preservation to be feasible, a museum use seemed to be the most natural and obvious use for such a building.
4. A suggested course of action of removing and re-erecting the Long Shop at the Museum of East Anglian Life at Stowmarket was rejected as being both undesirable in itself and unrealistic on cost grounds.

5. It was recognised that local authority support in terms of finance is an extremely unlikely prospect at present, and that any proposals that might in due course be evolved would be dependent upon support of a private and voluntary nature.

6. Messrs. Cannons and Clarke, for Richard Garrett (Engineering) Ltd., indicated that the Company was extremely sympathetic to the idea of preservation of the Long Shop as a museum, and was willing in principle to donate the building to a suitable recipient. This must however be contingent on:

    a) the sale, with the necessary planning permission for redevelopment, of the old works site as a whole.
    b) the agreement of any acquiring developer to the inclusion of the preservation of the Long Shop in the development.
    c) the approval of the Planning Authority to such an inclusion. (Mr. Talbot indicated that the proposals for redevelopment of the whole site were still under consideration by the Planning Authority, but that on the particular aspect of a "Long Shop Museum", this would be compatible with the Authority's views).

7. It was agreed that the Suffolk County Architect should be approached for his assistance in undertaking a feasibility study as to what would be necessary and at what cost to render the building, as a first step, sound and safe.

8. Mr. Wilding offered to seek the advice of the Area Museums Service for South Eastern England on the concept of a museum use of the Long Shop, and this offer was accepted with thanks.

9. It was noted that the building was not a listed or scheduled building, and it was agreed that as a first step application should be made to the DoE to have it listed. Mr. Popham undertook to do this in collaboration with Mr. Talbot.

10. The objectives which might be appropriate to a museum were discussed, necessarily in fairly general terms, and the broad consensus appeared to be that the emphasis should be on the Richard Garrett enterprise, its products and their manufacture, with particular emphasis on the mid- and later 19th century. The obvious and important links with the development of Leiston as a town and community should also find a place, as should the Garrett family history.

    It was considered that examples of suitable machines, e.g. road steam engines, threshing machines, seed drills, steam tractors, could fairly readily be found, and the Company has an excellent archive, including very good coverage of photographs and engineering drawings.

11. It was agreed to place responsibility for further study in more detail, and action on the various points raised at the meeting, with a Coordinating Group comprising Mr. Lightfoot (Chairman), and Messrs. Mason, Popham, and Serjeant, the Group to report back by November 1976.

12. Other matters noted were:

a) That if the Museum project shows promise, a Trust body of some kind would become necessary, and that one possibility might be to look to the Trustees of the Museum of East Anglian Life for this role.

b) Mr. Whitehead drew the meeting's attention to the fact that 1978 would be the bicentenary of the founding of the Company, and would therefore be a very suitable occasion to launch at least some part of the project.

c) It would be desirable to investigate in due course the availability of volunteer labour.

d) Mr. Cannon kindly undertook to see whether any steps could be taken to repair the roof of the Long Shop at a point at which it was observed that rain was leaking through into the building.

13. The thanks of the meeting were expressed to Messrs. Richard Garrett (Engineering) Ltd. for providing accommodation, as also for the Company's welcome offer to do so on any future occasion.

W.R.S.

Ward & Son's bus timetables, 1948

Traffic Commissioners' Report

F./R.866/1 (N. & P. No. 453).—Ward & Son (Aldeburgh) Ltd., High Street, Aldeburgh, Suffolk, a service of stage carriages between Aldeburgh (Ward's Garage) and Thorpeness (Boat House), subject to the following conditions:—

Route: Via unclassified roads.   Return by same route.

Time table:—	a.m.	a.m.	p.m.	p.m.	p.m.	p.m.	p.m.	p.m. *	p.m. *
Thorpeness (dep.) . .	8.30	10.15	12.15	2. 0	3.45	4.15	5.50	7.30	10. 0
Aldeburgh (arr.). . .	8.40	10.25	12.25	2.10	3.55	4.25	6. 0	7.40	10.10

	a.m.	noon	p.m.	p.m.	p.m.	p.m.	p.m.	p.m. *	p.m. †
Aldeburgh (dep.) . .	10. 0	12. 0	1. 0	2.20	4. 0	5. 5	6.15	8. 0	10.15
Thorpeness (arr.) . .	10.10	12.10	1.10	2.30	4.10	5.15	6.25	8.10	10.25

*Operates on *Tuesdays, Thursdays, Saturdays and Sundays* only. †Operates on *Saturdays* only.
Fare table:—4d. single; 6d. return.
Period of operation:—*Daily* from 1st June to 30th September.
Date of expiry:—30th June, 1949.

F./R.866/3 (N. & P. No. 453).—Ward & Son (Aldeburgh) Ltd., High Street, Aldeburgh, Suffolk, a service of stage carriages between Aldeburgh (Ward's Garage) and Aldeburgh (Golf Course), subject to the following conditions:—

Route:—Via High Street and Saxmundham Road. Return by same route reversed.

Time table:—	a.m.	a.m.	p.m.	p.m.	p.m.	p.m.	p.m.	p.m. *
Ward's Garage (dep.). . . .	9.20	9.45	12.25	12.50	2.10	4.55	6. 0	7.40
Golf Course (Club House) arr	9.25	9.50	12.30	12.55	2.15	5. 0	6. 5	7.45

	a.m.	a.m.	p.m.	p.m.	p.m.	p.m.	p.m.	p.m. *
Golf Course (Club House) dep.	9.25	9.50	12.30	12.55	2.15	5. 0	6. 5	7.45
Ward's Garage (arr.) . .	9.30	9.55	12.35	1. 0	2.20	5. 5	6.10	7.50

*Operates on *Saturdays* and *Sundays* only.
Fare table:—6d. single.
Period of operation:—*Daily* from 1st May to 30th September.
Date of expiry:—30th June, 1949.

Bibliography

Books

Arnott, W. G. *Alde Estuary*. Boydell Press, 1973.

Banbury, P. *Shipbuilders of the Thames and Medway*. David & Charles, 1971

Beattie, S. *The New Sculpture*. Yale University Press, 1983.

Benham, H. *Down Tops'l*. Harrap, Second Edition, 1971.

Biddell, H. *The Suffolk Stud Book*. H. Biddell, 1880.

Bristow, J. P. *Aldeburgh Diary*. J. P. Bristow, 1983.

Brown, R. J. *Windmills of England*. Robert Hale, 1976.

Cable, J. *A Lifeboatman's Days*. Lovett, 1928.

Carr, F. G. G. *Sailing Barges*. Peter Davies, Second Edition, 1951.

[Clodd, E.] *A Guide to Aldeburgh*. J. Buck, 1861.

Clodd, H. P. *Aldeburgh, the History of an Ancient Borough*. Norman Adlard, 1959.

Cope, R. K. *Comrade Bill*. Stewart Printing (Pty) Ltd (Cape Town).

Dobson, E. *A Rudimentary Treatise in the Manufacture of Bricks and Tiles*. George Street Press, Reprinted 1971.

Evans, G. E. *Ask the Fellows who Cut the Hay*. Faber & Faber, 1956.

Evans, G. E. *The Horse in the Furrow*. Faber & Faber, 1960.

Fairbairn *Fairbairn's Book of Crests*. T. C. & E. C. Jack, 1905.

Flint, B. *Suffolk Windmills*. Boydell Press, 1979.

Gordon, D. I. *A Regional History of the Railways of Great Britain Vol. 5—Eastern Counties*. David & Charles, 1968.

Hele, N. F. *Notes or Jottings about Aldeburgh Suffolk*. John Russell Smith, 1870.

Helps, A. *Life and Labours of Mr. Brassey*. 1872.

Higgins, D. *The Beachmen*. Terence Dalton Ltd, 1987.

Ivimey, A. (Editor) *Westleton from the 1830s to the 1860s*. Workers' Educational Association, 1968.

Jarvis, S. *Smuggling in East Anglia*. Countryside Books, 1987.

Jobson, A. *Aldeburgh Story*. Flood & Son, 1954.

Jobson, A. *Victorian Suffolk*. Robert Hall, 1972.

Kieve, J. L. *Electric Telegraph*. David & Charles, 1973.

Malster, R. *Saved from the Sea*. Terence Dalton Ltd, 1974.

Manton, J. *Elizabeth Garrett Anderson*. Methuen, 1965.

March, E. J. *Sailing Trawlers*. Percival Marshall, 1953.

Mogg, E. *Paterson's Roads*. Rivington (and others), 18th Edition, 1829.

OFT *Aldeburgh Golf Club—The First Hundred Years*. East Anglian Magazine Ltd, 1982.

Pipe, J. *Port on the Alde*. Snape Craft Shop.

Simper, R. *East Coast Sail*. David & Charles, 1972.

Simper, R. *East Anglian Coast and Waterways*. East Anglian Magazine Ltd, 1985.

Simper, R. *Suffolk Sandlings*. East Anglian Magazine Ltd, 1986.

Simper, R. *Over Snape Bridge*. East Anglian Magazine Ltd.

Simper, R. *Woodbridge and Beyond*. East Anglian Magazine Ltd, 1972.

Spielmann, M. H.   *British Sculpture and Sculptors of Today*. Cassell, 1901.

Thompson, F. M. L. (Editor)   *Horse in European Economic History*. The British Agricultural History Society, 1983.

Thirsk, J.   *Suffolk Farming in the Nineteenth Century Vol. 1*. Suffolk Record Society, 1958.

Wailes, R.   *The English Windmill*. Routledge & Kegan Paul, 1954.

Waddell, J. S.   *Illustrated Memorial of the Great War in Relation to Leiston and District*. J. S. Waddell, 1919.

Wilson, G.   *The Old Telegraphs*. Phillimore, 1976.

Woodforde, J.   *Bricks to Build a House*. Routledge & Kegan Paul, 1976.

Papers

Adrian, L.   *Richard Garrett. Railway Enthusiast 1846*. East Anglian Daily Times, 1985.

Irving, R.   *Snape*. R. Irving, 1945.

Lane, T. & G. E. and others   *Quakers of Leiston*. T. & G. E. Lane, 1960.

Morris, J.   *The Story of the Aldeburgh Lifeboats*. J. Morris, 1980.

Wailes, R.   *Suffolk Windmills Parts 1 and 2*. Newcomen Society, 1941/42.

Wright, R. A. & M. J.   *Friston Mill*. R. A. & M. J. Wright, 1980.

William Morris Gallery (Curator Peter Cormack Esq.)   *Women Stained Glass Artists of the Arts and Crafts Movement*. William Morris Gallery, 1985.

Index

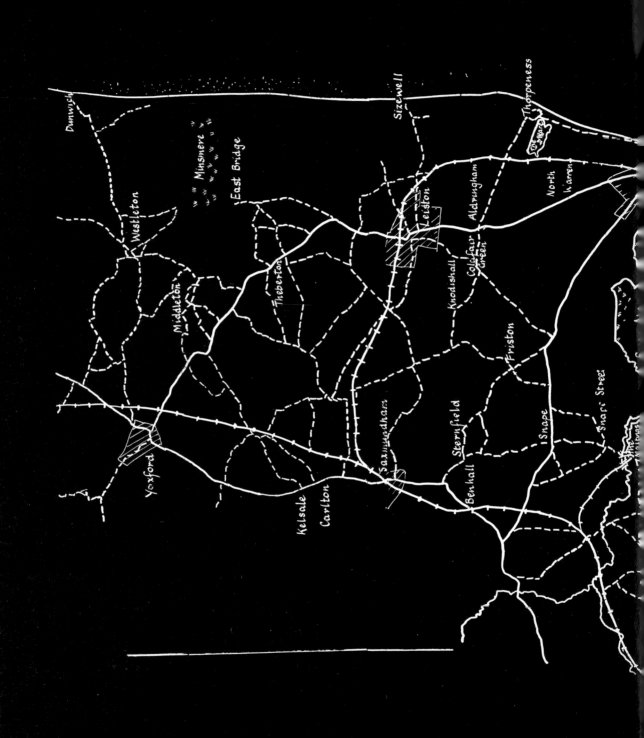